Praise f

The Size of Everything

"There are many heroic lives that are so unusual, or traumatic, or full of tribulation, that we cannot imagine living them ourselves. But like the best tales of those who find themselves in the grimmest circumstances, Erin Cole's life story is one of triumph and wit and sheer determination to survive. This beautifully written narrative will have you thanking your lucky stars for whatever happened in your own childhood, and cheering out loud for Erin, who like all exquisite lilies that tilt toward the golden sun, had to first push her way through a lot of muck to get there."

~W. Bruce Cameron, bestselling
author of *A Dog's Purpose*

"*The Size of Everything* isn't just yet another memoir about a dysfunctional childhood. It's the story of how one woman not only survived the most God-awful childhood imaginable but managed to find humor in it all and go on to thrive as a renowned bridal designer. Where other kids would have ended up in prison, on drugs or dead, Erin Cole demonstrated a remarkable resilience at every turn. After reading her book, you'll cheer for her and feel inspired."

~Jane Heller, bestselling author

"Tell you what—I'll wager my mother that Erin Cole's life is wilder and weirder than yours. That, in and of itself, doesn't mean you ought to read this book. But the combination of grace, hope, and beauty with which she and Jenna McCarthy tell her story elevates it so far beyond the traditional memoir that they've practically invented a new genre. A mixture of minimalism and extravagance, this punchy book covers an insane amount of ground, with every chapter just *daring* you to pick your jaw up off the floor. If the very best memoirs inevitably teach us something about ourselves, *The Size of Everything* could realistically be considered a graduate level class in you. At turns heartbreaking, sweet, and inspirational, this book reveals new pockets of reality while slowly and slyly making you fall in love with one of the toughest protagonists you'll ever meet."

~Travis Sentell, author of *Fluid* and
In the Shadow of Freedom

"Reminiscent of *The Glass Castle* and *The Sound of Gravel*, *The Size of Everything* is a searing account of a broken, devastating childhood and the triumph that emerged in spite of — and because of — the wreckage. I cheered, and I cried. What a book, what an inspiration."

~Allison Winn Scotch, bestselling author

"I was captivated by *The Size of Everything* from the very first page. With a magical blend of moments funny, uplifting and unforgiving, Cole and McCarthy have managed to turn a gruesome past into poetry. Get ready to fall in love."

~Elizabeth Lyons, bestselling author

"In *The Size of Everything*, Erin Cole's life is stunningly documented by Jenna McCarthy in short but powerful chapters that describe the pain of an unimaginably brutal childhood that eventually becomes a life-changing message of hope. Cole's amazing story is raw, honest, often heartbreaking, sometimes laugh-out-loud hilarious, and guaranteed to warm your heart. I love, love, love this book."

~Vikki Jensen Claflin, author of
Who Left the Cork Out of My Lunch?

"The story of Erin Cole is told in eloquent slivers of time that will, at times, jar the reader from complacency. Reading about the atrocities that Erin endured is sometimes hard, yet the poetic way in which her tale unfolds makes it impossible to peel your eyes from the page. This is one you'll read again and again."

~Tamara Doris, author of *Casey's Quest*

"From tumultuous to triumphant, you will be mesmerized by Erin Cole's story from the very first page. The misplaced child of alcoholics, Erin's life was filled with unimaginable abuse and neglect. This story, told with candid honesty and grace, chronicles one girl's desire to create a better life for herself. Erin's resilience and strength will astound you. That she came out unscathed is a miracle in itself; her story is a lesson to us all, to never give up no matter what obstacles are in the way."

~Stephanie Elliot, author of *Sad Perfect*

"*The Size of Everything* captures the feeling of childhood wonder and nostalgia for a bygone era of running wild and free, while giving the reader shocking glimpses of the horrors going on behind closed doors (and sometimes literally spilling out into the streets). As a series of tragic events unfolds, the desire to save Erin and her siblings is tempered with the realization that Erin never once views herself as a victim. We root for her, and there is solace from the beginning in knowing that she will overcome these seemingly insurmountable obstacles. The powerful message that one can not only survive, but succeed, despite exposure to death, addiction, and abuse is one that will serve the world."

~Kim DeVenne, Producer, Highway 101 Entertainment

"This book is like a roll of butterscotch candy... once you've started, you can't stop; each short chapter seduces you into 'just one more' until sadly, it's over. Many details of Erin Cole's upbringing would be too horrific to bear if they weren't so skillfully written through the optimistic eyes of a child destined to rise above it all. A story of love, loss and silver linings, *The Size of Everything* is a sweet treat you won't soon forget."

~Melodee Meyer, bestselling author

"I devoured every page of this book and was sad to see it end. Like *The Glass Castle* and *North of Normal*, *The Size of Everything* captivates the reader from page one and stays with you long after you finish reading."

~Cindy Bokma, author of *The Blondes of Bel Air*

"I found myself completely engrossed in Erin Cole's memoir, *The Size of Everything*. The author shares vivid, heart-wrenching details of parental neglect as she is bounced from one unstable home to another. Despite the abuse she suffered from the adults who controlled every aspect of her life—down to the way she dressed and how much she was allowed to eat—Ms. Cole sprinkles her stories with bits of humor to avoid leading us down a rabbit hole of pity and remorse. What struck me most about this memoir is the author's ability to overcome her cringe-worthy, troubled past. Her story is one of endurance and hope, and her resilience is an inspiration to all who read this amazing book."

~Marcia Kester Doyle, bestselling author of
Who Stole My Spandex? Life in the Hot Flash Lane

"I received an advance copy of *The Size of Everything* and planned to read a few chapters, but I was so touched by Erin's story that I read half the book in one sitting. The descriptions are so vivid that I was drawn into Erin's childhood like a moth to light. The pain of addiction in her family is so raw, yet the simple joys of childhood shine through. This book will rock you, break your heart and shine a light for a brighter future. I highly recommend it. Thank you, Erin, for sharing your life with us."

~Anne Bardsley, author of *Angel Bumps*

the size of
EVERYTHING

ERIN COLE
with
JENNA MCCARTHY

ISBN 10: 0-9799135-1-9
ISBN 13: 978-0-9799135-1-8

Library of Congress Control Number: 2018906549

BELLA LUNA PRESS

www.bellalunapress.com

For Isabella and Holland.
I wouldn't change one thing that happened to me in my
life, because every bit of it led me to you.

CONTENTS

DISCLAIMER

"You own everything that happened to you. Tell your stories.
If people wanted you to write warmly about them,
they should have behaved better."

~Anne Lamott

This is my story.

Everything that happens in this book happened in real life; *my* real life.

I consciously chose to write this book in love. For that reason, a handful of names and identifying characteristics have been changed. That is all. Details have not been enhanced or exaggerated. The dialogue is accurate to the best of my recollection, which some have called extraordinary. Conversations I could not recall verbatim have in places been recreated for readability but are one hundred percent based in fact and sentiment. As the nature of memory is personal, other people reflected in this book may recall events differently, a possibility I honor and respect.

This is my story.

ABOUT JERI MAC'S DIARIES

"Life can only be understood backwards;
but it must be lived forwards."

~Soren Kierkegaard

My mother kept diaries religiously throughout her life. When she died and I was informed by the police that her home was being condemned, I salvaged a worn stack of them along with her cat and some of her artwork. I couldn't bear to read them then, so I tucked the tattered, yellowing pages away in a box of old photographs and promptly forgot about them. As I was searching for pictures to include in this book—after the first draft of the manuscript was completed—I found the box. Reading through her journals was both enlightening and heart-wrenching. Her grammar and spelling were poor at times but her handwriting was lovely, at least when she was sober. I am including select excerpts within these pages to help the reader better understand her state of mind during these difficult years.

A NOTE FROM THE CO-AUTHOR

E rin Cole is one of the most inspiring human beings I have
ever met.

We first crossed paths over a decade ago when she was
the subject of a magazine article I was writing. We became
fast virtual-friends and great fans of one another's work, and
even though we had yet to meet in person before we began
collaborating on this book, Erin seemed to always know it was
going to happen. "Someday, we're going to write my story,"
she'd say from time to time, and I would look at her elegant,

xx | *Erin Cole with Jenna McCarthy*

glamorous life and think—but never say aloud— "Oh, pretty princess, I have a feeling your story isn't all that interesting."

I am happy to admit that I don't think I've ever been more wrong.

When Erin finally began revealing the details of her painful past to me, I was mesmerized. Not just by her incredible memory for details or the events themselves, but by the dichotomy between such a gruesome upbringing and the powerful, poised, secure, warm, generous, emotionally intelligent woman I was getting to know. When we were finished, I felt as if someone had handed me a tiny, defenseless newborn and asked me to shepherd it into the world and then guide and protect it and keep it from harm. *The Size of Everything* is that baby, and being entrusted with it has been one of my life's greatest honors. Thank you, Erin, for your confidence, your strength, your real-life friendship and your remarkable resilience. You have changed my life in ways I can't begin to explain. I love you with all my heart and I can't wait for our next adventure.

Jenna

A NOTE TO THE CO-AUTHOR

"Walking with a friend in the dark
is better than walking alone in the light."

~Helen Keller

To my Jenna,

I knew I had to write this memoir and all along I wanted it to be you. I waited ten years for you to breathe life into my story with your wit, compassion and crazy intellect. You have given me such insight into my past and taken so much of the pain and fear away. You are my soul and I can't imagine my life without you.

Thank you for giving me the opportunity to finally put my truth into print.

Thank you for trusting without knowing and taking the time to listen a little closer.

Thank you for paying attention in English class and for always keeping me on task. Your organizational skills are mind-blowing.

Thank you for being patient with me and allowing me to enter your very special world of creativity and artistry. You truly have a beautiful gift.

Thank you for never making a single comment about my atrocious grammar, spelling or punctuation. That was a lot to overlook.

Thank you for holding my hand when it was too scary to go back and too hard to keep going. You stayed at my side even when I had to get up and walk away wondering how I would ever be able to finish what we started.

Thank you for endless hours of laughter during some of the most difficult times of recall. You were my cheerleader and champion, guiding me carefully through each of my scary-ass homes, encouraging me to hold on and finish, always assuring me that we were so close to being out of there.

Thank you for your childlike curiosity; for taking on my story as your own, feeling it deep within you and then translating that onto every page.

Thank you for letting me tell it my way.

Thank you to Joe, Sophie and Sasha for welcoming me into your family and sharing your beautiful wife and mother with me. I had no idea how much I needed all of you.

Friends should leave you feeling like you want to be a better person, and that's what you have done for me. I am not sure how I even lived my life before you and I can't wait to go forward and create amazing new stories together. I love you, my beautiful friend. Thank you.

PROLOGUE:
REACH FOR THE STARS

When Mom was drinking, I'd wish with all my might that she would stop. But sometimes when she did, it was even worse.

It was only afternoon but of course she was in bed, the curtains pulled as tight as they would go. Our new house on Ramona wasn't like the one on Stardust—it didn't face the sun the same way or the curtains were made of a different fabric or maybe it was both—so making it feel like midnight in there wasn't an option. The best she could hope to recreate was dusk.

I was playing some quiet eight-year-old game in my room when I heard her talking. She didn't have a phone in her bedroom, not that she had any friends she might be chatting with anyway, so I went in to see who she was talking to.

The door was cracked. Mom was lying in her bed, on top of the covers. Her eyes were open and she had both arms outstretched toward the ceiling.

"Grab my hand," she was saying to the air, her tone desperate. "Come on, I have you. Just grab my hand!"

"Mom, who are you talking to?" I asked, trying to make my voice light.

She turned to me sharply. Her eyes were glazed and almost unrecognizable.

"You can't see him?" she shouted, as if I were blind or crazy or some combination of the two.

"Who?" I asked. My old friend panic slipped his fingers around my neck and began to softly squeeze.

"ERIN, HE'S RIGHT THERE! GRAB HIM!" She was frantic; adamant.

"There's no one there, Mom," I told her.

"YES, THERE IS," she insisted. "It's Kelly, he's here. He's really here. Grab his hand, Erin. Grab him! Get on the bed. Stand up on it and reach. You can get him, honey, I know you can!"

She was gone and I knew it. I didn't want to upset her any more than she already was so I did what she asked. I climbed onto her bed and I stretched out my arms as far as I could and I tried to grab Kelly.

"Reach straight up. Yes, right there! You've got him now, grab him. Come on, Erin, you can do this!"

Over the next few years, my sister and I would be subjected to this torture over and over. Mom would try to quit drinking dozens of times, each attempt marked by periods of intense hallucinations. And every time, we'd stand on her bed and reach and grasp just like she asked us to, but we could never get our dead brother back for her.

THE WHITE HOUSE WITH THE GREEN SHUTTERS

THE BUMS ARE COMING

I was five the first time I slept outside alone. It was a Saturday and my sister and I spent the day the way we almost always did on weekends: barefoot and unsupervised, running rough-shod around the bowels of our Southern California neighborhood. Jenny was two years older than me so she was in charge.

Most kindergarteners probably don't dread weekends, but I did. Two days off work meant our mom and stepdad would be home and drinking all day. My siblings and I knew it was best to stay far, far away. So whenever we could, we did.

"You two better get your asses home or the bums will eat you for dinner," my brothers would say when Jenny and I tried to follow them into the canyon. Kelly was nine and Patrick was thirteen, and they were right about one thing: the canyon was no place for my sister and me.

The canyon was our name for the endless, open space behind our house. It was filled with tall brush and giant boulders and was a magnet for curious kids and homeless people. That's not what we called them then, of course; they were bums — and they were terrifying. They didn't keep us out of the canyon, though. Nothing could have.

We loved it down there. We would dig holes and build forts and come home exhausted and caked in dirt. We kept going even after the time Kelly and Patrick were pushing massive rocks down a steep slope and knocked Jenny out, breaking her leg in two places. I wasn't with them when it happened, but I remember my brothers carrying her home with her mangled leg dangling and I remember them getting beaten severely even though it was an accident; they hadn't even known she was there. But what I remember most is that Jenny didn't even cry. She was tougher than any boy I knew.

Jenny and I would follow our brothers in secret, hiding behind trees and rocks and spying on their teenage conversations.

"Whistle while you work, Hitler is a jerk. Whistled while you bit his weenie, now it doesn't work," Kelly would sing at the top of his lungs, and I had to bite the inside of my cheek to keep from laughing. I looked those lyrics up decades later and it turns out the real words are "Mussolini bit his weenie." I'm not sure which version is funnier.

"I'm going to tell on you," Patrick would say if he saw us. At five years old, I understood this was an idle threat. Who was he going to tell? Our passed-out parents? And even if they were awake and sober — which wasn't a likely combo — there was a solid fifty-fifty chance the boys would get the same walloping as me and Jenny, just because. Tattling never worked out in our house and we all knew it.

Jenny and I came home that day once to pee. Mom and Donald were in the middle of a particularly sloppy fight—one of the ones where they'd punch and slap each other in between slurred insults—so we hurried back out as quickly as we could. Later we snuck back in to get a snack. The house was already dark and quiet, which meant they were asleep even though it was the middle of the afternoon. We grabbed two mushy, bruised bananas from the wicker basket on the floor that sometimes had rotting carrots and potatoes mixed in with weeks-old fruit. This was a risky move, because if we got caught taking food without asking—anything, ever—Mom would make us sit at the table and eat an entire raw onion. Your stomach would burn and you'd have bubble-guts for days, so you really wanted to avoid this punishment whenever possible.

We scarfed our bananas in secret, tossed the peels into the bushes behind our house and then went to Jenny's friend Rachael's house. Rachael lived two doors down and her mom was very kind and gave us mind-blowing snacks like Ding Dongs and Twinkies and Little Debbies. Their cupboards were always filled with a dozen or more boxes of these delicious, individually wrapped desserts, and Rachael and her brother Paul didn't even think this was amazing. Sometimes I wondered why some people got to live in houses with enormous and reliable supplies of food and others didn't, but I didn't dwell on it. It wasn't like you got to pick where you lived anyway.

Jenny and Rachael and I had the best time playing tag and jumping rope and riding our bikes. I'd pedal my tricycle as fast as I could—so fast that the front wheel would wobble—while they chased me until I couldn't pedal anymore and would have to ditch my bike and roll into the grass. I wore head to toe grass stains as a badge of honor; proof that I could hang with the big kids.

That Saturday, Rachael invited Jenny to spend the night. This was another dangerous proposition, because when our parents were drinking they'd forget they had allowed her to go anywhere. She'd come home the next day and they would say she was lying, she'd gone without permission, and it would end in a beating. Because of this, even when my parents said yes, my brain heard, "NO, don't go, don't do it, it's not worth it."

But that night, Jenny decided to risk it. To be honest, I might have risked it right along with her—anything to avoid going home—but Rachael's mom had a one-kid-per-night rule, which seemed totally unreasonable to me. The three of us played until it began to get dark, at which point my inner panic button started to go off. If my stepdad was awake, he'd start doing his cattle call, the one you could hear a mile away. It always sounded exactly the same, so my brothers and sister and I would often shout it along with him as we bolted home.

"PATRIIIIIIIIIIIIIIIIIIIIIICK, KEEEELLLLLLLLYYYYYYY, JENNNNNNYYYYYYYYYY, ERIIIIIIIIIIIIIIIIINNNNNNNNN!"

He'd call each name exactly one time and you'd better have your ass in a full-on sprint upon approach or you were being disrespectful, and you could get a beating for that. You could get a beating for lots of things in our house, and half the time you had absolutely no idea what grave and unacceptable offense you'd committed this time. Not that you would dare ask.

As the sun began to set that night, Jenny and Rachael ushered me home and watched me run down the sidewalk to my house. I was used to being alone, but I hated the dark. I waved goodbye from the sidewalk and watched them turn and take off, stuffing the jealousy deep down in the dark place I kept all my bad feelings. The sky had turned blue-black and it was getting colder by the minute, and I couldn't wait to get inside because I was filthy and barefoot. It hadn't occurred to me at this point that I had never heard the cattle call, which could only mean one thing.

I ran up the front porch stairs and twisted the doorknob, but it wouldn't budge. It was locked. I knocked on the door and waited. No one came. I waited a few minutes longer and knocked again, louder this time. Still nothing. It was pitch-black inside the house, and nearly as dark outside. I knew Pat and Kelly couldn't hear me from their rooms, where they'd hide every waking minute they could. My house wasn't the type where kids hung out in the living room playing Monopoly.

It may have taken five minutes or an hour — I'm honestly not sure — but eventually it hit me: my parents weren't coming. They'd gotten drunk, locked up for the night and gone to bed. Normal parents would make sure all their children were safe and sound and securely *inside* the house before doing this of course, but I didn't have normal parents. To them, I was no different than our ratty old dog Pierre. I might be inside, I might be out. I may have eaten, I may not have. Someone might give a rat's ass if bums ate me for dinner, someone might not. Either way, it was all my fault. I was always doing everything wrong.

Our house was white with green shutters and sat on top of a big hill. The front faced a street called Elberon, but I didn't know street names back then. The garage was on the downhill side of the house — along with my bedroom — so it was almost underground. There was a door down there, but it was always locked because it faced the street where anyone walking by could have just sauntered right in. Still, I ran back down the stairs and around to the downhill side, hoping against hope.

That almost never worked out for me.

The door was locked. Shaking with fear, I ran back up the darkened hill, through the backyard to the side of the house that had a basement window close to ground level on the outside. It was locked, which was probably a blessing as that window was way over my head on the inside and surely I'd have broken a bone had I been able to get through. I went to the front door one more time and knocked again, fully knowing the futility of this move.

I was five years old, filthy and terrified. The only neighbor I knew was Rachael, and I certainly couldn't go there. Her parents had already said I couldn't stay the night, and terrible things happened when you argued with parents. Everyone knew that. Plus, since I was to blame for this predicament, alerting other adults to my crime would have been a terribly misguided idea. No, I was in it alone. I had learned at a young age not to have needs—or at least, not to express them—because nobody was going to help me anyway. I had to figure this out by myself.

I crawled around in the dark, looking for some sort of shelter that felt even a tiny bit protected. Finally I lay down in an empty flower bed near the house, as far from the street as possible where the canyon bums couldn't see me if they decided to take a midnight stroll. You never knew what bums did to the little kids before they ate them. That was the part that scared me the most.

The night lasted an eternity. Slivers of moonlight peeked through the trees and cast gigantic, menacing shadows around the yard. I tried closing my eyes but that was even worse, fear filling my tiny body with the unequivocal knowledge that I was about to be ambushed. Every breeze, every car no matter how far in the distance, every buzz of a mosquito or flutter of a bird's wing was an army of bums coming to get me. Maybe I'd freeze to death before they did. The thought was mildly comforting.

The sun began to rise. I waited for the sound of the front door opening; willed it with every atom in my body. After what felt like days I heard my stepdad stumble out the door

and to his car, on his way to the handyman job that made zero
sense to me seeing as the man couldn't hammer a nail into
a stick of butter at home. Praying my mom was still sleeping off the previous day's bender, I slipped inside, made a
beeline for my room and tucked my filthy self into my bed.
I passed out within seconds, and had a nightmare that Jenny
came home and was brutally punished for sneaking out without permission. When I woke up hours later, I found out it
wasn't a nightmare.

GRANDMA KATIE
ON FIRE

My mom hated the white house with the green shutters, but I loved it. It was on the corner of Elberon and Hanford Avenues in San Pedro, and it sat high up on a steep embankment. This meant you had to slog up thirteen stairs to a landing, and then up another nine steps to get to the front porch. From there you had a perfect, unobstructed view of the bright green Vincent Thomas Bridge. I could sit out there and stare at the twinkling lights across the Los Angeles Harbor for hours. The view was breathtaking. I didn't know it at the time, but that was the best house we would ever live in.

We had moved in after my mom left my dad. I was around three years old and Grandma Katie came with the house. She'd raised my mom and my Uncle Jimmy there and stayed there by herself after my grandpa died of a heart attack in the basement bedroom that would be mine. Grandma Katie was a fabulous woman who loved to draw, drank Olympia beer and smoked Belair cigarettes by the carton. The box had a picture of heaven on it and I was convinced you were going to see Jesus in the clouds if you smoked enough of those things.

Grandma Katie also loved her tea. She had this ancient aluminum teapot that she'd just add more water to each time she used it, never rinsing it or dumping out the old water.

"What are those things in the bottom of your teacup?" I'd ask her. It turned out they were little chips of metal that came off the bottom of that old pot. She'd shrug and laugh and say she thought they were delicious — this was before people worried about things like dementia and BPA and TCP or even cancer — so I thought it was funny, too.

We were living with Grandma Katie when my mom started dating Donald Blomgren. I was four by that time, and I don't even remember what my own first impression of him was. All I knew was that Grandma Katie did *not* like him. He'd come over all the time anyway and late at night I'd hear them arguing.

"Over my dead body will you live in my goddamned house!" Grandma would shout.

"Well I'll be damned, because if you keep it up you might just get your wish," Don would bellow back. He always finished his retorts with, "And that's about the size of it!" As if that were some universal and definitive clincher.

I'm not sure how, but Don won that argument. He and my mom got married in Barstow and he moved in, even though Grandma Katie's body looked very much alive to me.

There was a lot of drinking in that house.

When Mom was home, things weren't that bad, but the minute Grandma Katie and my stepdad were alone, they'd be at each other's throats. Once I walked into the kitchen to find her waving a butcher knife in his face.

"Go ahead, you sonofabitch, try me," Grandma Katie taunted.

"You don't have the guts to use it," he snarled.

I quickly left the room, positive I didn't want to hear any more swearing or see anyone's guts. The funny (not funny) part was that neither of them batted an eye that a five-year-old was standing there witnessing this exchange.

Grandma Katie adored us kids and had infinite patience for our stories and games. The problem was, she was losing her marbles. It started off with small things; forgetting to turn off the stove, or letting her cigarettes burn all over the house and lighting a new one in the next room and then another in the next. I knew things were getting really bad when she poured Clorox into the pot of soup my mom was making for dinner one night. Fortunately she dumped the whole bottle in there—you could probably smell the fumes two streets over—so nobody accidentally ate it and died.

One of my most vivid memories of her in that house was the night she set her hair on fire. I was coloring at the kitchen table while Grandma Katie baked cornbread. My stepdad had just limped through the door after a long day at work and was making his way through the room when Grandma Katie opened the oven. Before any of us even knew what was happening, a big whooooosh of fire came flying at her. My stepdad shot out the door and in a second came running back in with the garden hose on full blast. He proceeded to aim the sharp spray nozzle at Grandma's lovely red Irish hair, which was fully ablaze. She stood there screaming bloody murder as Don pounded her with water like a prisoner in solitary confinement.

"*Are you outta your goddamn mind?*" she screamed, while he aimed the spray right in her face. She lunged at him, swinging and shouting and cracking him right across the jaw. He dropped the hose, which flew wildly around the kitchen like an angry, hissing cobra, spraying everything in its path. I sat in shock as the water whipped across their faces, down the walls and through my lopsided bowl cut, soaking me to the bone.

It wasn't long after that that my mom decided to send Grandma Katie to live with her sister, my great aunt Vivian, in Washington DC. That might have been one of the only times I ever saw Donald Blomgren smile. He never said anything, but I knew he was celebrating inside.

I missed Grandma Katie every day. She actually cared about us, and you could really feel that. Which is more than I could say for my stepfather. He only tolerated us because he had to, and you could really feel that, too. Down to your core.

JERI MAC

Geraldine Lorraine McPheeters was born on March 24, 1930; her brother James arrived four years later. To Mom's dismay, he would turn out to be the apple of her parents' proverbial eye. Mom always told us kids our Uncle Jimmy "could do no wrong." Sometimes it seemed as if she was determined to do enough wrong for both of them.

My mother did well in school and was incredibly artistic — sketching and painting and sewing from an early age with no instruction — although she would deny her talent at every turn. She wasn't being modest; she simply couldn't see what everyone else saw. I loved to watch over her shoulder as she drew, marveling at every careful stroke and wondering how she did it; how she could just think of something out of thin air and then lay it down on paper. It was mesmerizing.

Mom was vague and tight-lipped about her childhood. I do know she was close to her dad and not so close to her mom, Grandma Katie. I'm pretty sure I loved my grandmother enough to make up for my mom. I never met her father. His name was James, and he died in my mother's arms of a heart attack when she was eighteen and he was fifty-nine. She couldn't talk about him without crying.

There was one story Mom seemed to relish telling about her and my Uncle Jimmy. She was around ten and my uncle was six or so, and they were playing outside. Jimmy was bugging her about something, the way brothers do, when Mom reached up and pulled down one of the stiff branches of this big tree in the yard and told him to have a seat. I always picture her doing this with a pretend-sweet smile that showed all her teeth. "I knew it would launch him," she'd tell us later with a wicked giggle. "I just didn't know it would launch him that far." When Uncle Jimmy landed, his arm was badly broken. My mother always shared this story with a combination of pride and defiance. *He should have seen it coming*, she implied, like she knew how serious it could have been but it was okay because it was his fault, too.

Jeri Mac, as she called herself, was tall and slender well into her thirties, with a tiny waist and legs that went on for days. She had an Audrey Hepburn air about her that was more than a physical resemblance, although she had that, too. She loved to sing and dance and was as graceful as a swan. Mom finished high school at the top of her class, and had her hopes pinned on getting a college degree. But when her father died, she stayed back to help Grandma Katie deal with the devastating loss. Within a year she'd met and married Kenneth Conway Cole, my father.

Despite the fact that they loved each other passionately, it was a match made in hell.

They were a pair of kids with no college education, a fondness for liquor and just enough money to get into trouble. My parents financed a bar in a rough part of East LA called the Dollhouse. Mom loved to cook and created a nice little menu she'd serve to her regular customers while they knocked back their cocktails. It was a small and relatively sweet family operation until Dad decided a topless barmaid would really boost business and hired a woman named Tracy to do the job. People said Tracy was surprisingly intelligent as well as musically gifted, although it's unlikely either of those were the reason my father was screwing around with her. Much later, when Mom referred to the Dollhouse days, she'd say, "Oh, that's when your dad was taking out the trash." Meaning Tracy, of course.

Despite his philandering, Dad was a kind man who couldn't turn a blind eye to anyone in need. When his friend Manny was looking for a place to stay for a few days, Dad set up a cot in the bar's back room. He brought in blankets and a hot plate so Manny would be warm and comfortable. Manny showed his gratitude by leaving that hot plate on and burning Dad's bar to the ground.

Mom felt strongly that my father's carelessness with the trash was the true cause of their loss, and promptly divorced him. She had four kids and no money, so Grandma Katie took us all in. Dad moved to Lancaster and took the trash with him.

I'm sure my mom was drinking back then, but I always assumed the real boozing started when she married Don a few years later.

Mom could be fun and even nurturing when she was sober. I remember one 4th of July when I was around five she took us to watch the fireworks up the street overlooking the canyon. She gripped my hand with her own with all her strength, terrified I would get lost in the crowd.

I remember thinking she must care a lot about me to hold my hand like that.

The white house with the green shutters had a beautiful garden filled with avocado and grapefruit and pomegranate trees. The smell of it all together was heavenly. On a good day, Mom would strip me down to my underwear and crack open a pomegranate and we'd sit together for hours picking out the tiny fruit with our juice-stained fingers.

Every once in a while, she'd go through her makeup drawer and fill an empty Wheat Thins box with deep red lipsticks and peachy creme blushes and liquid eyeliners she didn't wear. I'd trot off to my room with this mysterious haul to experiment, and return as a cross between a call girl and a clown. She'd get the biggest kick out of my messy, inept attempts at playing grown-up. Being the one to make my mother laugh was one of my greatest joys in life.

Those were the early years, before things got really bad. Later I would cling to the memories of those days—of that mother—often. I'd pray that God or Jesus or the Universe or Yogi Bear or anyone, really, would please bring her back to me. But by then, she was too far gone.

WHITE GO-GO BOOTS

As the youngest of four kids, I remember my brothers and sister always whining about school. It was hard. They had to get up so early. Homework sucked. Their teachers were mean. Naturally, I wasn't exactly thrilled about starting kindergarten at Bandini Elementary.

That was until I got there. I couldn't fathom all the complaints, or why half my classmates cried every morning at drop-off. That place was amazing! You got to play with other kids. You got free breakfast in the cafeteria, which was my favorite. (Even the eggs were insane, and I hated eggs.) Then you got to have a snack. And lunch on top of that sometimes, when my mom remembered to pack me one or gave me money to buy pizza. It was fifty shades of fabulous, as far as I was concerned.

I wanted to live there and dreaded the one o'clock dismissal bell with all my heart.

One morning, Mom told me she was going to be a few minutes late picking me up because she had to work until just when school got out. She told me to wait on the playground, and that she'd be there before I knew it.

"I can just walk home," I told her. You'd think I had offered to chop off all the legs of Grandma Katie's dining room table or wash the windows with vodka.

"Over my dead body!" she roared. Apparently, my school was two solid miles from home—far too far for a kindergartener to walk by herself. I'd get lost. Or run over by a truck. And honestly, there was *"absolutely no way"* I could ever hope to find my way home from there in the first place, she was sure of it. So, it was settled. Walking was out of the question.

I nodded in agreement, hoping my cheeks weren't blazing red with guilt. I was pretty sure I knew my way around town as well as she did by that point. I could have drawn her a map to Bandini Elementary, the convent up on the hill, the liquor store, or my grandparents' house if she'd asked. I hadn't realized until then that my parents truly had no idea how much ground we kids routinely covered while they were drunk or sleeping. If Mom didn't want me walking home from school, she certainly wouldn't want me walking to my favorite park, the one where there was always a family or a mom with kids having a picnic. If you gave them just the right look—not too sad, just a soft, wistful smile and eye contact that lasted for maybe a moment longer than it should have—they'd immediately offer you some food. I got really good at that look.

For the record, I could have led my mom to that park with my eyes closed.

One school day she didn't tell me that she might be late picking me up. She just never showed up. I was the last kid on the playground, after one-by-one my classmates had been whisked away in their Pontiac station wagons or Chevy Chevelles, and my teacher, Mrs. Mueller, came out to check on me.

"Should we call your mom?" she asked kindly.

"Oh, she said she was going to be late today," I lied, wanting to protect my mother. I knew she wasn't coming, but I didn't want Mrs. Mueller to know that. It was too embarrassing. "She'll probably be here any minute."

Mrs. Mueller seemed satisfied with this explanation and trotted back off to our classroom. I figured the sooner I left the better, before she came back out to check on me again, so I bolted toward home.

About five blocks from the school, I saw my friend Theresa playing outside. She had told me she lived right up the street from Bandini and she did; literally. Theresa was wearing these white, knee-high patent leather boots that I coveted like nothing else I'd ever encountered, and when she invited me inside to play I didn't hesitate for one second. Her mom gave us a snack (Fig Newtons — a first for me — and grapes that were hard and fresh) and then Theresa showed me her closet. I adored fashion even at that age, and my jaw must have been on the floor.

Theresa had an amazing closet. She had clothes hung neatly on hangers and a whole dresser to herself with everything stacked neatly in drawers. Jenny and I shared a dresser — we even shared drawers — so it was always a pigsty. This was before Grandma Blanche, Don's mom, began making beautiful dresses for us, so I didn't have anything to put on hangers. My one corduroy dress was stuffed in one of those drawers somewhere. Theresa had enough hanging clothes to outfit an army.

But it wasn't Theresa's flowery frocks or her tidy stacks of t-shirts or even those go-go boots I envied the most; it was her socks. She had the most beautiful socks I'd ever seen in every color and style imaginable, from pale pink cable knit fold-overs ringed with ruffles to simple white cotton anklets with a darling scallop edge. I would have been happy with *any* socks. I had none of my own, which was shameful enough, but any time I stole a pair from Jenny's section of the drawer (completely off limits), they'd be huge on my little feet and would slide down into my shoes and drive me crazy all day long. So mostly I didn't wear them. Other kids teased me about this mercilessly.

I ogled my friend's finery for maybe a half hour before I decided I should go. Theresa told me I could come back and play anytime and I promised her I would. I said goodbye, and then I made my way easily home.

I crept in quietly, not sure what I was going to find. My mom was asleep on the couch. I felt bad for her because she'd worked late the night before and early that morning, so it made sense that she'd be so exhausted. I tried to tiptoe past her but her mom-radar must have been on full blast. She leapt up, wild-eyed and confused.

"What's the matter?" she shouted.

I apologized for waking her up and told her nothing was the matter, I was just coming home from school. I hoped she wouldn't ask me *how* I got there, but she did.

So I told her the truth.

Mom was furious, shouting that there was no way I could have done that (despite undeniable evidence to the contrary) while at the same time scolding me for being so foolish. I assumed a big-time spanking was coming but she must have been too tired.

"Go to your room and take a nap," she finally ordered, collapsing back onto the couch.

I didn't argue with her, ever. I said okay and padded off to my boring bedroom and crawled into bed. I wasn't tired and I couldn't sleep. After God-knows-how-long of lying there being bored out of my mind, I began to weigh my options. Theresa had invited me to come back and play "anytime." My siblings didn't get home until dinnertime. My stepdad, too. Mom would likely sleep at least until then. Finally, I decided she'd probably never find out if I went back to Theresa's house. I didn't let myself think about what would happen if she did.

I got out of bed, tiptoed down to the garage and let myself out the side door. Then I took off. I ran the entire way to Theresa's because I knew I couldn't stay long and I wanted to have as much time there as possible.

Theresa's mom seemed surprised but happy I came back. She didn't ask where I lived or if my mom knew where I was. Theresa and I played Barbies and dress-up, and at one point she offered to let me wear the white boots. She didn't have to ask twice. I paraded around Theresa's house in those things and I was Nancy Sinatra and *I Dream of Jeannie* all rolled into one. It was a-mazing.

Even though I wanted to stay forever, I reluctantly told Theresa I'd better go home. As I went to take off the boots, she stopped me.

"Wear them home!" she squealed. "You can give them back to me tomorrow at school." I couldn't believe my ears or my good fortune in finding this friend, and again I was not about to argue. She smiled and shoved me out the door; a tiny, shiny fashion plate in dirty cutoff shorts and blinding white patent leather boots.

As much as I wanted everyone in the world to see me in those things, still I ran all the way home, Theresa's boots making the most amazing clicking sound with each frenzied step. The enormity of what I'd done—sneaking out without permission, "gallivanting" around the neighborhood, as my parents would say—was starting to hit me. I knew that if my mom had gone into my room, I would be one dead kid.

I entered the house the same way I had left it, through the garage. My stomach in a giant knot, I went straight to my room and slipped into my bed, boots and all. Mom wasn't standing there with her arms crossed ready to kill me, so I was pretty sure I was in the clear.

This time I actually was tired. I was asleep in a matter of minutes.

The very next thing I saw was my mother's face; her words were loud and angry.

"Where in blue blazes did you get those boots?" she demanded, using one of her favorite Irish expressions.

My mind was a blank. I was still half-asleep and also, I hadn't thought that far ahead. We blinked at each other for a bit. She raised her eyebrows, waiting.

"My friend Theresa let me borrow them," I said finally, trying not to flinch. You really never knew what was going to set her off or what she'd let slide. "I'm going to give them back to her tomorrow."

Mom stared me down, as if trying to decide whether or not to believe me.

"You're a nutty kid," she finally said. "Don't forget!"

I promised I wouldn't, and that was the end of it.

That was the first time I snuck out and logged a few miles around town on my own, but it certainly wasn't the last.

THE QUEEN OF ELBERON

Defiant.
Challenging.
Difficult.
Liar.
Cheater.
Thief.

These are the labels my parents put on my sister Jenny over the years; the labels they created and the ones she seemed compelled to live up to. She couldn't escape them no matter what she did, so she began to believe them. It was brainwashing of the most vile and villainous sort.

The labels I would have given her are intelligent, intense, caring, compassionate, funny, remarkable, misunderstood.

Jenny didn't want to argue; she wanted to be heard.

Jenny never meant to hurt anyone; she had more than enough pain to go around.

Jenny didn't need to be disciplined; she needed to be supervised, to be engaged, to be understood, to be loved.

None of those things were happening in our house.

Bored and lonely one day, Jenny decided she would go out and make some new friends. But how? Maybe she could give them something, a gift of some sort. But she was all of seven years old, and frankly didn't have much to offer. Our parents weren't big on toys, money and food were damn near impossible to come by, and our wardrobes certainly weren't anything to write home about.

Then she had an idea. When she played it out in her own mind it must have been nothing short of brilliant. In fact, I imagine she was probably quite proud of herself.

Jenny went to our mom's jewelry box and started filling her pockets. When there wasn't room left for so much as a cameo brooch in there, she found one of Mom's purses and dumped the rest of her bling in there. Then she headed outside.

Most of it was probably costume junk, but the few nice things Mom owned—except her diamond wedding ring, thankfully—were in that haul. She came up with the Robin Hood plan on her own, mind you; there were never any sober, discerning adults around to guide, engage or re-direct any of us. They'd show up for the shouting and spanking that would come later, though. That you could count on.

The neighborhood kids played in the street back then. Jenny trotted out with her bag of baubles and began handing them out; a miniature blonde Robin Hood. Up and down the street she pranced —"*One for you, two for you. Oh no, really, take it. I insist!*" — until every last piece had been given away. For five whole minutes, Jenny was the Queen of Elberon Drive.

Good times for Jenny never lasted long.

CAPTAIN JACK

There was a liquor store on Pacific Coast Highway our step-dad liked to frequent. Jenny and I would sit in the parked car and wait while he went in and refilled his stash of Club vodka. From the parking lot, we had a clear view of the bar across the street, Captain Jack's. I don't remember if it was Jenny's idea or mine, but somehow Captain Jack became our private nickname for the miserable man with the hideous limp our mother had married. Oh, how we relished having a secret from him; something he couldn't control or take away. To this day, it's the only way we refer to him. Obviously he never found out, or odds are I wouldn't be alive to write this book.

Captain Jack was born Donald Max Blomgren. He grew up in San Pedro just two blocks from the white house with the green shutters. His parents, Blanche and Sam, were kind and generous and doted shamelessly on their only son. Blanche Blomgren could sew like Coco Chanel, and her husband Sam loved listening to baseball on his transistor radio and eating the breadsticks and cheese that my grandmother made for him. Grandpa Sam also was an incredible craftsman and a skilled gardener, producing lettuce, sweet peas, carrots, apples, turnips, potatoes and countless other fruits and vegetables for his family. All in all, Captain Jack's childhood was simple and sweet and far from extraordinary.

That was before the draft.

Captain Jack served in the Marine Corps and fought in both WW2 and the Korean War. His unit was stationed in the Chosin Reservoir in a province of North Korea when UN forces were overwhelmed by hundreds of thousands of Communist Chinese soldiers. He lost countless friends and in all likelihood, killed as many enemies. I may not know much about large-scale life-or-death military combat, but I do know this: you don't come out of it unscathed.

Things had gone from bad to worse, as they do in a war. Captain Jack already had lost his entire platoon when a bomb exploded, sending shrapnel into his calf and nearly severing the leg completely. He lay in a widening pool of blood, fading in and out of consciousness, probably begging for death to take him I would imagine, while frostbite consumed the foot of the mutilated leg.

To his great surprise, he was rescued and despite his grave condition, my stepdad survived. He was sent home like so many others: broken physically and emotionally, yet somehow expected to slip easily back into the civilian life he'd lived before, even though he bore little resemblance to the man who had once inhabited it. Donald Blomgren had left the safety of American soil a bright-eyed boy filled with confidence and conviction and returned as Captain Jack: crippled, angry, and capable of cold-blooded murder. Think Lieutenant Dan without the hippie hair or washboard abs.

A few years after my parents divorced, Mom and Captain Jack met right there in McCowan's, the little neighborhood market where she was a cashier and he was a customer. My mother never said as much, but I'm pretty sure she married him out of a sad combination of desperation and pity. I genuinely can't think of any other compelling reason she would have done it; it certainly wasn't for his money or his charming personality. He was short on both in equal measure.

In all fairness, Captain Jack was saddled with four stepchildren he never wanted. Worse still, he had endured untold, unmentionable atrocities of war and the injuries he sustained caused him chronic and unbearable pain. He had a lift in one of his shoes and walked with a severe limp. The frostbitten foot never fully healed. Winter and summer, he wore these thick wool socks that my mom would help him peel off at the end of the day. One sock would be heavy and crimson; soaked with blood. *Every single day.* It was a wretched sight.

On the best of all sober days, Captain Jack was brooding and angry. His was a festering sort of fury that made you feel guilty for existing, as if all the world knew you did so only to annoy and enrage him. When his state of mind was particularly vicious, Mom would shoo us outside. "I'll call you in when he's in a better mood," she'd whisper. I was always more than happy to go, and often figured I might never hear from her again, which would have been great because then I wouldn't have to come back.

It was clearly in everyone's best interest to get this man a drink... so everyone did. By the time we were five and seven, "everyone" included me and Jenny.

"There's enough brown in here to knock me on my ass," he'd chuckle approvingly. The "brown" was bourbon, and all we knew about it was that the right amount put him in a better mood.

The problem was, it was a delicate balance—maybe even a science—finding the "right amount." Not enough and the edge wouldn't get taken off at all; too much and he'd find a reason to beat the shit out of you. Giggling in bed might get you ripped from the thing and tossed around the room like a ragdoll; tiptoeing to the bathroom could end with a kick in the rear and being dropped like a bag of wet cement into the bathtub.

Jenny and I tried keeping careful track of the Captain's consumption, but invariably Mom would join in and they'd be having a great old time until they passed out (preferred) or ran out of booze (never good). When the latter happened, it would turn into the interrogation scene from *The Usual Suspects*, with the two shitfaced adults grilling each of us kids in turn to figure out who the hell drank all the Jim Beam. *Because it certainly wasn't them.*

Every once in a while, they'd doze off for an hour or four, then wake up and get a second wind. "Someone's in the kitchen with Dinah," we'd hear them crooning, loudly and off-key, from our beds. "Someone's in the kitchen, I know, I know..." It wasn't just folk music that lit their drunken fire; they were also fond of Irish pub tunes (Mom) and war songs (Captain Jack) that I can't quite recite but would recognize if I heard. Their late-night karaoke often escalated into verbal and physical fighting, with garbled barbs and lots of sloppy hitting and shoving—almost always initiated by Mom. Other times, they might wake and summon all four of us kids from our beds to sing songs, perform a fashion show or choreograph a dance routine for them. We always did what they asked, silently willing unconsciousness to overcome them sooner than later so we could go back to sleep ourselves. It never happened quickly enough.

PULLING RANK

As the oldest brother, Pat took his role as protector seriously. When our parents' drinking got out of hand, Kelly, Jenny and I would hang out in his room. It was safe in there. We would listen to music and he would let us play with the two hamsters he kept hidden in his top drawer. Eventually, any activity we engaged in escalated into a rank fight, which was basically team trash-talking on steroids. This is when I first began to curate my articulate foul mouth as a kid.

It was always me and Pat against Jenny and Kelly, and Pat and I would usually throw the first rank. Pat would whisper into my ear exactly what I was supposed to say, and then I'd hurtle it back at our opponents with the meanest sneer I could muster.

"Kelly, you and Jenny smell like you took a bath in shit!" innocent-looking five-year-old me would blurt, and all three of them would collapse into fits of hysteria. Half of the time I didn't even understand what I was saying, but I loved making my brothers and sister laugh more than anything in the world. Then it would be their turn.

"Pat, your breath is so bad it would make shit cry!" Jenny would squeal, igniting another round of convulsions. We would do this until our bellies ached, or until Pat pinned one of us to the ground saying, "Who's the greatest in the world?" or, "Who's the best on the planet?" and not letting up until we agreed it was him. We were dancing with danger all the while because our parents would never approve of us using such vulgar language *or* having so much fun. On an unfortunate night, Pat's door would fly open and hit the wall behind it with a loud CRACK and Captain Jack would be standing there, his beady eyes burning with rage; his breath heavy with exertion. He had limped all the way down the stairs just to yell at us, goddamnit, and he was going to make us pay.

"What in the hell is going on down here?" he'd roar, his broken hands waving in the air. His fingers were as mean and gnarled as his personality; maybe worse. They looked to me as if someone had broken every one of them by bending them backwards and letting them set any which way. They were painful to look at.

His was a rhetorical question that none of us—not even Pat—would have had the nerve to respond to.

Depending on how many drinks he'd had, Captain Jack would either stare us all down menacingly before turning back around and hobbling away with a look of complete disgust or he'd grab the nearest one of us and start swinging. Even when you got an ass-whooping for pulling rank, it was totally worth it.

GROWING PAINS IN THE ASS

"We're leaving in fifteen minutes," Mom told me with a look. "And don't you dare cross that street."

She didn't need to say that last part; not crossing the street was a non-negotiable rule, always. The white house with the green shutters sat on the bend of a busy throughway, and cars were always flying by at crazy speeds. Mom was sure it wasn't a matter of if but when one of us would get run over.

One of my front teeth had a painful, visible abscess and we were heading to see a dentist. My Aunt Gloria, a dental hygienist, had been the one to notice it in the first place and insisted Mom take me in promptly. Since I'd never been to a dentist before, I knew it was a special occasion and had donned the single dress I owned, a flowered corduroy knee-length number.

With fifteen whole minutes of freedom before me, I ran outside and hopped on my rusty old tricycle, the one with the ribbed platform between the two back wheels. You could go a lot faster if you stood back there on one foot and pushed yourself with the other, so that's what I was doing.

Rachael's pesky little brother Paul was outside their house, just two doors down, playing in the yard with a hose. I said hi or I waved or I did whatever a five-year-old girl does when she sees another kid she knows, and Paul said hello back the way only a six-year-old boy ever would: by aiming that hose right at me, in all my dentist-dress glory.

I pushed by him as fast as I could, but he got me anyway.

I wasn't soaked, but I still knew I was dead meat. At that point I had two choices: I could turn around and ride back past that little jerk, effectively giving him the chance to finish the job, or I could cross the street and stay out of his reach.

The split-second debate in my brain went like this: *Which one would make her madder, breaking the rules or getting soaked, having to change and being late for the dentist?* It was a hard call.

I chose wrong.

Right about then, something caused Mom to look out the kitchen window — maybe it was mother's intuition; maybe she caught a flash of that flower-powered dress out of the corner of her eye — and she came out shouting.

"Get into this house right now," she bellowed, scaring the wits out of me. *Oh, no! She'd seen me!* I hopped off my tricycle and ran to the front door, where she stood looking like an angry teakettle about to explode.

She grabbed me by the arm and dragged me to the kitchen, where she ripped my underpants down to my ankles. Usually it was Captain Jack doling out the blows, and old-fashioned rear-end beltings were rare. His style more closely resembled street-fighting — think punching, pummeling, thrashing — than open-palm spanking.

"I *told* you *not* to *cross* that *street*," Mom shouted, emphasizing every other word with a good, firm whack across my naked backside.

It stung like crazy but she was right. She *had* told me that, not once but probably a million times, so I couldn't even argue. I was trying to protect my pretty dress but that didn't matter a lick. Neither did the fact that I'd looked carefully both ways before I crossed that street, or even that I had tried — I really had — to pick the less-awful of the two terrible choices I'd had before me.

She spanked me pretty good that time, and in the end I decided not to be mad at myself. Either way I was getting an ass-whooping that day. By that point I already knew that some things in life just weren't fair, and this was going to be one of them.

The dentist wore a white lab coat and barked commands at me in a thick Asian accent. "Move your hands! Stop crying! Hold still! Move your hands!" He twisted and tugged and I cried and screamed until he yanked out my tooth with no anesthesia at all, not even a swab of topical Novocaine.

I figured I deserved it.

THE WAITING GAME

Dad was supposed to be there at three. He hadn't shown up last time, or the time before, but this time he was coming. We just knew it.

I'm not sure how long we sat on that curb, the four of us spit-shined for the occasion. I know we were there early, just in case. And then we'd wait and wait. My stomach would start to ache and I'd watch every last car go by, thinking maybe he got a new one or had forgotten where we lived. We'd sit there hoping and praying until it started to get dark and Captain

Jack came out to do the cattle call. Then we'd all try to hide our heartbreak as we slunk into the house.

I was eighteen before my dad told me that almost every single time he was supposed to come get us for a visit, Mom would call him at the last minute and tell him we were sick and would have to reschedule.

As much as it hurt, I believed him.

JENNY AND THE WEEDS

Rachael's brother Paul—the same one who sprayed me in my dentist dress—was a bossy little jerk. "You have to do what I say because I'm way older than you," he'd tell me. And since he was six and I was only five, his was a pretty airtight argument.

"Hurry *up*," Paul snapped at me. I was walking too slowly for his liking, and the canyon in all of its infinite possibility was waiting. I picked up my pace, closing the gap between us and Jenny and Rachael up ahead.

"Hey, do you think you guys could help me? Please?" The guy was around thirty (my best adult guess, in retrospect) and he looked worried and frantic and the four of us kids stopped in our tracks. He was clean-cut and had all of his teeth which meant he wasn't a bum, so we weren't scared of him. We were just curious and concerned.

"I lost my dog," he told us, panting, and he proceeded to describe the little guy. Of *course* we'd help him, we told him, excited to have an adventure, a purpose. Why wouldn't we be?

There were no cell phones back then to call someone and ask permission; no internet teeming with news stories of children who'd been kidnapped or killed by perfectly average-looking sociopaths; no Safety Town summer camps to teach us about "stranger danger"; no sternly repeated warnings about *guys who pretend to lose their imaginary pets to lure unsuspecting children into God-knows-what sort of danger*. A dog was missing, and we were being called on to help! What a glorious and grown-up honor!

"Why don't we split up, so we can cover more ground," he suggested. He nodded at me. "We'll go this way, and you guys go that way." He pointed down the path he wanted the other three to follow.

"I'll go with you," Jenny told him, hands planted on her hips to let him know it wasn't up for discussion. Jenny was in charge of me and she knew that our mom would have a conniption if she let me get separated from the group. The man agreed to take her instead and they took off in the opposite direction.

Rachael, Paul and I called and called for that stupid dog — Rex or Rover or some other cliched, make-believe dog name — until our throats became hoarse. After covering our own tracks twice, we decided to return to the spot where we'd split up. I was hoping Jenny would be there playing with that scruffy little fluffball, but no such luck. I started calling for her, and soon Rachael and Paul joined in. We didn't know the lost dog guy's name, so it was just JENNNNNNNNNN-NNNNNNY over and over and over.

It came out of nowhere, a terrifying choke.

"Run, Erin! RUN!"

It was Jenny. But where? We looked up, down, around; confused. Then there was a rustle in the brush and she was hurtling toward us, a blur of hair and earth and tears. We stood stock-still, paralyzed and confused.

"Run, *now*," Jenny cried as she sped by. In an instant I took it all in: her words filled with rage and fear; her cheeks streaked with dirt; her clothes and hair covered with weeds poking out in every direction; her eyes wild with I wasn't sure what. The three of us took off behind her. She was sprinting so fast the distance between us got wider and wider until she was barely a speck. I had no idea my sister could run so fast. We followed her the best we could, up and out of the canyon and all the way to Rachael's house, where we found her heaving and panting in the shade of the side yard. She ordered Paul to go inside and instructed him not to say anything to anyone about anything or we'd all get in big trouble. Paul obeyed.

Jenny was fighting back tears and holding her private parts.

"What happened?" we asked, incapable of imagining.

"He hurt me," she whispered, crying. She couldn't look at me or Rachael.

"How?" we asked. "Where?"

"My back and... down there," Jenny said. "It hurts, it really hurts." She was on the ground now, curled on her side into the fetal position. Her arms and legs were scratched and bleeding.

"Do you want us to look?" Rachael asked. Jenny shook her head no.

"We can't help you if we can't see what's wrong," Rachael said softly, sounding so much like a grown-up. A choked sob came from my sister. We waited.

"Please, Jen?" Rachael pleaded. Finally my sister nodded, still not looking at me or her friend. Rachael knelt down so I did the same. I watched as she gently pulled my sister's flowered cotton panties down and pried her knees apart.

What I saw could never be unseen or forgotten.

It was a mess. There was blood and weeds—so many weeds—coming from my sister's privates and some other cloudy liquid I couldn't recognize or identify. I don't know how long Rachael and I spent trying to rid Jenny's parts of debris, but it felt like hours. We worked in silence, the only sound Jenny's occasional muffled gasps of pain. I tried to imagine what on earth had happened to her, but I just couldn't. My brain was a merciful blank.

When we told her we were done, Jenny sat up. Her face had no emotion at all.

"I'm going home, and I'm going to tell mom I fell playing out front," she said sternly. "You guys stay outside. I'll take a shower and come back out. We're not going to tell Paul or anyone else about this, *ever*. Got it?" Rachael and I nodded. This was after the broken leg, so we both knew the sentencing would be harsh if our parents found out we'd gone back into the canyon.

Rachael and I followed Jenny back to my house in silence. The pain was evident in my sister's limp; in the curve of her back and the tight set of her jaw. We never spoke of that day again.

JESUS IN MY ROOM

My parents were not religious, to say the least. In fact, the only time the name *Jesus Christ* was spoken in my house was when somebody did something wrong. And since there were four of us and Captain Jack despised us all, that was often. Similarly, God was evoked almost exclusively in the context of "Goddamnit, get your ass in here right now!" A handful of times Grandma Blanche did take me to church, where they spoke of this mysterious Jesus person who was so nice he *died for our sins*. I remember the mass being sort of peaceful but also painfully long and boring. Sometimes I'd see Grandma Blanche praying, but as I understood it, God was a word you used when you were really pissed at someone. Whether it was because of this or despite it I'll never know, but it was around this time that Jesus came to visit me.

As far-fetched as that sounds, I can only say what I saw. There was no question who it was or why I was allowed to see him. All I can say is that it happened.

I was sound asleep in my basement bedroom when something woke me up. I opened my eyes and rather than being engulfed by darkness, half of my room was drenched in sunlight. Puffy white clouds stood out against the bluest sky I'd ever seen, and the air smelled distinctly crisp and fresh. Yes, the smell of the air in my bedroom was *that profound* that it nearly took my breath away.

But that wasn't all.

He was there. *Jesus was there*, in my bedroom. He hovered directly above me, within arms' reach; ethereal and glowing with what I immediately knew was pure and infinite love. There was nothing ambiguous about it. Very clearly he said, "Do you remember me?" And I replied simply, "Yes." I'm not sure why I remembered him, nor did I spend time wondering about it; I just gave into the fact that I did.

"Do you still love me?" Again, I softly but clearly told him that I did.

"I will always be with you and love you." He said this with so much conviction that it literally would have been impossible not to believe him.

"Okay," I said. (Yes, I replied to Jesus's vow of eternal love and protection with the verbal equivalent of a shrug. I was five; cut me some slack.)

And just like that he was gone, my room thrust back into darkness. Still I felt absolutely no fear. I basked in the knowledge that I was loved to my core by the reason I existed in the first place. I wondered if Jesus was like Santa; if he visited everyone once a year or maybe even every night. I fell asleep replaying our conversation over and over in my head—*I will always be with you and love you*—wrapped in a feeling of peaceful contentment I'd never experienced before.

In the morning, I told my mom that a man had come to my room during the night. I did this the way you'd tell a parent about the potato bug you squished on the sidewalk at school or the squirrel you saw on the fence: casually and definitively. After all, it was true, and I was just in there sleeping when it happened. I certainly hadn't done anything *wrong*.

Mom completely freaked. In retrospect and in her defense, her reaction was one that any parent would have if their child said they'd seen a man in their bedroom. She wanted to know if I knew him; if he was with anyone else; if he'd touched me or hurt me. Instinctively I knew I could not tell her the truth—*Of course I knew him and of course Jesus didn't hurt me!*—so while she continued to fire questions at me, I tried to think of a way to backpedal my way out of this.

What exactly had he said and why hadn't I yelled and screamed or come to get her? Had Patrick left the back door unlocked? Was it one of Pat's friends? IT WAS, WASN'T IT? She fired her angry questions at me and I shrugged and bit my tongue. I was frying in the hot seat, paralyzed with fear. I'm not sure how long the interrogation went on but eventually she let up on me, convinced by my silence that it had been one of my brother's stoner friends sneaking in looking for something to steal or a place to crash. The inquisition turned to Pat, allowing me to escape the spanking I had been positive was coming. The next day my grandpa was at my house installing deadbolts on all the basement doors.

So much for my "handy" stepdad.

I knew it that night on a cellular level and I am still sure of it to this day: it wasn't a dream, and it wasn't my damaged, deprived psyche fabricating a divine drive-by. Jesus was there with me, wanting me to know that while this life of mine was not going to be easy, he would be with me through the very difficult times I would endure in the very near future.

He was right about that not-being-easy part. I believe he came that night because he knew the crazy train was about to come barreling through my life, and he wanted me to know that he would always be with me. Trust me, I needed that.

DOWN THE HATCH

We were moving, they told us.

In the sovereignty ruled by Captain Jack, you took your orders like a good soldier: you accepted and then you obeyed, and you never, ever questioned.

Our new house was in Westminster, which was thirty-five minutes away over the Vincent Thomas Bridge. It was a nondescript single-story in an unremarkable neighborhood, but it was on a street called Stardust Drive which I thought sounded fancy, plus it had brand-new green shag carpeting in almost every room *and* a pool. I didn't know how to swim or even own a bathing suit, but everyone else seemed to think this was a big deal, so I tried to be excited, too.

My parents borrowed a friend's truck for the move. Mom was already at the new house trying to organize things and Pat, Kelly and Jen were allowed to help load boxes, but every time I tried to get in there I was told to "get the hell out of the way!" They'd pack that truck to the gills and then Captain Jack and Pat would run it all over and unload it. After I don't know how many trips, finally there was enough room in the back of the truck for three kids, so we piled in.

(*I know.* But this was the 1970s. Back then you could strap your children to your roof and drive to Alaska and back in a snowstorm and nobody would have batted an eye.)

Patrick, being the oldest, sat in the truck bed with me and Jenny while Kelly got to ride shotgun with Captain Jack. I had my back up against the cab window, Jenny was leaning against the hatch and Pat was perched on the wheel well. With his gorgeous, waist-length hair flowing in the wind, he looked like he was filming a Breck shampoo commercial up there. We were having the time of our lives. It was summer, we were about to see our brand-new home for the first time, and we were getting to ride in the back of this huge pickup truck. It was turning out to be one of the greatest days ever.

Gaffey was a wide street that ran north and south through San Pedro. We sped past sandwich shops and pizza parlors and tackle stores, Jenny leaning back on that hatch and hooting with her fists pumping in the air. She had her knees pulled up to her chest and was tapping her feet with excitement and she had the best smile I'd ever seen. I wanted to freeze that moment in my mind forever. It wasn't often that we felt anything like pure joy.

Maybe we hit a bump, maybe we didn't. It happened so fast it was almost like nothing happened at all—except a loud BANG. One second Jenny was there, the next second she wasn't. The hatch wasn't there either. There was just a big, empty opening at the back of the truck bed.

"STOOOOOOOOOOOP!" Patrick shouted before my brain could even process what had happened. I could see Kelly's face in the window, confused and terrified, as Captain Jack slammed on the brakes. He parked right there, half in and half out of the road, and jumped out of the truck, red-faced and furious. Limping faster than I would have dreamed was possible, he reached Jenny, who was sitting stunned in the street as cars swerved and honked all around her. It was a miracle she hadn't been run over.

Captain Jack was on fire.

"GODDAMNIT, JENNY, SEE WHAT HAPPENS WHEN YOU SCREW AROUND? YOU HAD TO RUIN IT FOR EVERYONE, DIDN'T YOU?"

He dragged her back to the truck and all but threw her back into the back, not letting up on his rant even long enough to ask her if she was hurt.

"YOU'RE LUCKY YOU DIDN'T CRACK YOUR SKULL! NOW SIT YOUR ASS DOWN AND KEEP YOUR MOUTH SHUT! AND THAT'S ABOUT THE SIZE OF IT!"

Nobody said a word for the rest of the trip. Jenny would smile her brave smile at Pat and me when she could see Captain Jack wasn't looking at her in the rear-view mirror. Since my back was to the cab, I would smile back. I prayed that my sister's legs would stop bleeding quickly, because that was only going to remind him what had happened and then he'd never let it go.

We finally got to the new house. It was much smaller than the white house with the green shutters with no fireplace or any kind of view, but it had nice grass so that made me happy. It seemed to me that all the people I knew with nice grass had happy homes. Maybe the house on Stardust Drive would turn out to be one of those after all.

STARDUST

SLIP SLIDING AWAY

Everyone seemed happy about the move, especially Mom. Maybe they'd made some money on the sale of the white house with the green shutters, or it could have been that Captain Jack's new janitorial job paid better than sporadic handyman gigs. Whatever the case, Mom didn't have to stand on her feet all day at McCowan's anymore weighing bags of grapes and calling for a cleanup on aisle three. I was happy for her about that.

After we were mostly unpacked and settled in, she spent her days doing stay-at-home-mom things like cooking and cleaning. She was a wonderful seamstress and would make darling clothes for my dolls. She and the Captain were still drinking heavily, but Mom almost always waited until he came home to start. We were away from Grandma Blanche and Grandpa Sam, so my parents didn't have to fight about them "popping over unannounced" and "judging their every move" all the time anymore.

Yes, life at Stardust was going to be good.

Even our cats Peanut and Sinny (short for Chosin, the battle that had crushed Captain Jack's leg and his spirit, because *that's* a sweet name for a cat) adjusted easily to their new surroundings. They were lifetime lovers and Sinny would pop out a litter every few months. We'd keep the kittens until they were weaned, then take most of them to the grocery store in a box and give them away. Sometimes we'd get to keep a kitten or two; Peewee was a favorite. This was before Bob Barker started ending every episode of *The Price is Right* with "don't forget to spay and neuter your pets," so maybe nobody in my house even knew that blocking their breeding was an option.

While the family felines sat in the sun and bathed one another and made babies, my siblings and I were clamoring to swim in our brand-new pool all day every day.

That first summer at Stardust was close to magical. My Uncle Jimmy's wife Gloria surprised me with an adorable floral hand-me-down bathing suit she'd gotten from one of her neighbors, and as long as Pat was home we were allowed to swim. I was supposed to stay in the shallow end because I had never had a lesson and couldn't even doggy paddle.

Pat would spend hours in there with me, encouraging and teaching. He was endlessly patient. He also was a total daredevil hell bent on turning me into one, too.

"Okay, Erin," he taunted one blistering day. "You ready for the slide?"

If you grew up in the '70s, you can picture this slide. Every house with a pool had the same one, which was a metal ladder with exactly seven rungs attached to a faded strip of blue plastic or fiberglass or whatever the slipperiest substance on earth was at the time. These slides were mounted to the ground (if you were lucky) at the edge of the pool, and anyone could tell you they were rickety death-rocket-launchers of unbridled fun.

But was I ready to go down one? I must have looked as terrified as I felt.

"I'll catch you, I swear it," Pat promised, over and over.

"She'll never do it," Kelly and Jenny goaded.

"Yeah, she will," Patrick told them. "Come on, Erin. Just do it."

Finally, I caved. Patrick could get anyone to do just about anything. I climbed that wobbly ladder and sat down. I already was an expert at not showing my feelings, which was fortunate because I really wanted to cry.

The top was so high.

The drop was so steep.

There was so much cement.

I still didn't technically know how to swim.

Everyone was watching me.

I might die.

I gave myself a little push anyway.

My breath caught in my throat as I flew down that slide like a buttered cannonball. Patrick was waiting at the bottom to catch me just like he promised—the diving board was in the deep end, and the pool at the slide end was only ribcage deep on him—but the force of me hit him like a freight train and pushed us both to the bottom of the pool.

I was drowning in panic and water. The chlorine burned my eyes. Poor Pat was trying to get his feet beneath him so he could thrust my head above the surface, but I was flailing and scratching at him like a drunk, slippery Edward Scissorhands. Instinctively, I took the deepest breath I knew how.

I was still underwater.

Breathing water feels horrible, for the record.

I sputtered and clawed and kicked and gasped. Somehow, despite my frenzy, my brother managed to stand up and pull me out of the water.

Patrick held onto me until I could breathe again. He was bleeding from where I'd scratched his face and chest and I felt bad about that, even though he was screaming obscenities at me.

"Easy with the goddamned knives!" he shouted. I yelled back that it was his fault for almost killing me.

"Want to go again?" he heckled, surely thinking I would say no when in fact my answer was *hell yes.*

Because I had to. I had to do it again right then or I knew I never would. I told everyone to back off. I took a few laps in the shallow end to make sure I could doggy paddle, then I got out and climbed that damned ladder. I didn't even pause this time. The minute my butt hit the slide I was airborne.

It was the most exhilarating feeling I'd ever felt—and it lasted about one whole second. I sliced through the water and popped back to the surface, grinning like a fool and anxious to do it again.

I loved everything about that slide, most of all the part where finally—finally—*I* was the one in control.

DINNER WAS A SHIT SHOW

It was time to upgrade from my wobbly tricycle to a real bike, Patrick said. But I was scared. I knew for certain that Mom and Captain Jack would kill me if I fell and broke my arm or chipped a tooth.

"I won't let you fall," Pat promised. And he didn't. He held onto the back of my yellow flowered banana seat and ran alongside me until I said I was ready for him to let go. I caught on right away and for the first time in my life, I actually could keep up with Pat and Kelly and Jenny. It was the greatest feeling.

There was a giant green bush at the end of our driveway, just by the sidewalk. It had cute, tiny white flowers on it and knife-sharp, inch-long thorns. Every time I'd get near it Patrick would yell, "Be careful, that bush is ALL STICKERS!" and I'd get so nervous and wobbly that half the time I'd drive straight into that fiery mess as if it had some sort of magnetic pull. Talk about manifesting your fears.

Still, those hours the four of us spent on our bikes were some of the happiest of my entire childhood. Eventually, though, Captain Jack would come out and do the cattle call and we'd have to come in for dinner. This was not our favorite time of day.

Dinner in my house was a shit show for a multitude of reasons, most of which centered around Captain Jack and his insatiable need to control and degrade us. As I saw it, the table rules in my house consisted of these:

1. If you didn't like what was being served, tough shit. You sure as hell better keep it to yourself.
2. Gagging got you nothing but an ass-beating. *Now shut up and eat.*
3. You couldn't touch your milk until all your food was gone (so much for washing that crap down). The only thing that was going to push the last bite down was another bite.
4. You'd sit at that table until you'd eaten. Period.

I had friends whose parents supposedly had that "sit at the table indefinitely" rule, too, but none of them actually enforced it. My parents did. I can't count the times I slept—or tried to sleep—all night long seated at that table. In the morning I had two choices: I could eat the ice-cold meatloaf or liver and onions... or I could go to school hungry.

I went to school hungry a lot.

Mom often fed us kids first, separate from my stepdad. He said (out loud, to us) that eating with us made him sick to his stomach. Even still, he'd hover nearby while we tried to choke back our food, either shouting at us to *"put the goddamned milk down and eat,"* or muttering insults under his breath. Dinner was a delight.

"I WANT TO EAT TOO!" was his battle cry, delivered in his meanest voice with the intention of making us feel as guilty as possible. Most of the time, Mom just let his comments slide, but every once in a while she'd get really mad and let him have it.

"You know what? You make *me* sick!" she'd shout. "You could have eaten with them but nooooooooo, you have to sit there and make them feel awful while they try to eat! What in the hell is the matter with you? Let them enjoy their food! You can eat by yourself!" And then all holy hell would break loose. If they were drinking, plates would likely fly. I sometimes wonder how it's possible that the only time a neighbor ever called the cops was the time Captain Jack threw Jenny out the window.

DANCING WITH THE SCARS

Kelly kept falling off his bike. Mom would tell him to stop being so clumsy, and I'd tease him about being a better bike-rider than he was, even though I was only seven and he was eleven. He was always covered in bruises and would complain constantly about how badly his leg hurt.

"Then quit falling! What's the matter with you? Now put an egg in your shoe and beat it, kid," Mom would scold, in a mildly joking way. Before too long it got so bad that Kelly couldn't even put any pressure on that leg and would cry in pain at night in bed. Even still, the only time *any* of us had ever been to the doctor was the time Jenny broke her leg, so when Mom said she was making him an appointment at the military hospital in Long Beach, I was more than a little surprised. The hospital seemed awfully drastic for a bruised leg.

Mom and Captain Jack took Kelly to the hospital together, which was disconcerting enough considering my stepdad wasn't particularly fond of any of us. Even worse, they came home without him. The doctors had drawn his blood and run a bunch of tests and decided to keep him overnight. This couldn't be good. What if there was something seriously wrong with the hilarious, silly-song-singing older brother I adored? There couldn't be.

But there was.

Kelly's white blood cell count was off the charts; there was talk of a tumor. I had no idea what a tumor was, but his was big and it was making my mom cry all the time. She had two moods: grief and hostility. The latter frequently felt directed at me and Jenny and Pat, as though what was happening to Kelly was because of something we had or hadn't done. I felt confused and alone, and the anxiety that was always there inside me grew like a festering blister threatening to explode.

My brother was tested for everything under the sun and sedated for pain with something called morphine. We waited. Finally, there was news: the tumor in Kelly's right leg was malignant. His doctors recommended transferring him to Children's Hospital of Orange County because it had a renowned oncology department. I didn't know what the words malignant or oncology meant, but I knew that Kelly wouldn't be coming home anytime soon.

My mom was taxed with the unpleasant task of telling our father—who we only saw once or twice a year and it was always ugly between them —that my brother had cancer. Dad and the topless table dancer came to the house so they could all talk about it. Of the many things I couldn't begin to fathom at the time, my parents sitting in a room together and *not* fighting was at the top of the list.

My siblings and I were not allowed at that meeting. In fact, nobody told me or Jenny or Patrick anything at all about what was going on. Our only sources of information were the snippets of conversation we'd strain to overhear after they'd sent us all to bed early, as if we'd done something wrong. I'd just about kill myself straining to hear their whispered words, but as soon as I did I almost always wished I hadn't. The news was never good.

The more I heard, the more scared I became — not only for Kelly, but for myself, too. Of all my siblings, Kelly and I were the most alike. I looked like him, I acted like him, I thought like him. If this could happen to Kelly, surely it was just a matter of time before it happened to me. There was nobody I could talk to about my fears; nobody to tell me any different.

Kelly's cancer was spreading. They were going to cut him open with a knife, starting at his tailbone and going all the way up his spine. I knew this because Jenny and I heard Mom and Captain Jack talking about it when we were supposed to be sleeping. At one point, the doctors wanted to cut his leg off from the knee down, but then they changed their minds. How could that even be a should-we-or-shouldn't-we thing? I decided right then that doctors were terrifying monsters; hell-raisers in white coats who were unpredictable and savage. I didn't want to even make eye contact with one, ever. At any moment they might say *Oh yeah, she has it too*, and want to cut something off of me.

When Mom said I was going to be allowed to visit Kelly, I was terrified of what I was going to see. But not going was not an option.

The hospital had an amazing waiting area filled with fun toys for kids and I remember wishing that I could just stay there and play. But far too quickly a nurse came to lead us to Kelly's room, and I had no choice but to follow her on wobbly legs. Orderlies pushed a parade of the sickest-looking kids you ever saw — they were bald and bruised and bandaged and lots of times missing limbs — up and down the hallways and I knew this was no place I wanted to be.

We entered Kelly's room and I tried to hide my shock. He looked so small, so sick he was almost green, so weak and lethargic, so *different*. I wanted to unsee all of it. I wanted to run out of there and never look back. I wanted to scream, *What have you done to Kelly?* But I couldn't do anything but stand there and try to pretend I wasn't horrified to the core.

After surgery Kelly was allowed to come home for two days. I was happy that he was home, and equally relieved that we didn't have to go to that smelly, scary hospital again. He showed me the scar on his back. It went all the way from the top of his neck down his spine and it was wide, too. I wasn't expecting that at all. Kelly was so strong and stoic and had almost an "it's no big deal" air about that scar, which was probably his way of protecting me because anyone could see it was intimidating and serious. It was puffy and I asked if I could touch it — a move I immediately regretted. Everything about that thing terrified me, and all I could think of was Frankenstein. I didn't know real people could have scars like that. I thought they were for zombies.

Kelly came home with a walker, which was the best thing that had happened around our house in a long time. It had wheels and handles on the sides you could hang onto and a seat you could sit on if you wanted to. Boy, did I want to! I rode it all over the house, down the driveway and around our pool. I pushed Kelly to China and back on that thing, too. I wanted my brother, my lookalike, my buddy, to have as much fun as he possibly could before going back to that awful sickhouse.

He moved slowly now, and he told me his back hurt a lot. I knew that already, because you can't have a scar like that and not hurt a lot. In a blink, Mom was taking Kelly back to the hospital. How could it be time for him to leave when he hadn't even gotten that sterile, chemical hospital-smell off him yet? Jenny and I kissed and hugged our brother and told him to get better soon.

At some point my real dad bought Kelly a tape recorder to pass the time. I heard Mom and Captain Jack say something about how this was a good idea because Kelly could record his voice and we'd "have it later." I thought they were talking about that recorder. When he felt well, he'd sing all his favorite songs into it, "Miss American Pie" and "Delta Dawn" and "Jeremiah Was a Bullfrog." It would be hilarious if he taped that "whistle while you work" song, I thought, but then I figured he was probably too smart for that—although at this point, he might have gotten away with it. You could get away with a lot when you were sick, it turned out. Kelly didn't have to do any schoolwork in the hospital, even though he was in fifth grade and they were starting on that fifty states project. I heard that was really hard and you didn't want to get behind on it. I even asked Kelly's teacher why she didn't send home any homework.

"Aw, he can just make it up later," she told me with a sweet smile. I thought she must be a really nice teacher. I hoped I would have her in fifth grade.

LOOK WHAT THE CAT DRAGGED IN

Sinny was an angry, cross-eyed blue point Siamese we picked up at the pound. She was moody and spastic and not the tiniest bit picky about where she slept or where she gave birth. Often I'd come into the kitchen to find her curled up in the cast iron pan that lived on the stove. It was one of those giant, deep ones that stayed warm for days after you used it, and she was so cute in there that I guess it never occurred to any of us to be horrified by the decidedly unhygienic sight of a cat sleeping in the cookware.

Once in the middle of the night, I awoke to what I was certain was a baby crying in my room. I sat up to see Sinny delivering a litter of kittens right there on the foot of my bed. There were two, tiny wet blobs already, and I held my breath as she bore four more right before my eyes.

At the time, it was the most incredible thing I'd ever witnessed. But that sight was trumped a year or so later when the very same cat jumped up on the stove and into her favorite cast iron skillet and brought six more fur-babies into the world. Right there, in that frying pan. I'd like to say we never used that thing again, but that would be a lie. That was Mom's good pan — the one she made eggs and fried chicken and pork chops in — and it wasn't like cast iron frying pans grew on trees.

GOING HOME

We were going to see Kelly in the hospital. All of us: me, Jenny, Patrick, Mom and Captain Jack. They usually said that was "too much" for him, so I wondered if maybe he was feeling better. As much as I was dreading the hospital itself, I missed my brother terribly and was excited to see him. It had been several weeks.

We made our way through the lobby and as we approached the play area my parents told us to stop. I thought, *gladly*, as my nerves were always a wreck when I was there, and my stomach was already in a knot.

There were some kids in the play area. One was chatting with his parents on the couch and I knew he was sick because he was in his pajamas. There was a girl sitting in her walker by the large beanbag cushions that littered the floor—she looked pretty normal, so maybe she was visiting, too—and there was another super skinny kid in a black wheelchair with something terribly wrong with his eye—

Whoa.

No way.

Oh my God, no.

OH MY GOD OH MY GOD.

NOOOOOOOOOOOOOOOOOOOOOOOOOOOOOOOOO OOOOOOOOO.

It was Kelly.

The kid in the black wheelchair was Kelly.

A sad, unfamiliar, so-very-sick version of Kelly. If not for the tiny flicker of my brother in this stranger's cute, crooked smile, I might not have recognized him at all.

His face looked like it was melting on one side and his left eye was sunken in and closed shut. He wore the pajamas he'd filled out perfectly when he got them for Christmas, but now they were hanging off his bony frame. My mind spun completely out of control. *What was happening? What had they done to Kelly? That's not my brother. I don't know that kid at all. It's too much. I can't be here. I'm so scared. I'm scared of this place. I'm scared of KELLY!!!*

In that moment, I didn't feel guilt or compassion or even love; I felt nothing but pure, irrepressible fear.

"I'm scared, Mama," I whispered. "Can we go?" She gave my arm a rough squeeze. I should have been thinking of him—my poor, sweet, sick brother—but all I could think of was myself, and how badly I wanted to leave. I looked at Mom, pleading with my eyes for her to understand; to take me the hell out of there. She gave me her own look right back; the one that said "I MEAN IT. NOT ANOTHER WORD, OR ELSE." I knew that look well, just as I knew what would happen if I defied it.

So I said nothing. I tried not to stare. I pretended I was invisible. I don't ever remember being so afraid. We stayed for what felt like an eternity while I imagined Kelly's sickness invading my body and taking it over completely.

When Mom finally gathered her things and said goodbye to Kelly, relief flooded through me like hot lava. I waved goodbye softly to the stranger in the wheelchair, not wanting to get too close or show my terror.

Sometimes Jenny and I would cry quietly at night in our bunk beds. We'd get in trouble if we made any noise so we kept our tears to ourselves and waited for Mom and Captain Jack to give us an accidental update. Then one night we heard them say something about Kelly coming home. *Kelly was coming home?* We didn't see how that was even possible, but for a magical moment in time my sister and I were filled with blind hope. After all, miracles happened sometimes! We lay in our beds singing *"Kelly's coming hooooome, Kelly's coming hooooome,"* quietly and joyfully.

It turned out we had it all wrong. They hadn't said Kelly was coming home after all. Our brave, sweet brother was *going* home. To our Father in Heaven.

Patrick told me later that Kelly would talk to him in the hospital. Pat said Kelly knew he was going to die and he asked if it was going to hurt. He told Pat he was afraid but he knew it was his time. Kelly Frederic Ellis Cole was just eleven years old when he left this earth on September 17, 1972, almost a half-century ago. I still miss him every day.

THE BLADE RUNNER

Things went from awful to worse after Kelly died.

None of us kids went to the funeral. This wasn't discussed or up for debate; it just was.

Mom was either drunk or sedated around the clock, and most days could barely drag herself out of bed. She ate next to nothing and grew weaker and weaker. The woman who used to make fresh bread from scratch and sing and dance around the kitchen, almost overnight had lost the ability (or the will) to perform basic everyday functions like brushing her teeth. My brother Patrick, fifteen and grieving just as hard as she was, couldn't take it anymore. I heard him yelling at my mom one morning—"*You still have three kids who need you!*"—and an hour later he told me and Jenny goodbye for good. I watched him walk down Stardust Drive in his Hang Ten t-shirt, brown cords and Wallabees, his long, golden hair swishing behind him.

Pat went to live with his best friend Jeff's family back in San Pedro. I would have given anything to go with him.

But I couldn't go anywhere, because I was dying myself. I had no symptoms and no medical diagnosis, mind you—I'd still yet to ever visit a doctor myself—but I knew that my demise was certain and imminent. I was just waiting for the ball to drop. My every waking thought was consumed with how it would happen, when it would happen, where it would happen. Morning and night I would look in the mirror and study my face. Was my eye sinking in? My face beginning to droop? My skin getting paler? Yes, all of it. I was sure of it. I was a ticking time bomb waiting to explode.

Seven years old and scared stiff, I did the only thing I could think to do: I tried to be perfect. I cleaned the house, kept my voice down, and pasted the brightest smile I could muster on my face whenever I was around Mom. I told her I loved her. I complained about nothing. I didn't want to give her one more thing to feel sad about. I would have done anything in my power to make her happy—or at least less miserable—but it was as if Mom had died with Kelly.

Captain Jack noticed my efforts and rewarded me by nicknaming me "Miss Sweetness and Light." Not in a nice way.

Mom stopped eating altogether and became so feeble that most days even walking to the bathroom was more than she could bear. Her legs withered to spindly sticks and her belly puffed out like a pillow. Captain Jack came home with two bedpans and showed me and Jenny how to change them. It wasn't like he could come home from work to deal with that shit—literally.

It was me and my sister against the world. We fed ourselves, got ourselves ready for school and put ourselves to bed. The first time I poured Raisin Bran into a pair of bowls and saw those flakes crawling with ants, I asked Jenny what we should do. I'd never bother Mom with something so trivial, even though anything else we had to eat in the house was rotten or stale. I knew no more food was coming until my grandparents could make it over to the commissary and then deliver it, because Captain Jack never went to the store unless it was to buy booze. And that was about the size of it.

"Just eat around them," Jenny told me. So that's what we did. They were black ants, and they were spicy and bitter. (You couldn't eat around *all* of them. It just wasn't possible.) The aftertaste was horrible and lingered until your next meal, too, and you never really knew when that would be. But we didn't have a choice. So Jenny and I would power through breakfast, trying our best to dodge those squirrely little suckers with our spoons. Every few bites, one of our faces would screw up in disgust, and then we'd laugh and try to see who could come up with the most hideous face. We could make a game out of just about anything.

Sometimes Mom would keep Jenny home from school to help her around the house or run errands. On one of those days, she gave my sister a grocery list and sent her to the market.

Milk, eggs, butter, booze.

Jenny was ten.

My sister obediently trotted down to Alpha Beta with a big bag slung over her shoulder. Like an efficient little assistant, she grabbed a cart and made her way about the store collecting the items on her list and putting them in it before sauntering over to the liquor aisle. With the skills of a Parisian pickpocket, Jenny slipped a fifth of vodka into her bag, just the way Mom had told her to. Then she proceeded to the checkout.

It was going to be easy as pie, Mom had assured her. Mom hadn't factored in a store employee becoming curious when a ten-year-old went down the booze aisle and spying on her to see what exactly she was doing.

Jenny was busted.

The store manager called Mom to tell her that her daughter had been caught shoplifting vodka. Mom did the second unforgivable thing of the day: she threw Jenny under the bus, acting shocked and appalled that her ten-year-old was stealing, and alcohol of all things. The manager explained that the cops had been called and that they would be bringing Jenny home. Mom thanked them and hung up.

There would be no apologies, of course; no admission of guilt or pleas for forgiveness. Mom said exactly nothing to Jenny about the incident. And then Captain Jack came home.

Maybe Mom wasn't planning to mention it at all, but when the Captain announced he was going to run up to Alpha Beta to grab some vodka, Mom stopped him with her third inexcusable act of the day. He couldn't, she explained, because Jenny had gotten into some serious trouble there. And then she told him the whole story. Her version of it, anyway.

Surely my stepfather knew that Jenny was only acting on command; that the real blame belonged on my mother. But he would never lift a hand to his wife, and *someone* was going to pay for the fact that he couldn't get his booze right-this-minute. Once again, it was Jenny. And unfortunately for her, sober beatings were usually worse than drunken ones.

During these bleak and interminable days, my sister and I would take turns coming home from school at lunchtime to clean Mom's bedpans and make her a lunch that she would never eat. The daily debate was *should we dump out the poop and pee first and then eat or vice versa?* There was no good answer. This was our new normal.

"I just want to die," Mom would moan, day after day. "Why can't I just die?" She begged us to help her; to bring her a knife so she could end her rotten, wretched, worthless life.

It was the worst form of torment I'd ever endured.

"Please don't say that," Jenny and I would plead. "We need you. We can't lose you, too. Please, Mommy, please!"

The more we sobbed the angrier she'd get.

"GO GET ME A KNIFE! NOW, DAMNIT!" she'd yell at the top of her lungs.

Eventually, we would bring her the knife. We had no choice. Because that's what you do; you obey your parents.

On the knife days, I'd say goodbye to her after lunch just like I always did and pretend I was going back to school. Then I would stand outside her door and listen and wait; wait for my mom to kill herself. With the weapon I'd just handed her.

I was in second grade at the time and my teacher was named Mrs. Moore. She had beautiful stick-straight brown hair and she wore fancy dresses and block heel shoes that made the best clinking sound when she skipped across the asphalt. Mrs. Moore had been my sister's teacher the year before and Jenny said she was the sweetest person she'd ever met. Jenny was right. Mrs. Moore would always ask me what I had for breakfast and bring me snacks I'd never seen before, like Pop-Tarts and Apple Jacks. I could tell that she liked me a lot, because she paid extra attention to me in class and never said a word to anyone when I didn't come back after lunch. Sometimes I wondered if she might be a sign that Jesus was watching me like he said he would. That thought got me through a lot.

Eventually Mom had to be admitted to a psychiatric hospital. That's not what Captain Jack called it. He told us she was going to a place for people who were sad because they had a kid who died, which I guess was a nice way to put it. But at the time I wanted to kick and scream and shout in her face, *You still have me and Jenny! What about us?* I never got the chance. One day I came home from school and she was gone.

Obviously, Captain Jack wasn't capable of—or remotely interested in—parenting me and Jenny on his own, so Grandma Blanche left Grandpa Sam at home alone and moved in with us. Even though they were both ancient, they got around remarkably well. Grandma made dinner and went grocery shopping and packed us big sack lunches. I'd never had anyone do that before — I was lucky to have the fixings to make myself a PB&J on stale Wonder Bread — and the irony was now that there was so much food around, I could barely even eat. My stomach was tied in a perpetual knot. And honestly, I was so grief-stricken about Kelly and worried about my mom and sad about Pat being gone, how could I possibly enjoy a turkey sandwich and some Cheetos? I wanted to ask someone if Mom was dying, but I was too scared of the answer.

Mangy, stinky Pierre the poodle was dying, too — only not fast enough. His fur was matted so badly it would bleed in spots, and he couldn't walk even a few feet without shitting. *All over the house.* We'd be running to the door to let him out, hoping to prevent the next pileup, and slide out in the last one. Crap literally was everywhere and impossible to see and sidestep on that awful green shag, so invariably we'd track it from room to room. The scent was permanent and pervasive.

Poor Grandma Blanche was trying to keep up with everything — me and Jenny, Captain Jack and his moods, the house, the pool, a nonstop parade of poop. I came home one day to find her on her hands and knees, trying to fish fresh droppings out of that rug. She was crying.

"How could you let it get this bad?" she asked Captain Jack. He started yelling something at her and then she was yelling back and I couldn't take it, I just ran out the back door.

I sat on the edge of the pool and tried not to cry. The pool itself was no longer a sparkling oasis. It was half-filled with a dark and terrifying tangle of leaves and algae and God-knew what else. If any of us had fallen in, you'd never have found us. I sat there and stared into the pitch-black pool of hell, wondering where was my mom, where was Pat, and most of all… where was Kelly?

FRUSTRATION

May 12/73

Frustration thats what
I feel today and alot
of disappointment in
the girls. mom
came last night
and I'd asked them
to pick up there
rooms and hang
there clothes and
clean the mess
they made in the
kitchen. When Don
and mom got home
everything was a
mess. I can't
stand this bed
any longer yet
my legs will
not straighten
out. I don't know
what to do. Cant
think straight this
morning.

IT'S A DOG EAT DOG WORLD

G randpa Sam would bring us boxes of food from the commissary as often as he could and Grandma Blanche was a decent enough cook, but sometimes she just had to make do with what we had in the house—which was never much. A regular dinner staple during this time was iceberg lettuce with a glob of Miracle Whip on top. Sure, it said "salad dressing" right on the jar, but I felt like that was taking it a bit too literally. Jenny and I used to joke that they named it "Miracle" Whip because it was a miracle anybody could eat it without puking.

And then there were her brussels sprouts. In Grandma's defense, this was long before the little mini cabbages were trendy restaurant fare, sauteed with pancetta or drizzled with a thick balsamic glaze that actually makes them palatable. My poor grandmother would simply throw a bunch in a pot of water, boil them until they were mush and then plop them onto your plate, a stinky, wet mess. I can gag just thinking about it.

I learned something amazing about brussels sprouts by accident one night when I tried to feed a forkful to smelly old Pierre. Even that mangy mutt knew better than to eat them and promptly spit that bite back out onto the awful green shag carpet—where to my great delight, they blended in perfectly. From that point on, I had a new tactic: toss them under the table, one brussels sprout-blob at a time, and then bury them in the pile with my feet. I'd always go back and fish them out the next day when nobody was looking and flush them down the toilet. I remember feeling so proud as they circled the bowl. *I had done that.*

I had figured out how to make my life better all by myself.

WE NEVER KNOW

continued 7-2-73

He told me he wouldn't say anything but he couldn't keep quiet and it all came out at the table. I just got in my chair & came to bed closed the door and let them scream, amongst my tears. No sense eating when your all upset. I just get sick and throw up anyway. I shall read & take my mind from it. It always calms me. I'm tired anyway & want to get a good nights sleep. Be good my little boy. I miss you. I won't be afraid because I just know you will be there. Don't mind dying when you have someone waiting. Maybe this will be the night. We never know.

BOOMERANG

10:00 pm. [handwritten] Sun. 13, 74. He will be 13. Born Fri. 13, died Sun 9-17, Birth in 74. Sun. 13, 74. Miss you so much Kelly, so does Dad, can't write now too many tears. Can't see.

I t seemed like Mom was gone forever. Days turned into weeks, then a month, then I don't even know how long. I lost all sense of time. Jenny and I walked around the house like naughty dogs waiting to be kicked and hoping not to accidentally annoy anyone, which you could do just by breathing. Captain Jack was a solid, constant ten on the tension scale and would snap at us for the smallest of transgressions. He'd mumble under his breath about how sick we made him if he heard us laughing or saw us playing a game. When we were watching TV and he came into the room, he'd change the channel as if we didn't exist.

Not existing was the best-case scenario when it came to our stepdad.

He got meaner and meaner. Part of the problem was that we couldn't even go make him a drink, because Grandma Blanche obviously had put her foot down. Although I never heard a word of the conversation, she must have made it clear that there would be absolutely no drinking on her watch because all of the booze that normally lived out in plain sight just disappeared into thin air.

Now the well was dry and Captain Jack was stone-cold sober and not at all happy about it. More than ever the man needed a drink. A big, stiff one. Without it, we got the undiluted, uncensored, worst-case version of him, twenty-four seven.

Mom called us once from the hospital. She told us she wouldn't be allowed to call again, but she would see us soon. *What was soon? A week? A year? Whatever it was, it wasn't "soon" enough.* I would lay in bed at night and shake like a wet cat. My anxiety was through the roof.

The silver lining in all of this was that Jenny and I no longer had to come home at lunch and do the bedpan dance. It was fun to stay at school and play on the playground during recess and feel almost like a normal kid. Not that anyone treated us like we were normal. We'd always been different, although I never understood why. When Kelly was alive, at least my sister and I had a safety net. He'd threaten to kick anybody's butt who messed with me or Jenny. Without him, my sister in particular got picked on a lot. Kids would call her names and sometimes even gang up and beat her up. I'm not saying she asked for it necessarily, but Jenny had something inside of her that just seemed to be a magnet for trouble. That never, ever went away.

The walk from school to Stardust Drive was far. I made the afternoon trek alone because Jenny got out of school later than I did. Sometimes it was good being the first one home, sometimes it was bad. Today it was good.

No, it was better than good; it was spectacular. Magical and magnificent, even. It was as if somebody had thrown me a giant surprise party—with balloons and presents and maybe even pony rides—and I hadn't even realized it was my birthday.

I walked in to find Mom sitting in her wheelchair in the kitchen.

She was back. Nobody had told us a thing. As far as we knew, she wasn't coming home for another year, or maybe never.

But there she was. I could hardly believe my eyes. She looked amazing, relatively speaking. She was still sad, I could see it in her eyes. But they were clear and she was sober and she was *back*; the buffer I needed between me and Captain Jack. Even at her most absent or melancholy or inebriated, having her there was better than not having her there by at least a million miles. Despite everything, I loved her. She was my mom.

They tried to kill her in the hospital, she told us. She was so glad to be home, and she never, ever wanted to go back. She was the same devastated human who had left and she was weak and needed a wheelchair. But she was alive and she was home. Who was I to complain?

Grandma Blanche said she'd stay for the rest of the week, while Mom got settled back in. I stayed glued to my mother's side while Grandma Blanche told us stories about her nosy neighbor, Mrs. Gorsky. Apparently, she was the Mrs. Kravitz of the neighborhood and was always gossiping about the other neighbors.

"Never trust a person who gossips," Grandma Blanche would say. "They'll be gossiping about you next." She had lots of other good advice, too. My favorite was, "Eat dessert first, because you never know if you're going to live through the meal." Whenever I stayed with her I would remind her of this, and she'd give me a treat before dinner.

The night Mom got back we had something close to a celebration. Grandma made an especially nice dinner and even Captain Jack seemed close to happy. Jenny and I told Mom over and over how great she looked, which made her smile. I felt better than I had in months. For a few magical hours, I even forgot that I was dying.

THE MISSING PONYTAIL

om's home.

M I remember waking up and having that thought floating in my brain before I even opened my eyes. School mornings were always a scramble, so I jumped out of bed instead of lingering there like I sometimes did. I wanted everything to be perfect for her.

Jenny obviously did not share that desire.

Mom had a rule that as long as Jenny and I insisted on having long hair, we would wear it in a ponytail to school. This order was as interconvertible as it was mysterious. To this day I'm not sure if it was simply a means of controlling us or something else entirely. Regardless, for some unfortunate reason my pot-stirring sister decided that on that day of all days she was going to defy this decree and wear her thick flaxen hair spilling down her back. Maybe it was a simple fashion choice, or maybe it was an intentional act of rebellion; a *fuck you* to our mom for leaving us at all, or for staying away for so long. Maybe Jenny just wanted to see if Mom had been bluffing all those times she promised that if we tried to go to school with our hair down she'd chop it right off. I still don't know and I can't imagine I ever will.

Don't do it, I wanted to hiss at Jenny that morning when I saw her free-flowing mane. *Please, don't.* Not only because in our house shit had a tendency to roll downhill, which meant when Jenny got in trouble I was often dragged along for the ride. I just didn't want her to rock the boat. Mom was back. We had a chance for a fresh start! Why would she do anything to jeopardize that? I hated conflict with all of my might and never would have dreamed of inviting drama into my life on purpose. But Jenny was a wild horse, the sort you could never tame.

Our mother called us into her room to say goodbye. Jenny entered timidly, as she should have. I followed, holding my breath.

Mom got one look at that hair and she flipped. In a split second, she was the crazy, ranting, screaming, out-of-control lunatic I had grown so deathly afraid of.

"WHAT HAVE I TOLD YOU FOREVER?" she roared, Joan Crawford without the blood-red lipstick and fake upper crust accent.

Jenny started bawling immediately. She said she'd put her hair up right this minute. She said she was sorry. Really, super sorry. She didn't mean—

"TOO LATE. GET THE SCISSORS," Mom screamed at Jenny. "GO GET THEM! NOW!"

Even if you were the sort of kid to push the envelope, you did what Mom said, or else you'd have to answer to Captain Jack later. So Jenny did as she was told.

I hovered in the corner, trying to be invisible. Jenny came back with the scissors.

Mom swept Jenny's hair into a makeshift ponytail and just started sawing at it, right where the rubber band would have been. *There was no way Jenny was going to start doing whatever she damn well pleased*, Mom hissed, *not as long as she was around.* Golden strands fell to the floor and covered my sister's shoulders, which heaved with her silent sobs. Jenny's hair was spaghetti-straight and thick, a beautiful horse's mane, and Mom really had to hack and chop at it. She was nearly breathless from the effort.

Why did you have to do it, Jenny? I thought, squeezing my eyes shut. *Why do you always have to go asking for trouble?*

Grandma Blanche tried her best to fix that mess, evening out some especially choppy spots here and blending in a few bald patches there, but there was not much that could be done. Jenny still looked like a scarecrow, with hair sticking up this way and that and none of it making any sense. I remember thinking that if Mom knew how badly the kids at school were going to tease Jenny, on top of how much abuse she'd already taken, she probably wouldn't have done it at all.

How could she not know that? I wondered.

How?

COOKING WITH COOL WHIP

Grandma Blanche couldn't stay forever, she told us. Grandpa Sam needed her, too. She'd come back and visit all the time, though, and we were welcome at her house whenever we wanted. We had our mom back now, and everything was going to be okay.

Except it wasn't.

Mom spent all day every day in the dark, depressing dungeon that was her bedroom. She had blackout curtains on the windows, so no matter what time you went in there it took your pupils several seconds to adjust to the complete darkness. I'd pop in to visit with her out of guilt and we'd talk for a few minutes, but I couldn't wait to get out of there and play in my brightly lit room with my dolls.

"Can I do anything for you?" I asked my bedridden mother one afternoon, hoping she'd say no so I could get the heck out of Dodge.

"There's a Cool Whip container of chicken broth in the freezer," Mom told me wearily. "Could you take it out and put it on the stove for me?"

She might as well have asked me to arm wrestle Freddy Krueger, but I said yes anyway.

It was an old gas stove you had to light with matches, and I was terrified. I'd seen what happens when the gas builds up and the oven doesn't turn on right away and you get that big flaming *whooooooosh* in your face and you accidentally light your hair on fire. You never had to worry about me playing with matches.

It probably took me a dozen tries but somehow I did it. Then I put the container on the burner and ran back to her room. We chatted for a while but I was nervous so I went back to the kitchen, just to make sure I'd done everything right. It looked okay to me, so I relaxed a little. I went back into her room and hung out with her some more. After a while she told me to go back in and check on the broth.

I couldn't believe my eyes. I had done exactly what my mother had asked me to do; I'd put the Cool Whip container on the stove. But obviously I'd done something wrong, because it was a train wreck. The plastic had melted not just on and around the burner but deep down into its deepest recesses. When it imploded, the broth had put out the flame, so parts of the plastic had already begun to cool and harden. It looked like one of Dali's melting clocks drowning in a puddle of broth, but worse, because it was all my fault.

I was furious at myself. All I wanted was for my mom to be happy. I wanted her to feel like I could take care of her, and that she could rely on me to get her through this. But none of that was true. I had completely let her down. I was an epic fail. A complete disaster as a person. Not that any of that mattered. When Captain Jack found out about this, he was going to kill me anyway.

I ran back to Mom's room in a panic and told her what I'd done. She was incredulous.

"You didn't put it in a pan?" she scolded. I shook my head.

"Never mind," she said. "I should have done it myself."

She was completely defeated; I could see that clearly. She wasn't angry at me for what I'd done, she was angry at herself for not teaching me how to do it properly, or maybe for not having the interest or the inclination to get up and do it herself. But no matter how badly she felt, I was sure I felt worse.

"What should I do?" I pleaded, my anxiety roaring to a head.

She told me to let it cool for a few minutes and then to "do whatever I had to do" to get it cleaned up, fast. I wasn't exactly sure what that meant, but if she thought I could handle it, then I was going to have to.

I paused at her door on my way out.

"Are you going to tell him?" I asked, afraid of her answer. But she shook her head, no.

"Now hurry up," she told me, making scooting motions with her hands.

I did as I was told and then I lived in greater fear than usual for several days. I kept waiting for Captain Jack to notice that I looked especially guilty, or that something in the kitchen was amiss. But he never found out about it.

A SAD CAT TALE

12-20-74 Fri

My little cat
Pee Wee became
ill about 2 days
ago & thought
he was still pout-
ing over his
father comming.
home.

He became worse
this morn &
(1:15) just died
in my arms
with one last.
cry. Dont know
whats wrong
with him. Im
sick. I loved

him so much.
He is laying here
beside me and
I just can't
move him. Dont
know what Im
going to do till
someone gets
home.

MAYBE A DEAD GOPHER WILL HELP

With Mom almost completely bedridden and Patrick gone, I was forbidden to go into the backyard. But when you're seven years old and you see something in the pool and you're positive it's an animal that's going to die if you don't get out there and save it, all bets are off.

I had to break the rules, I just had to. Mom was the biggest animal lover on the planet. She'd understand. She might even praise me.

I crept outside and gasped. I was right! It was a gopher and he was bobbing in the pool. I moved without even thinking, grabbing the skimmer that was lying by the diving board at the deep end and dragging it over to where the little guy was swaying in the water. I tried to scoop him up but the skimmer was heavy and unwieldy and it was harder than I thought it would be. I'd get that thing under him and try to lift it, but he'd roll this way or that as I tried to scoop him up, edging just out of my reach each time I almost had him. I'd move over a few feet, extend the pole a little farther and try again. I felt the familiar sense of panic rising. His little life depended on me. I was desperate to save him.

He started to sink, and I managed to get the skimmer beneath him. I lifted it as carefully as I could until his tiny body emerged from the water. I'd done it! He was in pretty bad shape but I was positive my mom could save him. I wasn't sure what she was going to do—perform mouth-to-mouth on him maybe?—and I'd have to wake her up to do it, but then she'd be so happy and so proud of me for helping save his life that it would be worth it.

But there wasn't much time.

I couldn't pick him up because if he was hurt and scared he might bite me and then I'd get in trouble for getting bitten. So I ran with that dripping wet skimmer straight into the house, through the shit-filled living room and down the hall to Mom's bedroom, where she was fast asleep. There was a perfect spot for him, right on the white pillow next to her head. I proceeded to plop the wet net, gopher and all, onto her bed and started to shake her.

"Mom, wake up! You have to save it! It's going to die, please save it," I cried, not imagining for even a minute anymore that she might get mad, or that I'd done anything wrong. Instead I was thinking, *I did it! I got him out! She's going to be so proud of me. Maybe we can keep him as a pet. Maybe now she'll even love me.* We were always saving lost or hurt strays. I secretly thought my mother liked animals more than she liked people.

Mom opened her eyes groggily and took it all in: the hysterical child, the sopping bed, the motionless rodent.

"WHAT THE HELL IS THAT?" she shrieked. "*AND WHY IS IT ON MY PILLOW?*"

I explained how I'd fished him out of the pool and that he was hurt and that I knew she could save him. Mom let out an exhausted sigh.

"Get it off my pillow," she told me. "It's dead."

"Are you sure?" I asked, not wanting to believe this. She told me yes, she was sure. Then she told me to put him in her trash can, take the whole thing outside and then dump him in a planter.

"You know you're not supposed to go outside," she reminded me as I was leaving, even though she'd just told me to go back out there herself.

I turned back to her and nodded.

"I know," I told her. "I'm sorry."

She closed her eyes, and I did what she told me to do.

It turned out that dead gopher didn't make her love me, although in her defense I doubt a live one would have, either.

Much later, after we'd locked the door on Stardust Drive for the last time, our family would get a good laugh out of the dead gopher story, especially me and Jenny.

PHIL IN THE BLANKS

> Ate sour milk with cereal didn't notice till I tried to drink the rest. Made me sick.
> Got thru lunch ok and no more vomiting just a headache.
> Dinner over ate too much. mended a little & tried to match sox.
> Losing battle.

When Kelly was alive, one of the things he always did with Mom was garden. It was sort of their thing. They both loved nothing more than digging in the dirt and planting neat little rows of seeds and marveling over the literal fruits of their labor. If she had asked me to garden with her, I'd have loved it too; pretty much anything she liked, we liked. But gardening was for her and Kelly. They were planning to build a big one at Stardust Drive, but then Kelly got sick and that plan — along with everything else in the universe — went to hell in a handbasket.

When Kelly got better, Mom had promised, they were going to plant a garden like you wouldn't believe. It was going to have tomatoes and strawberries and onions and watermelon and it would be the most amazing garden anyone ever saw.

One thing was clear: that garden was never going to happen on Stardust Drive. That place was toxic and we needed to get out of there; everyone knew it. The shit-stained living room, the bedroom of death, the backyard cesspool... it was all too much. There was no coming back from that much decay and despair; no way to make it sanitary or even suitable again. The only thing we could do was leave it behind.

It was settled. We were going to sell the house.

I was beside myself at the thought of a fresh start.

My parents met with a very nice real estate agent from Walker and Lee. His name was Phil, and he wore a brown polyester leisure suit just like the ones I'd seen in the Sears catalog. He was very handsome and had nice hands and a kind voice. It was a Saturday and we'd done our very best to tidy up, but there's only so much perfume you can put on a pig. The place reeked of Pierre's incontinence and bedpan spillage and misery, but to Phil's great credit, he managed to hide his revulsion. We took him on the not-so-grand tour, during which I knew with every ounce of my being the poor man was struggling not to puke. Then my parents offered him the listing.

Maybe Phil had eight kids of his own to feed. Maybe he felt sorry for us. Maybe he was just *that good* at his job; the kind of guy who could sell ice to Eskimos. For whatever reason, he accepted this flatly unappealing challenge.

"We definitely have some work to do," he mustered without gagging. Phil proceeded to make my parents a handy to-do list: they were going to need to replace all of the carpeting, throw a coat of paint on all of the walls to give it a fresh, new-house smell (hint, hint) and drain and fix the pool, which surely would be one of the home's greatest selling features.

"Let's get her in tip-top shape and get her sold," Phil said. I was skeptical. Who was going to do all of these things anyway? My parents? Me and Jenny? Phil? I didn't think it would be possible to make that house look or smell fresh or new, no matter what anyone did to it. But the adults all shook hands and agreed that this was a fine plan. Phil said he'd be back in two weeks' time to check on the progress.

I could have seen what happened next coming from three states away.

Phil came back, just like he promised. My parents hadn't done a single thing to put his plan into action. The carpet reeked; the pool festered; the walls were as grubby as ever. Phil didn't seem all that surprised. Clearly if anything productive was going to happen at that house, he was going to have to take the reins. So that's exactly what he did.

Phil told my parents that he knew people who could get the work done. He said he would take care of it all and even pay for it himself if they agreed to pay him back with the proceeds from the sale.

Who could say no to that?

Again true to his word, Phil sprang into action. A new set of strangers showed up each day with sponges and paint buckets and power tools. They ripped up that carpet first and left the floors bare while they painted the walls. I thought this was so cool, because it looked like we had a skating rink right in the living room. Phil was there every other day, overseeing the work and offering suggestions. I wondered if he had children, or if he ever got mad. I tried, but I just couldn't picture Phil getting angry or upset about anything. If he did have children, they were lucky and I was jealous of them.

One day I came home from school at lunchtime and I got to the house at the same time as Phil. I led him inside and went back to check on Mom. She was asleep as usual, so I returned to the kitchen where Phil was. He started asking me questions:

Did I come home for lunch a lot, what sort of stuff did I like, what did I usually eat, was I hungry right then? I probably mumbled a bunch of nonsense, because what did it matter what I liked or if I was hungry anyway? We had what we had, and whatever it was, it wasn't fresh or much.

"Let's see what you've got," Phil announced anyway, and started opening cabinets. He pulled a few hard heels of bread from the fridge along with a wilted head of lettuce and some mayo and mustard, and looked around hopelessly; a condiment-salad sandwich would have to do. He arranged this sad entree on a plate and cut it in half, looking almost guilty. I pointed to a cabinet way up high, out of my reach. Sometimes my parents hid snacks up there, I told him. He found a bag of chips and added a healthy serving to the plate.

I smiled at this near-stranger, thinking how good it felt to be cared for, and how strange it was that he barely knew me at all, and yet he liked me way more than Captain Jack did or ever would. I didn't have the words that day to tell Phil, but it was a special lunch I would never forget.

RAMONA

IT MAY OR MAY NOT BE EYE STRAIN

Feel good this morn, feel good about house on Ramona. Don will take pictures today & sign more papers. Sat up by myself and know I'm stronger.

3:30 Headache back, must be too much eye strain or something in the medication.

CAROL BURNETT
SAVES THE DAY

hil did everything he said he was going to do and more, and Stardust actually was shaping up to be the cute house I remembered moving into. The yard was lush and green and the pool sparkled, although we weren't allowed in it anymore. There was beautiful cream-colored carpet throughout the house that smelly old Pierre wasn't allowed to set a single paw on. We made him a bed in the garage and he was perfectly fine with this arrangement. Why hadn't anyone thought of this before?

Mom was shaping up somewhat as well. She was strong enough to get out of bed to go to the bathroom even, so the bedpans — and the stench that went with them — were gone, too. The house on Stardust Drive finally was livable again, so naturally it sold about five minutes later. That was the way things worked with us. There was never a time we moved into the nice house and it stayed that way. Everything got ugly, always. We'd only ever try to make it nice again when it was time to go.

We moved the last box out of the house that taught me how to swim, rescue dead gophers, deep-clean melted plastic out of a stove, remember to keep my hair pulled back, and say goodbye to both of my brothers. So much had happened in our two years there, it was hard to wrap my eight-year-old brain around it all. I tried to imagine a new family living there but I just couldn't. Would the mom drink or sleep all day? Would their dog shit all over that brand-new carpet? Would anyone die?

Our new house on Ramona Place was twenty-five minutes away, up and inland, in Garden Grove. Ramona featured a string of nearly identical, mid-century cinder-block homes in various states of disrepair with matching chain-link fences. Without numbers, you might not even know which house was yours. It wasn't like you could just say, "It's the sad-looking one with the flat roof and the broken-down carport."

There was only one bathroom for the four of us to share, but since both Kelly and Pat were gone, Jenny and I got our own bedrooms for the first time ever. The backyard was huge, nearly a quarter-acre filled with dead grass, dirt, and a tall planter box that was completely choked with weeds. The front yard was just as bad, which made me sad and embarrassed, even though every other yard in the neighborhood was in the same, sorry state.

We moved in with a month left of summer. Jenny and I spent all day every day cruising our cul-de-sac and the one around the corner. It was very much a family neighborhood, so on any summer night there would be a dozen or more kids running around the street playing dodgeball, kickball, tag or hide-and-seek. That was the most fun we would ever have with other kids. Of course, Captain Jack would still do the cattle call every night—even though we were down to just two cows—and after the neighbors got over their shock, everyone would mimic him in real-time.

"JEEEEEEEEENNNNNNNNNNNNNNY! EEEEEERRRR-RRRRRRRRRRRRRIN!" the whole entire neighborhood would howl, hands to their mouths like a megaphone. It was hilarious.

Mom was still mostly wheelchair-bound but she was getting stronger. She launched a quasi-health kick (as much as one can down bottomless bottles of booze and still be "healthy") and began grinding her own meat and baking bread and making dinners for us again. She discovered Adelle Davis and became a devotee, buying every one of the nutritionist's massive books. Adelle believed that most medical problems could be cured or avoided entirely if you just chose the right foods. She was extremely anti-processing and pro-exercise and vitamins and I guess she didn't have much to say about alcohol because as into Adelle as Mom was, the liquor never seemed to stop flowing.

Salt, Mom believed, was the enemy. It's what made her bones ache and her joints swell and her stomach balloon up like a giant marshmallow. *It certainly wasn't the alcohol*; that thought never entered her mind. She became obsessed with counting sodium and calories, monitoring and documenting her every morsel. Days were deemed good or bad depending on how restrictive she'd been with her diet; how much deprivation she had been able to force herself to endure.

In the evenings she and Captain Jack would sip their drinks and watch *Gunsmoke* and *The Carol Burnett Show*. I became an expert at mimicking the comedian's booming voice and hilarious faces and let me tell you, my variety-show antics came in handy when the night started heading south. No matter how much they drank, those two never tired of a good show.

AT LEAST THE VICE
PRESIDENT CARES

ARCHON

May 14, 1973

Mrs. Jeri Blomgren
5521 Stardust Drive
Huntington Beach, California 92647

Dear Mrs. Blomgren:

Thank you for your recent letter addressed to El
Molino Mills inquiring about CaraCoa Carob bars. Archon
Pure Products is the parent company for El Molino Mills;
your letter has been referred to me for response.

The CaraCoa carob bars have a calorie content of
approximately 150 calories per bar. I am sorry that
we do not have an analysis for its sodium content, but
we do not add salt to this product. However, there may
be residual sodium in the natural carob powder which is used
as a base.

The fats which are used in this product are not hydro-
genated, but have a natural level of saturation which gives
the bar its excellent melting characteristic and mouth feel.
We also use milk solids in the bar which may contribute to
the sodium content and provide a small amount of protein.

I regret that I cannot be more helpful than this, but
perhaps you can discuss these results with your physician.
I certainly hope that your health can improve so that you
can carry on more effectively as a mother.

Sincerely,

William E. Marshall, Ph.D.
Vice President Operations

/agg

Archon Pure Products Corporation
9595 Wilshire Boulevard, Beverly Hills, California 90212
(213) 278-1600

KUNG FU DRIVING

Every Sunday we'd drive from our new house in Garden Grove over the Vincent Thomas Bridge and back to San Pedro to have dinner with Grandma Blanche and Grandpa Sam. Captain Jack would watch the football game on TV while Grandpa listened to baseball on his transistor radio and my mom and my grandma cooked. They'd chat about gardening and pattern-making and recipes, and Grandma would have a stack of interesting articles she'd clipped out of the paper or her magazines to give to Mom. It was almost always a good time, until the drive home.

We had a little blue Toyota truck with a camper shell on the back—surely it came with the thing and wasn't purchased to keep us from falling out—and Jenny and I got to ride in the hard, dirty bed. Captain Jack would drive straight from his parents' house to the nearest liquor store to stock up on his cans of Club, which he would proceed to pound the entire way home. Jenny and I couldn't hear their conversations up front and they couldn't hear ours. All we knew was we were almost always in for a wild ride.

Each time we left San Pedro, my grandpa gave my sister and me the same three things for the trip home: a pack of Dentyne gum, a bag of Cheetos and a can of root beer or 7-Up. We were enjoying these treats in our isolated compartment one memorable evening, singing songs and looking out at the lights on the bridge, when all of a sudden the truck swerved hard to the right—probably Captain Jack trying to open one of those cans—throwing me and Jenny into a tumble and spilling our drinks and snacks everywhere. Bits of crunchy, cheese-flavored cornmeal bobbed in the sticky soda that was sloshing up and down the truck's grooved bed, and I was positive we were going to go right off the edge of that bridge and plunge to our deaths.

But somehow, Captain Jack managed to regain control of the truck. When Jenny and I realized we were going to live to tell the tale, we shrugged and started scarfing down the soda-soaked Cheetos, laughing because they were still crunchy. They tasted amazing; salty and sweet and tangy all at once, and we ate every last crumb. It had become a challenge, almost a game, to see if we could make the best of whatever fresh hell our stepdad dished up. In my head, I shouted at my miserable stepdad between bites, *Don't try to ruin our fun… we'll just have more! And that's a promise!*

Other drivers were constantly cursing at the Captain about his squirrely steering, but one night things escalated to a whole new level. A guy in a little green four-door rode next to us for blocks, pointing and yelling angry obscenities at Captain

Jack. Jenny and I could see him out the camper windows, and we thought this was the funniest thing we had ever seen. Captain Jack just swerved along, mostly ignoring him.

We stopped at a light. The guy pulled up right next to us, threw his car into park, jumped out—he had his whole family in there—and started kung fu kicking Captain Jack's door like he was Bruce Lee. Over and over he kicked, all the while shouting at my stepdad about his *"crazy goddamned driving"* that was *"going to kill somebody for chrissakes!"* He was gun-raging mad; like Captain Jack before a blackout, and it was scary but also awesome. *Finally, FINALLY, someone was giving it back to Captain Jack!* After a good minute of thrashing, the karate guy turned around with his back to the truck and we thought he was finished, but he gave that door one more good back-kick with his heel before storming off. Jenny and I were dying. We almost didn't want it to end, but then the guy was in his car and the light changed and my stepfather sped off, no doubt spewing a string of profanities of his own.

When we got home, Captain Jack's door was dented in so bad that he had to climb over the center console and get out Mom's side. Jenny and I made sure to hide our amusement. He hadn't killed us with his driving, but he'd have murdered us for that for sure.

DIGGING, DRINKS AND DIAMONDS

5-1-74 Wed.
Just walked to the
store with Erin push-
ing the wheelchair.
I made it but just
barely. Don't think
I'll try that again
for awhile. I can't
believe the price of
groceries I hardly
bought anything.

"I know what we can do today," Mom said in a playful, conspiratorial tone I barely recognized. It was a Saturday and it was just the two of us, and Mom told me she was ready to start Kelly's garden. She wasn't just ready; she was *excited* about accomplishing it. I couldn't remember the last time she was excited about anything, so I thought this was a great sign.

I ran around gathering things — gardening gloves, rakes, hand hoes and shovels — while Mom fixed herself a drink. She was in and out of her wheelchair — Kelly's old one — at this point, but she asked me to get it because she thought she'd be more comfortable sitting while she worked. Before she could sit down, I pushed the wheelchair onto the patio. The patio was basically a cracked concrete slab with an ugly awning above it, but Mom had filled it with dozens of planters she'd collected over the years. They were tall and short, skinny and fat, and filled with a variety of plants that she was pretty good about watering every week. The green was always a welcome sight when I stepped outside.

Mom got herself situated in her chair so that I could wheel her over to the overgrown planter. Sweat trickled down my cheeks — it was hot out there already — as I pushed and I panted and struggled to roll my 135-pound mother over the rough, rocky earth. I might have been fifty pounds myself at the time, dripping wet. Even though I regularly pushed her to the grocery store a mile away with no problems, the terrain back there was making the task impossible. Eventually Mom offered to get up and walk the short remaining distance, probably to keep from spilling her drink. I pushed the empty chair over to the edge of the raised garden bed and she sat back down.

It was a mess. Tall, tough vines shot out of the cement-hard earth at every angle and danced above my head. These weren't wimpy little wisps of sourgrass or delicate sprigs of dandelion that slide out of the ground with a tiny tug. Oh, no. These weeds had hard, thick trunks and the sort of roots that grew deep and spread wide and held on for dear life. There was no way in hell we were going to make a dent in that backyard disaster with just our small tools, so Mom sent me back to the shed for the big shovel. She wasn't even angry. In fact, she looked so happy sitting there in the sun with her drink I wanted to freeze that moment in time forever.

When I returned she was working away at one end of the planter with her small hand shovel so I started at the other. We decided we'd meet in the middle, and see who could make the most progress.

It was grueling work, and no job for an eight-year-old or a lady in a wheelchair. We sawed and hacked and dug in that dirt for hours before we agreed to call it a day. I was disappointed in our progress—we weren't even close to the middle—but Mom was in such a good mood and I'd enjoyed spending time with her so much I told myself this just meant we would get to do it again. And again. And probably again.

It wasn't until several drinks later, when Mom was cooking dinner, that she realized what she'd done.

"OH NOOOOOOOOOOOO," she sobbed.

"What in the hell is the matter now?" was Captain Jack's compassionate reply. I can still see the disdain all over his face.

"My diamond ring! It's gone!" She put her hands up to her face and screamed into them. "Damnit, what the hell could have happened to my ring?" Her milky arms—the vitiligo she'd suffered for decades had stripped them nearly completely of color by this point—were bony and shaking. Mom had lost the one thing of any value she owned—the single piece of jewelry that had been spared in Jenny's Robin Hood adventure at the white house with the green shutters—out in that awful tangle of weeds and dirt.

It was dark outside, so obviously a search would have to wait until morning. We never had money for batteries so there was no use having a flashlight around. I was always amazed when I'd go to other kids' houses and they had Indian Joe or that cymbal-clapping monkey or some other battery-operated toy. I thought that was such a waste, because once the battery was dead so was the toy. In my house, you might as well throw it away.

I heard my mother cry herself to sleep that night. If there were any soothing sounds or sentiments coming from my stepfather, which I highly doubt, I missed them.

At dawn I dashed outside, determined to find Mom's ring. I combed through every square inch of that dirt and dumped out the bags we'd filled and sifted and sorted for hours, but it was no use. Her ring was as good as gone.

THROTTLED

I t didn't take long for me and Jenny to find out that Ramona was in a rough area, to say the least. And once we started school, it became crystal clear that the kids in our neighborhood, the ones we had been so excited to play kickball and tag and hide-and-seek with over the summer, were basically a bunch of thugs.

Still, they were our neighbors, so we all took the same bus to school in the morning and we all rode the same bus home in the afternoon. Mornings were usually fine, because lots of moms took their kids to the bus stop every day. That meant there could be a parent around at any second, so everyone was on their best behavior. It was the afternoons that could kill you. Or I should say, get you killed.

I'd wind up getting beaten up dozens of times by the same three boys, but the first and last were by far the most memorable.

They lived on Ramona, too, but at the very end of the cul-de-sac. We all got off the bus at the same spot that first day, and I'd walked about twenty feet or so — just far enough for the bus to pull out of sight — when the boys started shouting at me and calling me names from behind. I ignored them and kept walking. Out of nowhere, Timmy Labonte, who was in my grade, ran up and punched me in the stomach, knocking me to the ground. Before I could even process what was happening or why, his two little henchmen joined in. They took turns delivering blows until the three of them decided they were finished with their unprompted pounding and took off laughing down the street.

I was equal parts hurt and humiliated, and I held my stomach as I cried my eyes out all the way home.

My mom's reaction was rarely the one you were hoping for. That day was no exception.

"What's the matter now?" she asked wearily when I walked in doubled over and sobbing. I could tell I was inconveniencing her with my pain and tears, that she would prefer I just say "nothing" and go to my room, but I couldn't help it. I told her the whole story.

"What did you do to them to make them do that?" she demanded. I promised her that I hadn't done a thing, I was just walking home, but she just kept shaking her head and saying, "Well, you must have done *something*."

Message received: this was my problem, not hers. It was my fault it was happening, and my responsibility to figure out how to stop it. And that was about the size of it.

The beatings went on for weeks. I tried getting off the bus in different spots, but those boys would almost always find me, whether they had to catch up to me or wait for me. I told the bus driver—a tough, no-nonsense lady who'd been doing the same route for decades—what was happening, and I could tell right away she wanted to help me. She made them sit at the back of the bus and let me ride up front. Then she'd open the door at our stop and shut it quickly after I'd gotten off, basically giving me a little head start before she released the hounds. If I ran really fast, sometimes I could make it home without being pummeled.

One day the boys weren't on the bus ride home. I was relieved until we got to my stop. The bus driver must not have seen them hiding behind a bunch of cars, but as soon as she drove away, there they were: my trio of tormentors, with their smug faces and balled-up fists. I took off running, but one of them grabbed the hood of my jacket and pulled me backward. *Here we go again.* I tumbled onto the asphalt, where they kicked and punched me until I was just a bloody heap on the ground before they ran off, calling me horrible names the whole while.

I was used to this by now, so I got up, dusted myself off and once again made the walk of shame home.

For once, luck was on my side. My brother Patrick picked that day—we hadn't seen him in I don't know how many months—to pop in for a visit. I saw his motorcycle first, but I was afraid to even hope that he was actually inside my house.

But he was.

"What in the hell happened to you?" he said, taking in my bloody nose and scraped-up arms and hands. I watched his face cloud over in fury as I told him about the boys who did this to me several times a week.

"Do you know where they live?" he asked. I nodded. Patrick didn't tell me to get cleaned up or wake up our mother to tell her what we were doing. He just threw me on the back of his motorcycle—without helmets of course—and drove straight to Timmy Labonte's house.

I wanted to crawl into a hole and hide, but Pat dragged me off the bike and up to Timmy's front door, roaring the whole time.

"TIMMY LABONTE, GET OUT HERE RIGHT NOW."

One of the other two boys who'd been abusing me, Jeff Jones, lived right across the street from Timmy. His dad was outside working in the yard when we pulled up, and now he started walking towards us.

"What's going on?" Mr. Jones wanted to know. He looked square at me. "What happened to you?"

"I MEAN IT, TIMMY, GET YOUR ASS OUT HERE *NOW*," Patrick was shouting through the screen door. I was trying to figure out how to answer Jeff's dad when Timmy's older brother opened the screen. He was around Patrick's age, eighteen or nineteen.

"Is your brother Timmy?" Pat asked him.

The kid at the door nodded.

"Well, he's been kicking the shit out of my sister along with two other kids on this street every day for the last month," Patrick fumed. Timmy appeared in the door next to his brother.

"That's not true, it wasn't me," Timmy stammered.

Patrick turned back to me. "Erin, who were the other two?"

Everyone was staring at me, waiting for an answer. Including Jeff Jones's father.

"Ricky Cardozo and Jeff Jones," I said softly.

Mr. Jones's face turned ripe-tomato red before he spun around to face his own house.

"JEEEEEEEEEEEEEEEEEEEEEEEEEFFFFFFFFFFFFFFFFFFFF," he shouted. Jeff came running outside. His father pointed angrily at me.

"Did you do this to her?"

Jeff immediately started bawling. "Yeessssssssss," he said between choked sobs.

"You better not be bullshitting me," Timmy's brother said, nudging Timmy in the back. "I mean it, you better come clean."

"Yeah, all right, fine," Timmy mumbled. And then his brother did the strangest thing. He shoved Timmy right into my brother and said, "Here you go. Kick his ass!"

Pat didn't need an engraved invitation. He grabbed the front of Timmy's shirt and gave it a good twist before pulling him in until their faces were just inches apart. "You see her?" he hissed, pointing at me. "You so much as *look* at her and I'm going to come over here and break both your legs. Do you understand me?"

Timmy whimpered something that sounded like yes.

"Now go tell her you're sorry," Pat spat, pushing Timmy in my direction.

"I'm really sorry, Erin," Timmy said, embarrassed. I didn't know what to say to that, but it didn't matter. Mr. Jones had launched into an ass-kicking of his own, slapping and cursing at Jeff right there in front of all of us, a scrappy mess of, "*Don't you ever hit a girl, you big sissy,*" and, "*What kind of idiots are you, anyway?*" While Mr. Jones yelled and swung, Jeff bawled and apologized all the way up their path and into the house.

Pat put me back on his motorcycle, took me home and helped me get cleaned up. I thought that was the end of it, but then our doorbell rang. Mr. Jones had dragged Jeff over to apologize. He looked like he'd gotten it pretty bad and I almost felt sorry for him.

After that day, the boys left me alone. Sometimes they would even say hi to me at school or the bus stop. I was gun-shy for a while, always looking over my shoulder whenever I walked alone to see if they were about to pounce. They never did again, not even once. Between Pat and Mr. Jones, they were basically scared stiff. Eventually we would all become friends, and when the boys wanted to get a team together to play a game in the street, they'd always come knocking on my door first.

DON'T LOSE
YOUR HEAD

Mom and Captain Jack would shop at the naval commissary in Long Beach on the weekends. Kids weren't allowed in for some reason, so if you went you had to sit outside on this boring bench. Without Jenny it was especially brutal, so when she wasn't around it was better just to stay home alone. I wasn't looking for trouble or life-changing trauma that day; I was just bored. Desperate to kill some time, I did what I imagine every nine-year-old does when she's left at home unsupervised: I snooped.

An expert investigator, I didn't waste a lot of time. I went straight to Mom and Captain Jack's room. I pawed through familiar sock drawers and bedside tables; scanned boring bookshelves I knew by heart. I rummaged through my mom's old coats and purses, hoping maybe I'd find some cool hidden treasure I'd somehow missed before that I could share with my class. But it was all been-there-done-that.

Be careful what you wish for.

I moved to Captain Jack's dresser. His was one of those old-fashioned kinds that had all the skinny drawers on top. The thing itself was tall—far taller than me—so when I opened those top drawers I had to stand on my tiptoes and really stretch to fish around in there. That day I was up for the challenge, breathing length into my arms and willing my hungry digits to find something noteworthy to extract. Within seconds I landed on a distinctly misshapen form that my fingertips recognized instantly: his ancient slide viewer.

It wasn't a particularly riveting find, I'll be honest. Captain Jack owned exactly two slides, and I had memorized every minute detail of both of them by heart. The first one freaked me out a little bit every time I saw it, not that that kept me from going back for more. The image captured an injured soldier in a naval hospital with his leg in traction; the rest of his body a tangle of tubes and bandages. He was propped up in this contraption that looked like some crazy person had put giant guardrails on a grown-up bed, and the vacant, faraway look in his eyes was nothing short of haunting. Something about that photo—the soldier's expression, his condition, my own intuition—said that he probably wasn't going to make it.

But there was a second, equally familiar photo; a harbinger of hope. This one showed the same soldier, still bandaged and bruised, but something about his face had changed. He was looking at the camera—and truly, maybe that was all that was different—but he appeared coherent and aware; alive.

This soldier was going to go home, you could just tell. That, the happy ending, made everything else okay.

Even though I'd secretly entertained myself with this same slide viewer dozens of times, out of nowhere my fingers found a third slide. A new slide. Something exciting; secret; unseen. I briefly held each small square up to the light to discern the new one; there was the soldier who was going to die, the soldier who was going to live, and a different shape altogether! I carefully slipped the unfamiliar image into the slide viewer and lifted the crude contraption to my eye, bursting with curiosity—

NOOOOOOOOOOOOOOOOOOOOOOOOOOOOOOO!

I threw the viewer across the room and squeezed my eyes shut tightly, as if this would somehow erase the image they'd just taken in. But that slide was now and forever burned into my mind's third eye; the one that never forgets anything.

The photo was one of young Captain Jack, dapper in his Marine Corps uniform. He stood tall and proud and ramrod-straight, one arm raised up high in the air like a statue or a trophy. He wore a look that was part anger, part vengeance and even part pride; a combination even more menacing than any I'd encountered in real life. In his uplifted hand he held a head.

A severed human head.

You know how you just can't help but sneak a sideways peek as you pass a car accident on the highway, even tentatively, furtively, ever-so-quickly? *That.* I couldn't resist. I retrieved the slide viewer and took one last split-second glance, one I instantly and deeply regretted.

The head belonged to a Korean man. His hair was long and he looked more like a warrior than a soldier. I had never seen a dead person before—let alone just the detached head part of one—and instinctively my hands went up to my own throat. Never have I wished more earnestly that I could rewind the clock, go back and have a do-over.

Chills danced up and down my spine with this new and horrific knowledge. My stepfather was a murderer—and proud of it. I had to get out of there.

I removed the gruesome slide and returned these things to the drawer as carefully as I could. Everything had to be exactly as I'd found it. If Captain Jack was capable of chopping off a man's head, what would he do to me if he caught me snooping through his things?

I remember gluing myself to my mom's side that night, my mind racing with questions. *Did she know? What if she didn't? What if he was planning to do that to her, or to me and Jenny, or to all of us?* I couldn't ask these questions, of course, because if I did, she might tell him. And then I would definitely be next.

ALIVE AND KICKING

No matter where we lived or went to school, my sister did not have many friends. The kids were cruel to both of us because we were different, but Jenny definitely got the brunt of the abuse. I was far from immune, but most of the time I kept my mouth shut and tried to make people like me or at least avoid confrontation. Not Jenny. Jenny spoke up when she should have kept quiet, and if someone pushed her buttons she'd push back twice as hard. She questioned everyone and everything. In our neighborhood, questioning things could get you beat up.

Jenny got beat up a lot.

I was in fourth grade at Stanley Elementary and Jenny was in sixth. Her grade started classes a half hour before me, so sometimes we took the bus together and other times I walked. That day, I'd decided to make the trek alone.

I dropped my soggy lunch off in my classroom and headed up toward the playground. As I rounded the bend at the end of the building, I saw a crowd of kids gathered around in a circle. They were yelling and clapping and I could see two figures flailing around on the ground — two girls.

Just as I reached the crowd, the girl with her back to me took a giant swing and slugged the other one right in the face. Suddenly there was blood everywhere. In the jumble of legs and limbs and hair and blood, it took me a minute to realize the other girl was Jenny. She was on the ground and she was getting the living daylights beaten out of her by our scrappy neighbor Rhonda Schafer.

Without even thinking, I ran right into that circle, hauled off and kicked Rhonda straight in the back with everything I had.

"GET THE FUCK OFF MY SISTER," I yelled like a crazy person as my Buster Brown thumped Rhonda's spine, and everyone got really quiet. Hands went to mouths around that group — nobody was used to even hearing me whisper, let alone shout obscenities — and Rhonda Schafer stood up, wild-eyed with arrogance.

"I'm telling on you," she growled with great conviction. *"You said the f-word."*

Before I could point out that I'd only been dropping f-bombs because *she was beating my sister to bloody shreds,* the recess captain appeared out of nowhere from behind me. She grabbed me by the arm roughly and spun me around.

"I heard what you just said, and that is *not* acceptable language!" she shouted. I couldn't believe she was chastising me over Rhonda, but apparently the captain wasn't finished. She turned and grabbed Rhonda's arm with equal force.

"Since when is it okay to punch someone in the face? Huh? ANSWER ME!"

Neither of us said a word as she dragged us to the office.

I was waiting to get my ass-whooping from the principal and find out how long I'd be suspended when Jenny came in to see the nurse and get cleaned up. She was a dirty, bloody mess. She mouthed S-O-R-R-Y to me, and I gave her a tiny smile and a shrug. It's not like you could watch someone kicking your sister's ass and not try to stop them. Jenny would have done the same thing for me.

For once, my sister didn't even get in trouble. Rhonda and I each got two days' suspension and neither of us got the whipping our principal was near-famous for. Instead, he called our moms, told them what we'd done and then loaded Stanley's two latest delinquents into his yellow Pinto station wagon with wood side panels and drove us home, because we were suspended and all, and because you could do that in those days.

My stomach was in one of its pretzel-knots on the way home, wondering how Mom was going to react when we got there, and if she'd be drunk, and if she'd yell at me or even hit me right in front of the principal.

He dropped Rhonda off first. A minute later, he pulled up to my dilapidated house. Mom had gotten out of her wheelchair and was standing in the doorway, holding the screen door propped open with her foot. She waved at the principal and then put her hands on her hips and scowled at me, like she wanted him to know I was about to get it. The principal turned to me in the back seat and told me he was surprised at my actions because he had only heard great things about me from my teacher, and that he hoped I would rethink my language and behavior at school in the future. I'm sure I thanked him for the ride home before I hopped out of his banana-on-wheels and made my way toward my mom.

She moved aside so I could enter, and then she closed the door behind me.

"Well?" my mom asked. She sounded tired.

I told her what had happened, how Jenny was getting beat up and I didn't mean to say the bad word but I was just so angry that it slipped out by accident. Mom was pretty big on defending yourself and not getting pushed around. She thought about this for a second and nodded.

"Want to make some popcorn and watch a movie?" she asked.

"Sure," I said quietly.

Mom made a giant bowl of the best, butteriest popcorn and we watched *Old Yeller* together. At one point, just as we were getting settled, she turned to me.

"I think we'll just keep this to ourselves," she said. I nodded my agreement. I didn't have to worry about Captain Jack finding out about my suspension on his own because a) he left for work at five a.m., and b) he'd never, *ever* ask me about my day.

Mom and I never spoke of the incident again.

THE NAKED TRUTH

> Day turned out miserable. Jenny hurt me very much, Don did to don't even want think. Will go to sleep soon; hope they both can stand themselves.

Down the street from us and around the corner on Paloma was an old, decaying Victorian. Its blue-gray paint was faded and chipping, and through the cracked, dirty or sometimes-missing windows you could see it hadn't been inhabited for years, maybe decades. Every once in a while someone would come and board up those windows to keep out the raccoons and the kids and the druggies, but another someone would always show up and bust them back out. The place was in rough shape.

At this point, there are two things that should be patently obvious about the gray house, as Jenny and I called it:

1. We were convinced it was haunted.
2. We were forbidden to go anywhere near it.

The first thing, of course, rendered the second one impossible. That and Jenny's insatiable thirst for trouble.

My mother's very last words before she and Captain Jack took off for who-knows-where one particular afternoon left little room for misinterpretation: "DO NOT LEAVE THIS HOUSE FOR ANY REASON."

But Jenny was Jenny, and as such she was hell bent on disobeying this explicit command. Not only that, she was going to the gray house, of all places. A double-breach! I begged her not to, but she just laughed.

"Listen, don't worry about it," she said, in that too-cool-for-school manner my sister could have made famous. "It's not a big deal and they're never going to find out." At ten I had no desire to stay home by myself, but going *with* her was out of the question. I watched her leave out the window, wondering if I would ever even see her again.

The next two hours were interminable. Finally, just as dusk was setting in, she sauntered in the door. I didn't even have time to ask her if she'd seen anyone shooting up or making out before the door flew right back open.

"WHERE WERE YOU?" It was Captain Jack, steaming mad, our mom hot on his heels. He made a beeline for my sister.

I felt faint; Jenny didn't flinch.

"WE SAW YOU RUNNING DOWN THE STREET," Captain Jack spat in her face. "WHERE THE HELL WERE YOU?"

"I just went over to Rhonda Schafer's for a minute." Jenny shrugged.

"I told you not to leave the house," Mom said, her voice low and scary.

"She's lying, Jeri! Can't you see she's lying?" My stepfather turned to me.

"I know you know the truth, Miss Sweetness and Light," he said, his voice dripping with sarcasm. That's what he called me, in the meanest manner possible, just because I was a good kid. "Tell me where she went or you're both getting it good."

The words tumbled out of my mouth before I could stop them. I regretted them instantly, even before I knew what was coming. But it was too late.

"The gray house, I think," I said, a barely audible choke.

It was Mom who spoke first.

"Go to your room and take off your clothes," she ordered Jenny slowly and angrily. "And then get back in here."

Jenny's mouth dropped open.

"GO! NOW! DO AS I SAY! OR ELSE!" Mom was shaking with fury.

My sister bolted down the hall to her room, and I wondered what on earth my mom was thinking.

"GET IN HERE NOOOOOOOW!" Mom roared when she felt Jenny had had enough time to disrobe.

Jenny was thirteen and she had a beautiful body. She had Mom's long legs and a perfectly flat stomach and her hips had just a tiny curve and she had new, perky breasts. She tried to cover all of this at once with her hands as she shuffled, red-faced with shame, into the living room. If I could have died for her, I would have.

Why would anyone do this? Why? My brain was spinning. My parents did reprehensible things to us on a daily basis, but for some reason this act seemed to make the others pale in comparison. It was hateful; unforgivable. And the very worst part was, it was all my fault.

Mom must have been shitfaced; that's all there was to it. She went off on Jenny, a crazy, furious, rambling rant. "*You want to have it your way? Do whatever you please even when it's dangerous? You want to go where I tell you not to go? Do you know what could happen to you? What could have happened to you?*" Jenny just stood there, her legs crossed in disgrace, her body bent and twisted and heaving. She sobbed and sobbed.

I silently begged my mother to stop, but she kept going. She was out of control, even Captain Jack knew it. My stepdad was a million and one horrible things, but he wasn't a pervert or a child molester.

"Goddamnit, Jeri, what are you doing?" he muttered. "What good is this going to do?"

Mom ignored him and kept up her rant. She was determined to humiliate Jen into compliance, and that was about the size of it.

"Get out of my sight," Mom finally slurred. I couldn't even watch Jenny's mortified retreat.

Countless times in my childhood, when witnessing one horror or another, I'd tell myself that whatever it was, was just life, and that life wasn't fair. This was not one of those times. This night went light years beyond unfair; it was the very definition of cruel and unusual punishment.

TAKE COVER

didn't know what PTSD was back then, but I sure knew what it looked — and sounded — like.

"GET DOWN, TAKE COVER, THEY HAVE US SUR-ROUNDED! THEY'RE ON THE ROOF GODDAMNIT, GET DOWN! GET DOWN NOW!"

When you heard that at two o'clock in the morning, your ass was taking cover.

Captain Jack would go from room to room, looking for the enemy and checking on his men. I could see his gimpy-limp from beneath my bed, where I would crawl with my blanket and pillow. Mom would be yelling from the other room for us kids to keep quiet, as if we might suddenly decide this would be a fine time to start telling jokes or singing "Crocodile Rock." Eventually the Captain would run outside, grab the garden hose and start shooting at his invisible adversaries. It was alarming but also pretty funny because he slept in tighty-whities and a t-shirt.

The war flashbacks always happened on big drinking nights.

Once, Jenny hadn't made it to cover yet. She'd been woken by his crazy rant but sometimes, if you were in a deep sleep or in the middle of an intense dream, you'd be taken so off-guard that you'd just be sort of frozen in place. We'll never know what the Captain was thinking, of course; whether he thought she was an enemy soldier, or a grenade, or one of his own men on fire maybe. Whatever it was, he picked her up off that bed and launched her straight through her bedroom window.

Somehow, my sister survived this act of war; the only visible damage a few cuts on her palms and knees from the broken glass. Her sweet soul was another story altogether.

Two cops showed up twenty minutes later. A neighbor had called to complain about the noise at our house. (Not about children flying through windows, mind you.) Adam-12 asked Jenny if she was okay — as if she would dare tell them no — and then they informed Captain Jack he'd be in *some serious trouble* if they had to come back.

And that was literally the size of it.

The day after a midnight raid, Mom would have to tell our stepdad what he'd done. The crazy part was, he'd actually apologize.

"All right, guys, sorry about last night," he'd say in the same tone you'd use to say "Okay guys, the party's over," or "There's never a good reason to throw a child out the window, but sometimes you can't help it."

I knew even then that he didn't have control over his flashbacks, but I wondered why he could bring himself to ask our forgiveness for *those* when he never once apologized for all the terrible things he did have control over.

PRAYING WITH THE NEIGHBORS

My salvation on Ramona Place, literally and figuratively, was the Fuentes family.

Their house was two doors down and across the street from mine and had the most beautiful garden. They grew guava and grapefruit and strawberries, and the kids could eat any of them whenever they wanted.

The Fuentes were a close-knit family who loved God and each other equally and passionately. The mother cooked amazing food and didn't speak a word of English, and the father was warm and generous, the sort who'd bring me a soda every time he brought some home for his own kids. The oldest brother Robert was twenty-seven and handsome and was studying to be a priest. I would have given anything to be a Fuentes.

There were eight Fuentes children in total, but the two I spent the most time with were Maggie and Patty. They were both far younger than I was—when I was ten, Maggie was seven and Patty was four—but I couldn't have cared less about the age difference. I adored both of them and for the first time, I felt like I had friends of my own. We played hopscotch and jumped rope for hours. I was way too tall for the only short rope we had and had to contort myself so that thing could clear my head, but I didn't mind. I was happier at their house than anywhere else on earth.

I thought Maggie and Patty were saints. After school, they weren't allowed to play until they had read their Bibles, so I'd go to their house and read with them until they were finished. They also weren't allowed to come to my house, ever—even before Captain Jack threw Jenny out the window—and I was fine with that. They'd laughingly ask me why my stepdad was always yelling throughout the neighborhood, and why didn't he just tell me when he wanted me to come home. I didn't have an answer.

They knew that my brother had died and that my mom was sick, and probed me only gently and with concern. Why was she in a wheelchair? Was she going to get better? Did it have to do with Kelly? Was it hard to push her around all the time? Had I asked Jesus to help her? It was important, they told me, to pray for my mom and my family so that we could all get better.

So we did; we prayed together. They even made me a list of the things I could pray about when I got home, so I wouldn't forget anything. They told me it was best to pray right before bed, and they promised they would pray for my family, too.

I did what they said. I prayed each night before bed, and as I did, I'd think about Maggie and Patty — the saints — in *their* beds praying for me at the very same time, and I would feel overwhelmed with love and gratitude.

One day Mr. Fuentes brought home a new jump rope. It was one of the really long kinds made especially for double Dutch, and he said he bought it so that I could actually fit under it. It was one of the nicest things anyone had ever done for me.

Sometimes their mom would make us tamales or empanadas and serve them with her homemade horchata. Other times we'd pick dozens of guava — they pronounced it "*why-yah-vah*" and it took me decades to realize the two fruits were one and the same — right from their trees and eat the sweet, flowery flesh until we felt sick. But mostly we just hung out, not doing much of anything except feeling safe and happy.

THE GUTTER AND THE CRUCIFIX

While the world celebrated the bicentennial, Mom was at a low point, even for her. She was back in her wheelchair almost exclusively and I often heard her crying in the middle of the night. I would have done anything to make her feel even a tiny bit better, but my options were pretty limited.

Every once in a while I'd skip lunch and squirrel away that money so I could buy a birthday present for Grandma Blanche or Mom or Jenny. I didn't have much, but I figured I probably had enough to get Mom a little gift. I'd ridden my bike a little farther than I should have one day and saw some shops I'd never seen before. There was a clothing store and an ice cream shop and a Goodwill and another store that sold Bibles and prayer beads and other religious paraphernalia. There was going to be something special for my mom in that store, I was sure of it.

She wanted to know where I was going, of course, and I told her it was a surprise. She pushed back, saying she needed to know where I was at all times. I reiterated the surprise bit and even came out and told her that it was for her, even though that was already spoiling it. Mom was already visibly buzzed, and she would not budge. I wasn't going anywhere without giving her a detailed itinerary.

"The little shopping center on the other side of Lucky, near the Goodwill," I told her. Finally she agreed to let me go, after making me promise to wear a jacket because it was still wet out from a big rain the night before. I grabbed a sweatshirt and bolted out the door before she could change her mind.

I was giddy with excitement both at being out on my own and the idea of surprising my mom with a present. I was going to wrap it up in construction paper and tie a bow around it and I couldn't wait to see the look on her face when I handed it to her. I wore a smile the size of the South Bay across my face as I cruised through our neighborhood, close to two dollars in change burning a hole in my pocket.

The God store was colorful and quiet, with walls of bookcases and candles and racks of rosaries. There were framed paintings of Jesus and the Pope, and statues of Mary and one whole case filled with crosses, the kind you'd wear on a necklace. Some were made of metal stamped with delicate designs and others were carved out of wood and had Jesus on them. I chose two of the wooden kind. They were fifty cents each and they were perfect. I counted out the money and handed it to the cashier, feeling proud and excited, and I told her they were presents for my mom and grandma. She said I'd made really good choices, which made me feel so great. I floated out of that store on cloud nine.

My rusty old Schwinn was right outside the door, but that wasn't the first thing I saw. The first thing I saw was our ugly blue camper screeching up to the curb in front of the store, with Captain Jack at the wheel and Mom riding shotgun. Before I could even begin to worry why they were there, I watched in slow-motion horror as my mother opened her door and tumbled out of it like human syrup, landing with a splat in the gutter that was gushing with rainwater. The dirty water raced over and around her legs and splashed right in her face. She was mumbling and sputtering—clearly three and a half sheets to the wind—and a few people moved toward her to try and help.

I was not one of them.

I was frozen. For a split second I thought about pretending I hadn't seen them, hadn't seen her; pretending that wasn't my drunk mother in the gutter not ten feet from where I stood. But by then Captain Jack had seen *me*. Our eyes met as he got out of the truck and hobbled over to Mom. At least he had the decency to look embarrassed.

I told you I'd be right back, I wanted to scream at her. *Why couldn't you trust me? Why couldn't you just stay home?*

"Aw damnit, Jeri, come on," Captain Jack slurred, shooing the Samaritans away and trying to drag my mom to her feet. I watched him struggle to get her into the truck; a soaking, shivering, incoherent blob. Then he turned to me. "Mom just wanted to see what you were doing," he said. It was the closest thing to an apology I'd ever get from him. Then he got in the truck and drove off. None of us ever said a word about her mortifying gutter dive.

Even though she had hurt and humiliated me, I felt like she needed Jesus more than ever. I had to give her that crucifix. When I did, she seemed surprised and happy. She told me it was beautiful and that it was so sweet of me to get it for her. She never wore it.

After that day I never told them where I was going when I left the house, and they didn't ask. I'd just say that I was going to ride my bike. It was a bittersweet victory and a high price to pay for a sliver of independence, but it was better than nothing.

HOUSEKEEPING

N eil Sergeant was a friendly man who lived with his wife
of thirty-five years in another ugly, run-down house just
around the bend from us on Ramona Place. He'd always
be outside when we got off the bus in the afternoons and we'd
say hi and sometimes stop to talk. Mrs. Sergeant was dying of
emphysema, he told us. After that, Mom would send Jenny
over with a nice dish she had made, or just to check on them.

One day, Sarge called and asked if Jenny could come over
and clean his house. He'd be happy to pay her, he said, and
Jenny was thrilled at the idea of making some spare change;
something we never had lying around. Before long she was
cleaning his house every Tuesday, and in exchange he'd ask

Mom if he could pick up anything for her at the store. Her answer was always yes, and anything always meant alcohol.

Jenny was spending more and more time at the Sergeants. I was jealous because she was making money and also because she had an excuse to get away from the torment at home. Sometimes she'd take me with her, and we'd hang out over there and clean and drink coffee. I would pretend we were both at work and I felt so grown-up.

One Tuesday, Jenny went to Sarge's like she always did, but she didn't come home. I waited and waited, but by nine o'clock I realized it wasn't happening. Captain Jack woke up shortly thereafter and had the same epiphany.

"DON'T TELL ME SHE DIDN'T TELL YOU WHERE SHE WAS GOING, MISS SWEETNESS AND LIGHT," he shouted in my face after I told him in all honesty that I had no idea where she was. "YOU KNOW EXACTLY WHERE SHE IS AND YOU BETTER START TALKING!" My parents screamed and I cried and you'd think maybe they would have called Mr. Sergeant or the police but they didn't.

If it were today, there would be an APB out for the missing beautiful, blonde thirteen-year-old girl. Concerned neighbors would comb the streets. Cadaver dogs would be called in. The family wouldn't sleep or eat; they'd be too busy giving impassioned news interviews and worrying themselves sick. But this was 1976, and it was my parents. The only thing they did was sober up for a few weeks while we waited for news and pretended everything was normal.

Nothing to see here, folks. Now just move along.

I was nauseous around the clock. Mr. Sergeant came by to ask about Jenny, since she hadn't been by to clean. Mom lied and told him she'd gone to stay with her father for a while, when the truth was none of us had a clue where she was.

"I guess I lost my housekeeper then," I heard him say. They were sitting in the kitchen drinking coffee; just two old friends shooting the breeze. "It's a shame, because she really did such a nice job."

"Maybe I can do it," I said shyly from the doorway.

"I don't know, you'll have to ask your mom," he replied.

Naturally Mom said yes, because it would get me out of her hair and because there was money involved and because he would continue to bring her booze. Sarge was a friend with her favorite kind of benefits.

I missed my sister terribly; what I didn't miss was the trouble that followed her everywhere like a hungry dog. Now that she was gone, Mom was up and cooking again and mostly sober; Captain Jack got another new job. The fact that they weren't searching for Jenny night and day notwithstanding, they were at least making an effort.

The first time I cleaned for Sarge, he was waiting for me out front after school. He fixed me a snack of coffee and Vanilla Wafers and then he showed me where the Pledge and Windex and Comet were and exactly how he wanted me to clean. He was very particular about things, and when I finished that day he told me I'd done such a great job he was going to pay me extra. I couldn't wait to tell my mom.

Later that night I was playing by myself in the backyard and heard someone at the back wall.

"Pssssssssssst."

I looked around but didn't see anyone.

"Pssssssssssssssssssssssssssssssssst."

There was a rustle in the bushes and in it I could see Jenny. I couldn't believe it! I knew right away she wasn't back to stay; she very clearly did not want to be seen. She was crouched down and waving at me frantically to come to her. I was so scared Mom would see and we'd both get in trouble but I went over to her anyway.

"Pleeeeeeeeeeease come with me, Erin," she whispered. "Please, you have to. You can't stay here. *Please*."

She kept saying it over and over but the problem was, I didn't want to go. Mom wasn't sleeping all day anymore and the Captain had a job and so did I, I told her. This seemed to upset her even more.

"You have to come, Erin. You *have to*."

I said I was sorry but I was fine and I was going to stay, even though I knew that wasn't what she wanted to hear and it was making her sad. Jenny begged and begged but I refused to budge. Finally she gave up. Before she left she made me promise I wouldn't tell anyone I'd seen her, so I did. Then she disappeared again and I was sad, too, because I thought she was making a huge mistake. Why would she leave when everything was just starting to get better?

DUSTING FOR THE DEVIL

Sarge was a nice man who would ask about my mom, about my day, about my friends. He talked to me about the other neighbors, once admitting he thought the Ramos family were weird and wondering what I thought. I told him I'd seen the father chain two of the kids together with a bike lock with my own two eyes, and we agreed that was a terrible thing to do. I felt flattered that Sarge would confide in me this way.

Every time I cleaned, I was that much closer to getting the darling little guinea pig I had seen at the pet store. I'd race from the bus stop to Sarge's house like a little girl chasing the ice cream truck. How lucky I was to have a real job and be earning real money and getting to escape my horrible home life for a few hours.

"Do you know where Jenny is?" Sarge asked me one day as I was dusting a bookshelf. He'd come up behind me and was just standing there; I could feel his closeness.

"No," I said nervously. The truth was I *didn't* know where she was, but I still felt guilty that I'd seen her and hadn't told anyone.

"I do," he told me. Before I could turn around he was pressing himself into me from behind, touching me in confusing and altogether inappropriate ways and places.

I was frozen; powerless. I said nothing.

Afterward he said all the cliche things that pedophiles say to kids; the things that have become cliche because they work. He told me that I knew I couldn't tell anyone about this, right? Because bad things would happen to me and my family if I breathed even a word about it to anyone. He knew where Jenny was and he wanted her to stay safe, but that meant I had to be on his side. If I told anyone anything, Jenny and I would both be sent to juvenile hall—that was like prison for kids—and my parents would go to jail and it would just make a huge mess of things. I didn't want that, did I?

I shook my head. Of course I didn't want that. What ten-year-old would?

"You're going to keep coming on Tuesdays, right?" he asked me before I left that first day. If I didn't, people might ask why and wonder if something was wrong and then me or Jenny might get hurt or taken away.

I told him I'd be back.

He didn't molest me every time I cleaned his house, and he took me to Disney and the race track and we even had my birthday party in his backyard one year. As long as I didn't say anything about what happened sometimes, everyone was safe and happy and nobody had to go to jail. He never yelled at me or hit me, not even once. The fact is it wasn't any worse at Sarge's house than it was at home.

STEP ON A CRACK

House payment due again. Money. money. Haven't heard one word from Soc. Sec. either. Probably won't get it anyway. Things don't happen that way for me. Sick & tired of scratching for every penny.

My anxiety was at an all-time high. It was three roundtrip miles from my house to Stanley Elementary, a trip that took me twice as long as it should have because I couldn't step on a single crack. The *last* thing my mother needed was a broken back.

MIDNIGHT RUN

I'm tired I guess been hard on the kids too, with reason. Erin ruined brand new pair cot, Jenny bad report from teacher refuses to work. Maybe that's Don now. Yes It. will quiet down now.

Jenny finally came home. It was "of her own volition" they said, and I was beside myself, partly because I felt like I'd helped to keep her alive by not saying anything to anybody about anything. Mom wanted to know where she'd been—with this neighbor and that friend, Jenny told her—and Mom said she couldn't just go running around living on the streets. My sister said Mom needed to act like she cared about us more, and Mom promised she'd try.

Mom's promises were about as good as an egg salad sandwich left out in the sun.

Within days of Jenny's return, things were back to the old normal. At least we only had to deal with the screaming, fighting and drinking for a few hours in the evening, we mused. As if on cue, Captain Jack got fired. Again. Apparently you can only show up to your handyman job drunk or hungover — or not show up at all — so many times before they tell you not to come back.

Life on Ramona was at an all-time low, and that's saying something. Jenny and I lived with two alcoholics who had nowhere to go and nothing to do, so boozing became their collective twenty-four seven job. Like feral cats or newborn babies, they stayed up all night howling and then crashed hard during the day, only to wake up and accuse us of stealing or pouring out their alcohol.

Fortunately for them, Sarge was always coming by with more.

There were bottles of liquor everywhere I looked, stashed in every nook and cranny imaginable: in the water tank in the toilet, at the bottom of the laundry basket in the bathroom, in the pillow cushions on the couch. We found booze in the TV cabinet, the china cabinet, the linen closet. One night, ravenous and desperate, Jenny and I picked the lock they kept on the freezer to forage for food and we found several bottles in there, too. Who were they hiding it from? Themselves? Us? Each other? It was like a never-ending Easter egg hunt for alcohol — *Oh, hoppy day, I found some more!* — punctuated by the occasional screaming match or four-day nap.

At school, things weren't much better. That place was nothing more than a way to not be at home. I couldn't focus to save my life. I never participated or did any of my work, and other than having one teacher move my desk to isolation in the far corner of the room (I couldn't have cared less), I never got in trouble for it. I was invisible, and that was exactly as I wanted it.

The only thing I had to distract myself from my parents' drinking was my own certain and imminent death.

I was dying, a conviction I carried around with me like a purse. Wherever I went, it went. It was as if all the tension, fear, sadness and loneliness in my life needed somewhere to go, and decided to bubble up into a frothy forecast of sure death. I couldn't breathe because I had cancer. My arm hurt because I was having a heart attack. Anxiety made my heart pound in my ears to the point that I couldn't hear people when they spoke to me.

I said nothing about any of it.

At home, my sister and I tried our best to roll with the punches, literally and figuratively, but there was just no light at the end of the tunnel. One night, Jenny told me that the only reason she'd come back at all was to get me, and that it was time for us both to go. This time I didn't argue.

With nothing but a jacket and a change of clothes each, we set out in the dark. It was past my bedtime but our parents had been passed out for hours. It could be days before they realized we were gone.

Pat had some hippy friends who didn't live too far from our neighborhood, a married couple named Carol and Bob. Carol had beautiful curly blonde hair and wore bell-bottoms and halter tops and Bob sometimes didn't wear clothes at all. You never knew when he might open the door buck naked, like it was no big deal. We'd been to their house with our brother a few times and I remembered Patrick telling us they loved kids and smoking pot. I'd only ever seen people cook *with* a pot; I had no idea how you'd smoke one and thought that would be a funny thing to see.

Carol answered the door, and looked surprised when Jenny asked if we could come in. We sat in their *Partridge Family* living room awkwardly. They wanted to know why on earth we were out so late on a school night, so we told them. Carol gave Bob a look, then she nodded and asked if we were hungry. Were we ever. She made us hamburgers on big squishy buns and Kraft mac-and-cheese, which I had never had in my life. I thought I might have died and gone to heaven.

After our feast, Carol tucked me into bed in a spare bedroom and told me she and Jenny were going to figure out a plan. I believed her and fell into a deep and peaceful sleep.

"Erin." It was a voice I knew; a man's voice. I opened my eyes but I wasn't sure I could trust what I was seeing.

"Come on, honey," he said, scooping me up in his arms. "I'm taking you guys home."

And then he did.

Our dad — my real dad — took us home.

THE FOUNTAIN OF MY YOUTH

Dad had been busy during the years we'd been out of touch, marrying Topless Tracy and fathering a fifth child, Lindsay, with her. Sadly for Dad, it turned out Tracy was only interested in men she *wasn't* married to, so Dad decided to let somebody else take the trash out after that. He told Tracy he'd take all of their debt with him if could have baby Lindsay, too. Tracy was fine with that arrangement, and nobody ever saw or heard from her again.

When I got there, Dad and six-year-old Lindsay lived with his girlfriend Betty on Walnut Street in Fountain Valley, fifteen minutes away. He'd just bought the house with money he made at his new real estate job. It was your basic Brady Bunch house, a two-story wood and stone square with a well-kept lawn and a marbled mirror foyer. Walnut Street had neat sidewalks and strategically spaced palm trees and there wasn't a chain-link fence on the whole block.

It wasn't that I didn't like it there. My half-sister Lindsay was one of the cutest, sweetest kids I'd ever seen and it was a relief to be in the company of sober adults for a change. Betty didn't seem to like children all that much and Dad's house wasn't spotless, but I'd certainly seen dirtier. All in all, it was a decided step up from Ramona Place.

The problem was, I was worried sick about my mom. She was all alone with Captain Jack and I thought for sure she would go off the deep end or they'd wind up killing each other if there was nobody there to keep an eye on them. Who else was going to do it? I had to go back; there was no other choice. Jenny, on the other hand, made it crystal clear she wasn't going anywhere.

Dad didn't want to let me go but Mom played the custody card. To appease him — or maybe because it was just easier — she said she'd "let" Jenny stay with him. As if anyone could control that.

"You call me if things get bad, or if you need anything at all," Dad told me when he dropped me off at my mom's less than a week after he'd rescued me from Patrick's hippy friends. He said Jenny had told him all about Mom and Captain Jack and I could see the guilt and sadness in his eyes. "You can't live like this, honey. I won't let you. I'm going to fight for full custody of both you girls."

I wanted him to and I didn't want him to all at the same time.

SHINY NEW TEN-SPEED GETAWAY

It was hard to leave Dad's, but I had to. I needed to watch out for my mom, and I thought that if I tried hard enough I could help her get sober, and maybe she'd even stay that way this time.

I missed Jenny every day, and now I missed Lindsay, too. After a decade of being the baby, I finally had a little sister. Lindsay was adorable and well-behaved and looked up to me like I was a movie star. I couldn't believe that even though we barely knew each other, we were flesh and blood and we

153

would be forever. We were *family*, and nobody could ever take that away.

At her house on Walnut, my half-sister loved nothing more than pedaling around on her Big Wheel. Since I didn't have a bike there, Dad had lent me his ten-speed so Lindsay and I could cruise the neighborhood together. After slumming it on my rusty, clunky Schwinn—the same one I'd had since I was six—straddling Dad's sleek ten-speed felt like getting behind the wheel of a Ferrari. I dreamed of having a bike of my own like that someday and had tried dropping a few hints to Mom, which I knew was mostly useless. We didn't even have money for batteries in that house; surely bicycles were out of the question.

Without Jenny, the days dragged. Three long, lonely months crawled by, and the only thing I had to look forward to was Christmas. Not the holiday itself; the Grinch had stolen that forever ago. Any Christmas tree fund was always blown on booze, so my parents would drag the same sad potted shrub in from outside, throw some tinsel at it and call it a day. Maybe they'd have a gift or two for us, maybe they wouldn't, but at the very least I'd get two weeks off of school and Grandma and Grandpa would come for dinner—which meant *we'd be having dinner*, and my parents most likely would even sober up for it. That was a Christmas miracle unto itself.

That year it was just me. Without Jenny, Pat or Kelly, I waited outside alone for Grandma Blanche and Grandpa Sam to arrive. They pulled up in their mint 1960 Chevy and I ran to greet them. They'd bought that Bel Air right off the assembly line and it still looked showroom-new, something I marveled at each time I saw it. Grandpa opened the trunk—the one you could have fit at least twenty dead bodies in—and no lie, it was filled with beautifully wrapped presents in every size and shape you could imagine. I'd never seen that many gifts all in one place in my life. We unloaded the trunk and stacked the stunning packages beneath our sad, saggy Christmas shrub. I felt stabs of guilt at the sight of their gift-wrapped love for me, knowing it was just a matter of days until I would be out of their lives for good.

See, I was getting the ten-speed. Mom was the worst secret-keeper in the world, and try as she might she just couldn't help ruining a surprise. This time I'd heard her on the phone with Grandma Blanche telling her to tell Grandpa to, "*Get the yellow one because it's the most like her dad's, and Erin specifically said yellow.*" She wasn't even trying to be sly about it. My grandparents probably paid for it, I told myself, so it wasn't like I was breaking my mother's heart with her own money.

I couldn't save her and I knew it. And it was all just too much. The drinking, the loneliness, the isolation, Sarge. If I even suggested I might want to skip a Tuesday, Mom would get irate. "You made a commitment," she'd say. "Sarge needs your help." The truth was, Mom needed booze and Sarge was her supplier. I was just a mule.

Once I had that shiny new bike, my plan was to get on it and ride away for good. Nobody could stop me. I had my outfit all picked out; I knew what time I would leave. I wasn't going to say goodbye to any of my friends, because they might tell their parents and then my brilliant plan would be ruined. I was leaving on Monday, because I couldn't handle one more Tuesday with Sarge. I just couldn't.

We ate Christmas dinner and after cleaning up every last napkin and fork, I said, "Let's open gifts!" I could barely contain my excitement. Captain Jack shot me his usual *HOW DARE YOU* look of hatred, but I honestly didn't care. I was getting that ten-speed and I was leaving! He couldn't burst my bubble with a red-hot poker.

I opened the red and blue Vans I'd been dying to have and thought I never, ever would. In that magical bounty there also was a jewelry box and a brand-new pillow (the one I had

at the time was older than me and wafer-thin) and a calico kitten Grandma had made with fur she bought at the fabric store.
It was nicer than any stuffed animal you could buy at Lucky
Supermarket, with eyes and a nose and a perfect little mouth
sewn on. I opened gift after thoughtful gift and tried my best
not to wish each one was a ten-speed. It wasn't long before
there were no more boxes to open and the last of the crumpled
paper had been cleaned up. Christmas was over. I hadn't gotten the bike after all. Disappointment crashed over me like a
suffocating wave, but I tried to hide my despair.

"Why don't you go see if Maggie and Patty can play,"
Mom said. I was used to her wanting to get rid of me, and my
grandparents would be leaving soon so there wasn't much to
hang around for anyway. I opened the door and nearly had a
heart attack.

It was there.

My ticket to freedom was waiting right outside the door.
It was shinier than I could have imagined; an actual dream
come true.

Even though I had heard her telling Grandma what
I wanted, I don't think I had let myself fully believe I might
actually get that bike—or ever get out of that life—until that
moment. Mom could have changed her mind or I could have
blown it. You never wanted to get your hopes up too high in
my house. I conjured my inner Faye Dunaway and pasted a
look of unbridled shock on my face before turning to Mom.
She was already holding the old clunky camera they mostly
pulled out on birthdays and holidays.

"Hop on it," she said, and I did. I smiled shyly for the
camera from the comfort of my gleaming two-wheeled get-
away car.

I was a pro at hiding my true feelings, so nobody was the
wiser. But for two days I walked around on air, because it was
happening. I was getting out of that hell for good.

Finally Monday came. My tiny bag was packed, the Captain was at work and Mom was still passed out from the night before. She hadn't been sober for five minutes since my grandparents had said goodbye. I felt bad leaving her, but I also knew she'd wake up and be wasted within the hour and I'd probably be forgotten anyway. I loved her and maybe she loved me too, but she loved booze even more. Even a ten-year-old could see that.

It was twenty minutes to Dad's by car, so I calculated that it would take me at least an hour by bicycle. I'd carefully noted as many landmarks as I could along the route the last time Dad drove me home, somehow certain that I would need this information. I rode slowly, afraid that if I looked as eager as I actually was, a police officer would stop me and take me back home. There was no way I was going to let that happen.

I passed the liquor store and amazing Mile Square Park, the former military airfield Dad had worked on with his water truck. After that was Fountain Valley Hospital, where I knew Lindsay had gone the time she broke her collarbone. A sharp right turn should take me straight to the freeway overpass that marked the way to Dad's street. As soon as I saw it, I knew I was home free. From there it was only two quick, easy turns. No longer terrified about being nabbed by cops, I raced to his driveway, ditched my new bike and knocked breathlessly on the front door.

Nobody was home. I went to Lindsay's friend Heather's house next door. We had played over there and Heather's mom recognized me immediately and gave me a big smile. I explained that I'd run away from my mom's to live with my dad and her face changed quickly. She brought me inside and told me I could watch TV while she made some phone calls. I wasn't worried about her calling Mom because she didn't even know her name, so I settled in and watched *Sanford and Son* and waited.

Soon enough Betty showed up and everyone seemed to be up in arms about my escape and the fact I'd gotten myself from Garden Grove to Fountain Valley after only ever making the trip twice in my life. All I could think was, *Wow, they're so proud and impressed. These people might really care about me!*

Betty took me and the neighbor out to lunch; the second time that had ever happened in my life. When Dad got home, he gave me the biggest hug and asked me if I was sure this was what I wanted. I said yes and I asked him the same question. We all agreed my being with him was for the best. And for the time being, that was about the size of it.

WALNUT

MAN OF MYSTERY

My father Kenneth Conway Cole grew up in Indiana with two siblings and their middle-class, conservative parents, Connie and Eleanor. Later they moved to San Jacinto, CA, to open a convenience store. Dad was generous and hard-working and had no interest in confrontation of any kind. He drove a truck in the Korean War and also served as a cook. I wish I could say I knew more about him, but this is everything I know.

UGLY BETTY

"When love rules, power disappears.
When power rules, love disappears."

~Paulo Coelho

etty JoAnn Hickey grew up in a trailer in Kentucky, but you weren't supposed to talk about that. She wore too-short shorts, and tops that showed her belly, and she was pasty and freckled from head to toe, all things I might not have even noticed if she were a tiny bit motherly—but she wasn't. She swore like a sailor and chain-smoked Kool cigarettes and I couldn't for the life of me figure out what Dad saw in her. Maybe he just needed someone to tell him what to do, because I could see the minute I moved in that Betty was the boss on Walnut Street.

My new house there must have been a stretch for them financially; the evidence of this was in the trimmings. We ate on office chairs around a table that was actually a giant spool someone had rescued from the junkyard. The top was raw, splintery plywood and we were always cutting our arms on it, until someone got the bright idea to staple some padding around the edges. The living room featured a hodgepodge of velvet and pleather and oak, while over in the foyer, visitors were greeted by a plaster statue of a naked lady. It was huge and out of place—clearly meant for a garden—and everyone cracked their toe on it at least once. I can imagine my dad's trailer-bred sweetheart thinking that hunk of cement was the height of upper-class elegance.

Unlike the free-range life I lived with Mom and Captain Jack, Betty was all about rules. I listened to each one carefully, because I wanted to be perfect. If I made a mess, I was expected to clean it up immediately. My room was to be immaculate at all times. Betty cared how we looked to an unnatural degree, demanding that we brush our hair even if we'd just done so, or insisting that Jenny "go put on some lipgloss" when she wasn't going anywhere at all.

And then there were the chores. Jenny and I were on dish duty — and there were lots and lots of dishes. If Dad ever got up to help us Betty would insist that he sit right back down.

"The fact is," she'd say, employing her signature phrase, "these kids need to learn how to do the dishes, not you."

Maybe it was because Lindsay was so much younger, or possibly because she came with Dad when he and Betty met, but for some reason my half-sister was more or less spared Betty's whip-cracking wrath. Jenny and me, not so much.

"I want this place spotless," she'd order as we scrubbed and scoured, even though we'd never seen her so much as wipe down a square inch of Formica. She'd inspect our work afterward and if she deemed the results subpar — and that could literally mean one glass still had a single smudge on it — she'd pull every last dish from the cabinets and we would have to start all over.

I was scared of Betty, as I should have been, and I was determined not to set her off. Unfortunately for me, and Jenny in particular, that didn't take much at all.

I soon learned that if you weren't around to do dish duty — even if it was because you were next door at the neighbor's getting help with your homework — Betty would take the night's dirty plates, still heaped with baked beans and chicken bones and whatever else had been on the dinner menu, and pile them right on top of your bed. Grease and ketchup would be pooling on your pillow by the time you discovered it, and your only choice was to schlep it all back to the kitchen and clean it up. She had to go quite a way out of her way to do this, mind you, when dumping those dishes in the sink five feet away would have been far faster and easier. The truth was there was no excuse for Betty's behavior, and no way we could make sense of it. Jenny had warned me the moment I arrived: this was just the way it was. We could take it or leave it.

Neither of us wanted to leave it. At least she was sober.

The dishes were just the beginning. I also was responsible for setting the table, doing the laundry, cleaning the living room and raking the shag carpet. The laundry was pretty simple, unless I wasn't there waiting the split second the spin cycle ended. Then Betty would pull it all out and drop it in a sloppy heap on the garage floor, forcing me to start the job all over. "The fact is, you should have done it when the cycle was finished," she'd say. "That's what the buzzer is for. Why don't you try using your ears?"

Raking the shag wasn't too bad, unless I forgot to do it. The first time I neglected that detail, Betty found me and beat me with the rake handle. She was ruthless. I had bruises all over my back and legs afterward, but I was used to those. That was what you got when you disappointed people or just weren't good enough. I vowed to do better.

Dad worked several jobs to keep Betty living the good life on Walnut Street, and he was up and out at five for his water truck job. After that he'd sell real estate, often coming home late into the evening. Between nonstop work and his battle with diabetes, Dad was tired a lot. But he took medicine to keep his insulin levels in check and never complained about any of it. When he was home for dinner he was always the one to cook, whipping up chili and burgers and breakfast for dinner and SOS while Betty stomped around looking for chores for us to do. SOS stood for "shit on a shingle" and it was basically salted, peppered ground beef sauteed with some sort of milk sauce and poured over white toast. It sounds dreadful, but Dad could make anything taste good.

Betty did nothing much to speak of, besides take a few classes here and there and dream up ways to make me and my sister miserable. Her abuse seemed to get worse by the day, although in these early years she mostly left Lindsay alone. Sadly that wouldn't always be the case, but Jenny and I would be long gone before Betty turned her venom on Lindsay.

In the meantime, life with Betty was brutal. If Jenny didn't have breakfast on the table at six a.m. sharp, Betty would belt her with a broomstick. Not the bristly broom part; the solid, hard, unforgiving handle. Although Jenny seemed to provoke Betty just by existing, I was no stranger to her cruelty. And unlike at my old house on Ramona, you never knew what was going to set Betty off. One day she'd make up a reason to be mad at you, and the next she'd offer to take you shopping for new shoes. It was garden-variety psychological warfare.

Jenny could be moody like any typical teenager, but Betty deemed her erratic and had her put on Ritalin. Anytime Jenny said or did anything to irritate Betty, which was a dozen times a day, she would roll her eyes and say, "Oh, go take your pill." She said it in front of our friends in the meanest, most humiliating tone she could muster.

"The fact is," she'd say, "you're acting like a basket case. Now go take your pill." In all actuality the fact was, Betty was a monster. She'd find something to fault us for whenever she and my dad had company so that she could make us stand, humiliated, in a corner. Betty was a textbook narcissist, deriving her entire sense of self from her ability to bully and belittle us. I simultaneously hated and pitied her.

166 | *Erin Cole with Jenna McCarthy*

For reasons I couldn't fathom, Betty had lots of friends who were always coming by the house. She loved to try to impress people with how smart she was, and how she could boss Dad around and call him names. She'd say, "How's it going, asshole?" to him in front of their friends and purposely pick topics of conversation he knew nothing about just to make him look foolish. Dad was actually very bright and knew a lot about history and politics. Every once in a while he'd snap and tell Betty to "go pound sand up her ass," but more often than not, he'd just let her antics slide. We'd sit there and watch as he shrugged and smiled and let her insult and demean him.

Maybe that was why he didn't even notice she was doing the exact same thing to me and Jenny.

LET THEM EAT CAKE

*"When hunger isn't the problem,
food isn't the answer."*

~Unknown

D ad enrolled me in Fountain Valley Elementary School under his last name, Cole. It was a fresh start, and as a mid-year transfer I got tons of attention. Everyone was so welcoming and sweet and curious about me, and I tried hard to fit in and stay out of trouble. As far as my classmates were concerned, I was the skinny, mostly normal new kid who sometimes forgot her own name and wrote Erin Blomgren at the top of her paper.

Lindsay's friend Heather next door had an older sister my age named Jane. Jane was in my grade but not the same class, and we instantly became inseparable. We'd roller skate and play horse in the street and sometimes she'd invite me over for sleepovers at her house. Jane had a heated pool we'd skinny-dip in at night, and a trundle bed and a wall of fancy dolls she kept in cases. You didn't play with them, you just looked at them, something I found equal parts weird and wonderful. It felt so good to have a friend my own age to hang out with.

I didn't just have a friend, I had food. After a lifetime of deprivation, suddenly I was allowed to go into the cupboards and take anything I wanted, whenever I wanted it. Betty bought yogurt and sliced cheese and Nilla Wafers and Cheerios, all the things we weren't allowed to have at Mom's. In my young mind, food was love. I couldn't comprehend how someone could be so cruel and yet buy all the best foods you could ever want.

Sometimes on Saturdays Dad would to go his friend Larry Lepley's donut shop and come back with a huge pink box of bear claws and apple fritters and chocolate bars and our very favorite, old-fashioned glazed donuts. We'd eat nothing but donuts all day long and nobody ever said I should stop or tell me that I'd probably had enough.

In fact, more often than not, they force-fed me like a goose bound for the foie gras factory.

After years of being ignored and neglected, now I had someone monitoring my every morsel. Even though my appetite was virtually nonexistent, Betty arbitrarily decided that I could—and should—be able to eat at least as much food as Lindsay, who was five years my junior. Not only that, Betty wouldn't let me leave the table until I'd matched my little sister bite for bite. I know lots of families had a sit-at-the-table rule for things like creamed spinach or liverwurst, but I was also being forced to eat foods I loved but just wasn't hungry for.

My half-sister was little, but the kid could eat. If Lindsay wanted a third pancake, I got a third pancake, too. It didn't take her long to catch on and realize she had control over me in this way. She was a good kid and I'm sure she thought it was harmless fun, but stuffing myself when I already felt full was miserable.

Jenny and I did our very best to hide our displeasure with anything edible, because as soon as Betty realized you didn't like something, it would automatically go into the regular rotation.

"Mmmmmmmmmmmmm, isn't it delicious, Erin?" she'd ask with an evil grin as I choked down the dehydrated scalloped potatoes from a box she knew I detested. I'd make myself swallow bite after nauseating bite and pray they wouldn't come back up. I knew first-hand what would happen if they did.

It was corned beef hash that time. Betty served the kind that came in a can that was mostly bits of salty meat suspended in some sort of gelatinous goo. It was the worst. My stomach was already stretched beyond its capacity, which made each bite painful. I gagged every time a morsel entered my mouth, as if my throat was trying to prevent further gastric assault.

"Keep going," Betty would sing-song sweetly, savoring my misery. I tried, I really did. But all of a sudden my insides just revolted on me and every bite I'd eaten came right back up and landed on my plate in one big, sloppy heap. Betty acted as if nothing were amiss.

"Keep going," she said again, deadpan. My plate was a sea of vomit that frankly didn't look all that different than it had before I'd swallowed it the first time. There was no arguing with her; no chance of crying out "no fair." So instead I blinked back tears and forced myself to ingest the regurgitated meat. If Dad had been home, he'd never have let that happen, not in a million years. At least that's what I liked to tell myself.

TAP DANCING FOR
TEAM GERITOL

Aside from the obvious, things weren't all bad at Dad's. For one thing, I was doing great in school, mostly because we had very strict rules at this house. As soon as you walked in the door, you sat down and did your homework. While this was foreign to me, it also made a great deal of sense. For the first time I was a star student bringing home near-perfect grades.

Betty signed me and Jenny up for dance classes with Lindsay, probably as an excuse to get rid of us for a few hours a week but I didn't care. I was obsessed with *Soul Train* and Maxine Nightingale and this was like winning the lottery to me. Our teacher was an ancient man named Mr. Baker whose son Eddie went on to have a successful Broadway dance career. We did tap and ballet and Polynesian dancing, but my favorite was jazz. I'd never been enrolled in any sort of extracurricular activity and I felt like a *Solid Gold* dancer every time we performed for what we dubbed Team Geritol at the neighborhood convalescent homes. Those hours on Tuesday and Thursday were the highlight of my week.

Lindsay and I were growing closer and closer. Betty wasn't nearly as hard on her as she was on me and Jenny — for reasons we never quite understood, she reserved a special sort of hatred for us — but she definitely kept Lindsay on a short, barbed leash. I could see the abuse taking its toll on my little sister's sweet soul as well, but we wouldn't speak of it until many years later. Sometimes we'd give each other a certain look — I get it; it's not you, it's her; we're going to be okay — and that was the best we could do.

Dad's house had a pool table upstairs and on weekends when Dad was home and Betty wasn't, Lindsay and I would sneak up there and play our own special sort of billiards; a pool-chicken game we made up ourselves. We'd divide the balls up evenly and stand at opposite ends of the table. One of us would wrap our hands over the edge of the green, so our fingertips were touching the table, and then the other would fire her half of the balls down as hard and fast as she could, one at a time, aiming straight for the knuckles. You were a wuss if you flinched or pulled your hands away and you were a champion if you struck your opponent's knuckles square on. We would laugh and cry and do it over and over, until it usually ended with one of us sending a ball over so hard that it cleared the lip, flew off the table and sailed straight down the stairs into the foyer. If you sent it hard enough and at just the right angle, it might even hit one of those marbled mirror panels. The resulting *CRASH* was exquisite.

"What the HELL is going on up there?" Dad would always yell.

"Sorry!" we'd reply, muffling our giggles. But he'd never come up there or punish us or even pad to the foyer to survey the damage. Lindsay and I knew the drill anyway. After we recovered from our hysteria, we'd go down to the garage and get the hated broom and clean up the mess, then we'd find the stash of replacement mirrors and stick a new one up.

For obvious reasons, we never played pool-chicken when Betty was home. But knowing what we'd done and gotten away with in her absence was a thrill unlike few I had ever known.

AVON CALLING

"It was a small but positive surprise."
~Stefan Bielmeier

B etty might not have had the capacity to care for her step-children, but she had just enough to care about how we looked and smelled. She'd chase us around with curling irons and nail polish and deodorant, as if maybe if we *looked* okay nobody would question our life at home. Jenny and I would pay close attention to her beauty lessons and thank her for the new shag haircuts and eventually learned to curl our own hair without incurring burns. If the one good thing we could get out of our dad's awful choices in women was a nice perfume sample or the secret to stubble-free underarms, we'd take it.

Once a month, the Avon lady would visit Walnut Street. Her name was Connie and she was tall, dark and lovely. Lindsay and I secretly wished she was our mom. She was so kind and sweet, we could never imagine her getting so angry that she would slap or humiliate us.

When we saw Connie coming we'd shout, "AVON LADY!!!" and race to open the door for her. Betty would spend hours at a time sampling Connie's delicious wares. Sometimes we were even allowed to sit with them at the giant spool kitchen table. Connie would show us necklaces with butterflies and hearts and tassels, and beautiful bracelets with your initials on them. She had gold knot earrings and a choker with a star right in the middle and a cameo ring that had a secret lid and perfume inside. I'd never seen so many sparkling, scented things in all my life.

Betty saw me trying on that cameo ring and smelling the perfume. "Do you love it?" she wanted to know.

"I do," I admitted, because of course I did. But I loved those knot earrings more than anything Connie had and I told her so. Betty laughed at me.

"You don't even have pierced ears," she said. I saw an opening and I took it; right there on the spot, I asked Connie if she could pierce my ears.

"Pleeeeeeeeeeeeeease?" I begged. Betty laughed even harder. She told Connie she should go door-to-door piercing ears because she'd probably sell a lot more earrings that way. Everyone got a big kick out of that. Then Betty told Connie that she'd take the ring and the knot earrings. I was afraid to ask who they were for.

Avon orders took three weeks to come and I think I held my breath the entire time. When Connie finally came back to deliver the goods, Betty made a big production of presenting Lindsay with that cameo ring. Then she turned to me.

"I guess we need to go get your ears pierced," she said.

And we did. She took me and Lindsay to Claire's in the Westminster mall that very day and we both got our ears pierced. (Well, Lindsay got one ear pierced. She freaked out after that and wouldn't let them touch the other side, so she walked around with one earring in for years.) I felt so proud and grown-up with my pierced ears; they were a special treat, a luxury, and I certainly didn't have many of those. It would be another long month before I could replace the plain posts from Claire's with those knots, but after that I would wear them forever.

FLOORED

'm not sure where I got the tenacity I had as a kid, or the drive to do my best and finish what I started. It certainly wasn't from my family.

At one point, Betty convinced my dad that we needed new flooring in the kitchen. They ripped up the nasty, soiled restaurant-grade carpet in there to find it had been laid right over another layer of Linoleum. It was old and cracked and faded, and Betty figured removing it would be a delightful project for her three young charges. Day after day, for hours at a time, she had us chipping away at that mess with chisels. Many years earlier the Linoleum had been affixed to the plywood subfloor with a thick layer of black glue that looked like tar and had the consistency of cement. You could only break off tiny brittle bits at a time, and it was backbreaking work that went on for weeks.

Either we gave up or Betty gave in, because eventually the project ground to an official and permanent halt. Half of the kitchen still had hideous, dated flooring, and the other was a tragic patchwork of tar-dappled timber. It was still that way when I left Walnut Street for good.

Pretty much everything in that house had half-assed written all over it. Another time the big idea was to wallpaper the kitchen. Tropical prints were all the rage and Betty picked out a palm leaf pattern that never ended; each leaf ran right into the next and the whole thing went on forever. That woman loved a good overhaul—as long as someone else was doing the heavy lifting. I volunteered for the task and they ordered the supplies, but I ran out of paper halfway through the project. By the time they finally got around to buying the second half, the part I'd already done had faded to a dirty grease color and the two halves never matched.

As awful as both of those things were, the backyard put them to shame. There was no grass, no planter garden, nothing in pots and no furniture to sit on. It was just a big, weed-choked field. One of Betty's favorite punishments for us was to dig holes out there. She kept a row of shovels propped against the side of the house for just this purpose. "That's the breaks," she would say with a shrug whenever she doled out this sentence. It happened so often that Jane would pop her head over the wall and ask, "How long do you have to do it this time?" Whenever Betty saw us talking, she'd come out there—often in her awful black negligee—and wiggle her fingers.

"Goodbye, Jane," she'd say, and my friend's face would lower like a screen and disappear. Jenny and I called it "grave-digging" because we were sure Betty's eventual plan was to kill us and kick us in one of those holes and bury us up.

The worst part was, Betty didn't even pretend those holes were for a fabulous garden she was planning to plant or the beginning of a pond we might someday fill with fish. The holes were pointless and everyone knew it. They'd cave in and the weeds would be back in a matter of weeks. They were just another way to control and humiliate us.

A NOT-SO-CINDERELLA STORY

Jenny might as well have been the mayor of our Fountain Valley neighborhood. She was friendly and outgoing and knew the name of every family on the street. She knew where the bullies lived and how to avoid them. She knew what everyone did for work and where they went to church and how many kids they had and probably even what they had for dinner last night.

One of the neighbors was a boy named Steve Sizzler. Steve was a senior in high school and he played football and he was handsome and muscular and always talked to me like I was his age and not somebody's baby sister. Even though Jenny was only in eighth grade, she looked much older. She was tall and thin and drop-dead gorgeous, too, so it wasn't surprising when Steve developed a massive crush on her.

They started spending more time together and soon Steve asked Jenny to his high school homecoming dance. Because he was practically a grown man and because Betty was Betty, I never in a million years imagined my parents actually letting her go, but they did.

The dance was more than a month away and I prayed that Jenny wouldn't screw up this amazing opportunity. But I could see that she was on her best behavior. She did the dishes without complaining and made sure Lindsay and I were up on time and didn't pick any fights with anyone. In Dad's house, if two of us were arguing or acting up, all three of us would get the same punishment. Lindsay and I understood this on a cellular level and also we knew what was at stake, so we tried our best to be perfect, too. Nobody wanted to ruin this for Jenny.

You could have knocked me over with a sneeze when Betty offered to take my sister shopping for a dress. I hadn't even thought about that. The only dresses we'd owned for as long as I could remember had been made by Grandma Blanche. Shopping for a brand-new one? This was like a real-life fairy-tale. We almost had the evil stepmother to prove it.

They went alone, just Jenny and Betty. I hoped the whole time that they were having fun and that Betty was being nice and maybe even taking Jen out to lunch. When they finally got home, Jenny was carrying two fancy, expensive-looking shopping bags (although to me, anything that wasn't a brown bag from Lucky Supermarket looked fancy). She told us that Betty had helped her pick out a dress and shoes, and Lindsay and I begged her to model her new outfit.

"Close your eyes, you guys," she shouted from down the hall. Lindsay and I buried our faces in our hands and waited for the big reveal. We could hear Jenny's heels click-click-clicking across the tile. It was all I could do not to sneak a peek.

"Okay, open!" Jenny finally squealed.

She was exquisite. Betty had chosen a long gown in a pale baby blue hue that brought out Jenny's amazing eyes. The dress had skinny straps and a fitted waist that hugged her curves and a swishy skirt that fell gracefully to the floor. The tips of Jenny's new strappy silver heels poked out from beneath the hem. I had never seen my sister look happier or more beautiful.

Everyone was beyond excited about the homecoming dance. Dad had even invited his parents to come over and see Jenny off. They lived an hour and a half away in Hemet and we didn't see them often, so it was a special occasion just having them over. My grandparents weren't fans of Betty but they were always polite to her face. In private Grandma would tell me and Jenny how much they loved and missed our mom and make us promise we'd tell her hello. I liked it when she did that.

Not to be outdone by the Cole family, Betty invited her brother Rob and his wife Stacy to watch the send-off as well. They were two of the biggest people I had ever met and they lived in one of the tiniest trailers I had ever seen, in a mobile home park right next to Disneyland. I'd spent the night at their trailer once and when I saw it for the first time I seriously wondered how we were all going to fit in that thing. But we did and it was really fun—the park had a pool and a game room for kids and we were allowed to walk there all by ourselves— and I thought it was nice that they'd come over for Jenny's big night.

It was practically a party, with me and Dad and Betty and Lindsay and my grandparents and Stacy and Rob. We all sat in the living room together and waited for Jenny to make her grand entrance. Finally Betty announced that she was ready.

Jenny floated into the room looking like a million bucks. Betty had dyed Jenny's hair a golden, buttery caramel color just for the occasion, and curled it in soft ringlets. Jenny had the perfect amount of makeup on, just some pink to highlight her cheeks, a swipe of pale blue eyeshadow across her lids and a light coat of mascara on her lashes. She looked absolutely perfect.

Lindsay and I waited for Steve just inside the front door. It was flanked by two glass panels and we wanted to see his reaction when Jenny opened it. We were not disappointed. His face lit up and his eyes opened wide and his smile nearly ripped his face in half and I remember hoping that just once in my life a boy would look at me that way.

He came inside and took a flower bracelet out of a clear box and slipped it onto Jenny's wrist. All I could think in that moment was, *I wish Mom could see this.* I had to hold back my tears.

After Jenny introduced Steve around to our family, Rob said he and Stacy had a present for Jen, too. He handed her a box all wrapped up with paper and everything. Jenny thanked him shyly while I could see my grandparents looking sort of embarrassed, like they didn't know they were supposed to bring gifts to a homecoming send-off.

"Actually, it's for both of you," Rob said, nodding at Steve. I couldn't imagine what it could be. "Go on, open it."

We all watched, excited, as Jenny pulled back that paper and her gorgeous smile faded into something else entirely. I heard snickers and gasps and I couldn't make one bit of sense of what I was seeing. All of a sudden Jenny was crying, mascara running down her cheeks and ruining her whole face. She was shaking her head; shaking all over.

It was Vaseline.

Rob and Stacy had given Jen and Steve a huge tub of Vaseline.

Betty was nearly rolling on the floor.

I didn't get any of it; not why the trailer people would give her something people put on babies' butts and chapped lips, or why Jenny was so upset about it, or why Betty and Stacy and Rob thought this was the funniest thing in all of ever. I didn't understand why my grandpa was so furious, or why my grandma ran out of the room, or why my dad was giving Betty the dirtiest look I'd ever seen him give anyone in my whole life. I tried getting answers—"Dad, what's going on? Why is Jenny crying? Why did they give her that?"—but I was told to leave the room.

"Oh, calm down everyone, it was just a joke," I heard Betty say as Lindsay and I left.

I didn't get the joke at all. All I knew was that Betty and Rob and Stacy had just ruined what was supposed to be the best night of Jenny's life and I hated all three of them because of it. It would be years before I understood the full force of the humiliation my sister felt that night, but to her great credit she refused to let them get the last laugh. Steve took her for an amazing dinner at the Velvet Turtle, which was elegant and expensive and famous for their chocolate mousse, and then they had a great time dancing with Steve's friends and their girlfriends and dates. Steve told Jenny she looked like a princess and treated her like one all night, opening her door and pulling out her chair and showing her all the respect she deserved; the respect that was nowhere to be found at home.

CURL UP AND DIE

Lindsay and I were going to Disneyland. Jane's mom had offered to take all three of us but Jenny couldn't go because she was on restriction. We were going to get to skip school and everything and I felt awful that Jenny was missing out, especially since it was obvious that she was depressed. I could see it in the way she was completely detached from everything, even me and Lindsay. That was the difference between me and Jen; we both had heard nothing but a nonstop chorus of "you're bad, you're bad, you're bad" from the day we were born, but Jenny internalized it. She believed it. I'd hear the same words and think, *No,* you're *bad.* I have no idea how I came to that conclusion, but I'd have given anything to be able to convince my sister to believe it, too.

One night we were washing dishes and I saw Jenny put something in her shirt. My eyebrows shot up in questioning; *what was that?*

Jenny shook her head and mouthed *nothing.*

But I'd seen her take something from the windowsill. I was sure of it. What was it? Why was she hiding it from me? Not knowing these things filled me with dread. I went to bed feeling sad and worried about my sister. If she took something she wasn't supposed to, especially something of Betty's, there would be serious consequences.

I woke up at 6:30 in a panic. Jenny must have overslept, because she always made sure I was up for breakfast at six. Betty was going to beat the living pulp out of both of us. I sprinted to my sister's room and immediately knew something was very, very wrong.

Jenny was sprawled on top of her bed like a starfish. She wasn't even under the covers. I ran to her and I shook her and shook her but she wouldn't wake up. I kept slapping her face and pinching her, whispering frantically, *"Wake up, get up, you have to get up!"*

Finally after what felt like a lifetime, she opened her eyes just barely. She squinted at me and I saw something register; she moaned a long, drawn-out, *"Nooooooooooooooooooooooooo."* That no said everything to me: No, I don't want to be here. No, I don't want to be alive. No to all of it, every last bit.

Just no.

I saw Dad's bottle of pills on the floor and grabbed it; it was empty. The fact that she wasn't dead meant that Betty could still kill her. I shook her again, pleading with her to get up.

"Please, she'll be down here any minute, you have to get up now, I'm begging you please," I whispered, when in reality I wanted to scream. I was terrified. It took all the strength in my tiny frame to do it, but somehow I got Jenny out of her bed and

to her feet. I pulled her down the hall, and she was dragging and gagging and heaving the whole way. Each time she stumbled she slammed into the wall and the sound echoed through the house.

"*Shhhhhhhhhhhhhh,*" I whispered, pleading.

I got her to the kitchen and pushed her into a chair. She sat slumped over the table while I ran around throwing together something that resembled breakfast. Because that's what you did when your sister had tried to commit suicide; you worried about being beaten for not doing your chores.

I put a plate by Jenny's lifeless face—so it might look like she was eating to someone half-blind—and dashed to Dad's room. Betty routinely got up at four a.m. to study—she was always taking classes at Golden West College, although she never got a degree and never worked a professional day in her life—so thankfully she was in her office upstairs clear on the other side of the house.

"Dad, wake up but *please be quiet,*" I begged. Dad sat bolt upright.

"What's wrong?" he asked.

"Jenny... took your pills and she's... she's not okay at all," I explained. "Please don't tell Betty."

Dad raced to the kitchen, where Jenny now lay in a lifeless heap on the floor. She'd fallen from her chair and was surrounded by vomit.

My father flipped. Despite my specifically asking him not to, he started yelling for Betty, *like that was what we needed,* and no matter how fiercely I begged him to stop, he wouldn't. He couldn't. Betty was the boss in that house, all day every day. Dad didn't have an ounce of authority. If we asked him for anything—a dollar for lunch, permission to play outside, details about what time we were doing something—he said the same thing every single time: "Ask Betty." He was a good man; he just liked to avoid conflict at all costs. He either didn't want to bother with us, or was worried about what would happen if he did.

Betty blew into that kitchen like a hurricane, bellowing at my dad. "What the hell is your problem?" she demanded, oblivious to my sister's condition. Dad pointed to Jenny and explained to his wicked girlfriend what she had done.

If someone had offered me one million dollars to dream up one million ways my dad's insignificant other might have responded, what happened next wouldn't even have made the list.

Betty marched over to Jenny and pulled her roughly to a sitting position. By now, sweet six-year-old Lindsay was awake and witnessing this atrocity along with me.

"If you're going to die," Betty hissed at Jenny, venom dripping from each word, "you might as well look good doing it." Then she dragged my sister to her feet. Jenny looked like a ragdoll. A giant, puke-covered, deathly sick ragdoll.

"What are you doing?" Dad asked, confused. I was wondering the very same thing, but I knew better than to ask.

Betty turned to him, furious. "You know she's just doing this for attention, right? Well, she needs to learn that it's *not* going to work on me!"

"Don't you think we should get her to the hospital?" Dad asked.

"We won't be long," Betty smirked, shaking Jenny. "We're going to go put on some makeup and curl her hair and she's going to look amazing in that ambulance."

Jenny couldn't walk on her own so Betty half-supported, half-dragged her, letting her bang into the walls all the way to the bathroom. Lindsay and I followed, terrified. "Wipe your face," Betty barked at Jenny in disgust as she thrust her into a vanity chair. I had never even hated Captain Jack as much as I hated Betty in that moment.

Betty wanted Jenny to die that day; I'm sure of it. Jenny was throwing up everywhere and Betty just went about her beauty routine as if it were any old average morning, while Lindsay and I cried quietly in the corner and Jenny heaved and gagged. "Don't miss," she told Jenny, handing her an empty Kleenex box to puke into before turning out another perfect ringlet.

Dad finally drove Jenny to the ER, so she didn't even get to show off her nicely curled hair to anyone in the ambulance. The doctors said if they'd waited thirty minutes longer, Jenny would have been dead.

My sister had downed an entire bottle of insulin, which threw her system into a hypoglycemic tailspin. Although Jenny was lucky to be alive, she was in bad shape and spent two weeks in the ICU. Afterward they transferred her to a psychiatric ward for evaluation and monitoring. They must have decided she was just fine, because another three weeks later they released her. Jenny came home to a bed piled high with sticky, crusty plates and my father's furious girlfriend who hated her more than ever.

SOAP SANDWICHES

"Siblings: your only enemy
that you can't live without."

~Anonymous

After Jenny came home from the hospital, some things were different and some things stayed the same. We didn't hang out much because Jenny spent most of her time in her room listening to music and writing in her journal. The writing part was part of her homework from the hospital, an ongoing assignment she had to complete if she wanted to be able to live at home. The hospital must have been pretty bad, because she did it faithfully.

The new Jenny was quiet and withdrawn—it was as if the fire she'd been born with had been doused—so most of my free time at home was spent with Lindsay. One of our favorite things to do was play practical jokes on one another. She put a spider on my pillow right before I crawled into bed, and I retaliated by smearing ketchup all over my neck and a long, sharp kitchen knife and then sprawling out on the floor at the bottom of the stairs and waiting for my half-sister to find my lifeless corpse. I could see my reflection in the marbled mirrors and it was amazing. I can still hear Lindsay's horrified screams in my head. In retrospect, it was a terrible trick to play on a six-year-old, but she always got me back.

When she was angry at me, Lindsay would pull the worst possible prank: she would slap herself on the arm or cheek, and I mean good and hard enough so that it would leave a bright red handprint. Then she'd start sobbing and shouting.

"Erin, stop! Don't hit me!"

Betty, of course, would come running. She'd never ask what had happened or who started what; she'd just start wailing on me, ironically punctuating her point—"You *don't hit* your *sister*"—with punches of her own.

After one such incident, I was desperate to get the last laugh. Betty was out and had told me to make Lindsay's lunch. I fixed my little sister a nice peanut butter, jelly and dish soap sandwich. I'd seen Spanky do that to Alfalfa on *The Little Rascals*, and every time Alfalfa talked, he burped a soap bubble. I was hoping so badly that would happen to Lindsay, and it was all I could do to keep it together as she bit into that thing over and over. She didn't burp up any bubbles, but eventually Lindsay figured out that there was something amiss. I fessed up between giggles and she was livid, spitting the soapy food out of her mouth and shouting obscenities at me. I knew I'd have to think of a really good bribe to keep her from telling Betty on me, so I took her out for ice cream afterward. To this day, I'm pretty sure it was the best fifty cents I ever spent.

WHISTLING DIXIE

*"The most revolutionary thing you can do
is get to know your neighbors."*

~Karl Hess

D ixie Merrill lived across the street with her husband Fred
in a house that was a reverse carbon copy of Jane's. Dixie
was a stunning and elegant former ice skating champion
and when she saw me and Jane outside on our roller skates
she'd come out and give us pointers. She taught us how to
skate backwards and spin in tight little circles and I thought it
was incredible that a grown woman would take the time to do
that for some kids. I couldn't imagine my mom or Betty ever
doing anything of the sort. I was pretty naive to the ways of the
world but I knew one thing for certain: Dixie Merrill was good
and she was safe.

Sometimes she would happen to be outside when Betty
and I were getting back from somewhere and she would casually ask if I could come over and help her with something.
Betty was always more than happy to get rid of me, so she
wouldn't even question what I might be over there doing.

"I have an idea," Dixie told me one of the first times this
happened. "I'm going to pay you for your work, but instead
of giving you the money, how about I save it for you until you
need something big? We can even open a bank account for

you, if you want." I thought this was an amazing idea, because that way I wouldn't have to hand my earnings over to Betty. After I'd helped Dixie unload her groceries or fold her laundry or complete whatever simple task she'd given me, she would tell me how much money I had earned and make a big deal out of pulling that precise amount from her wallet and putting it into an envelope she kept tucked in the back of a kitchen drawer. I never asked how much was in there because I didn't care. I wasn't doing it for the money, I just liked being with Dixie — and away from Betty.

When we were together, Dixie would show me how to iron shirts and sew on buttons that had fallen off. She told me all about her daughter Sherri who was off playing tennis at UNLV with big-time movie stars and loving every minute of it. Dixie talked to me a lot about college and the future and she asked me lots of questions about my family. I didn't dare get into any specifics, but I did say that Betty was pretty hard on me and that sometimes she wasn't a very nice person.

"I never take my eyes off your front door," Dixie told me once. "You know you can always come to me if you need anything." I wondered if she had heard or seen something, or maybe she just had a sixth sense about us. Regardless, I didn't want to drag Dixie into our drama, so I never took her up on that offer. But I liked knowing there was someone right across the street who was watching out for and cared about me. That thought got me through a lot of dark days and nights.

HITCH YOUR WAGON

*"Whatever good things we build
end up building us."*

~Jim Rohn

L indsay and I were perfectly typical sisters. We'd fight like cats and dogs one minute, and the next we'd be drawing plans for the side-by-side houses we were going to build one day and nobody could stop us. I loved her dearly.

I have no idea where or how I got the idea, but one Saturday morning I decided I was going to build her a wagon. I had found some wood in the backyard and I was pretty sure I had enough for the four sides and the bottom. I asked my dad if he could help me with this project, but he was in the middle of a show. I told him I had what I needed for the box, and that I was sure that I could get wheels and a handle and the rest of the stuff I needed at the hardware store in the shopping center up the street. He nodded his vague agreement, so off I went.

There was a nice older man working at the hardware store and I told him I was building a wagon. He raised his eyebrows at me and asked me what materials I had so far. I explained about the wood and he asked me how much I wanted to spend on the rest. I told him I wanted to spend as little as possible but that I still wanted it to be great. He seemed satisfied with that answer and took me around the store, pointing out everything I was going to need.

192

"Do you have a drill?" he asked. I told him I did not. Again, he raised his brows. "Then how will you attach the handle?"

"That's what I'm here to find out!" I explained.

"Can you bring me the wood?" he asked. "That way I can see what you're working with and maybe I can even drill the holes for you." I said that I definitely could, and I raced back home to get the wood.

I must have looked like quite the sight; a skinny, scrawny kid in patchwork hand-me-downs carrying her weight in wood down Fountain Valley's main drag. I couldn't have cared less what anyone thought. I had a wagon to build, and I had someone to help me build it.

The hardware store man laid out all of my wood and assured me that I was right; I had what I needed. He drilled the holes for me right there and then helped me put the box part together, so I could carry my other purchases back home in it.

Back at home, I brought all my supplies inside and began assembling Lindsay's wagon. Dad heard me clanking around and came down to see what the ruckus was all about.

"What are you doing?" He laughed when he saw the elaborate construction site I was manning.

"I told you I was making Lindsay a wagon!" I said.

"I didn't know you meant a *real* wagon," he said. "I thought you were just going to tie a rope to a cardboard box."

He couldn't believe I'd carried that wood to the store and figured out what I needed to buy. The wagon came out so cute it was all I could do not to keep it for myself. I presented it to Lindsay when she got home from her friend Heather's house and she jumped right in and begged me to pull her around so I did. When Betty got home and saw the wagon, she said it was really sweet of me to do that for Lindsay. It was one of the rare glimpses of kindness I'd see in her over the course of many years, and her words filled me with pride. That was one of my favorite days ever on Walnut Street.

THE SHORT END OF THE STICK

*"And for once bravery looked
a lot like running away."*

~Kat Savage

It was clear that Betty detested me, and she went to great lengths to make sure I never forgot it. Everything I did was wrong; no small offense went unpunished. And anything at all could be an offense.

One morning before school, Betty walked by my room and saw some clothes lying over my chair. I had just gotten out of the shower, and she started screaming that she'd already told me to put them away. She ran off in a fury, and I thought that was the end of that.

I was wrong.

Betty came barreling back into my room with a large, bare tree branch in her hand. She swung at me over and over with that stick while I tried to cover myself, but she wouldn't let up. I could see the hatred in her eyes as she did it; she was Captain Jack in a jumpsuit. I heard screaming; terrifying, unfamiliar, carnal sounds that I didn't recognize but were coming from deep inside me. I didn't understand her rage; all I knew was that I couldn't fight back. That would be like begging her to hit me longer and harder. Instead I turned from her and cowered in a corner while she lashed at my back and legs until she felt she'd made her point and then left me there, aching and ashamed.

That day I wore my mint green "GIMME FIVE" t-shirt and baby blue hand-me-down Dittos bell-bottoms. It was like any other normal day at school until a call came into my classroom.

"We'd like to see Erin Cole in the office, please," the disembodied voice said.

My stomach wrenched. What had I done? I grabbed my backpack and hurried out, avoiding my classmates' curious stares.

The secretary brought me into the Assistant Principal's office. She was plump and kind and had a million confusing questions for me. She asked how I liked school and I told her I loved it there because everyone was so nice and my teachers were amazing. She asked how I was adjusting at home, and I said it was great, I had my own room and lots of good snacks and everything was really good. She pressed on: Did I feel like everything was the way it should be there? Was I ever scared? Was I happy?

Yes! No! Yes! I told her. My yardstick was pretty warped at that point, and I genuinely couldn't understand where she was going with this line of questioning.

"Is something wrong?" I asked her.

"No, not at all," she told me. "May I have a look at your legs for a minute?"

I pulled my pants up to my knees and she asked me to turn around. For the first time I felt fear. What was happening? What had I done? Was Betty there? She was friends with the principal; maybe she'd come to humiliate me here, too. Warning sirens were screaming in my head: *Something's wrong, don't trust her, you can't trust anyone.* But she was an adult, and the Assistant Principal at my school, so I slowly turned until my back was to her.

She gasped.

I looked back at my own legs and could see the wild stripes where the branch had ripped through my skin. The whip marks weren't only visible to the naked eye but had left bloody trails across my pale blue Dittos. They were a dead giveaway.

The AP wanted to know what had happened to me but I couldn't hear her words because hot blood was filling my head and all I could hear was the pounding of my own heart. *Betty was going to kill me, that was all there was to it. What could I tell this lady that would get me out of trouble? How could I save myself? Think, Erin. THINK!*

"I'd like to call your father," I heard her say from ten million miles away. And then she was gone.

I didn't sit there and consider my options because there was only one. I grabbed my backpack, bolted out the door and out of the office, and I ran as fast as I could right off that campus.

I didn't slow down until I reached the bus stop over the freeway. I checked the schedule; the next bus would be there in fifteen minutes. I'd learned how to read the timetable when I was still at Ramona with Mom. It was my backup plan in case they didn't come through with the ten-speed. I was leaving one way or another.

Those fifteen minutes were some of the longest of my life. I thought for sure they'd come looking for me, but nobody did. The bus finally came and I gave the driver my lunch money and asked her where I could get off in Garden Grove.

"I stop at Trask," she told me.

I knew exactly where that was and how to get home from there.

Home. They alternately say it's where the heart is; there's no place like it; it's the nicest word there is. To me, it was the lesser of all evils, one tiny step above living cold and alone out on the street.

At least for now.

RAMONA AGAIN

WHO'S ERIN COLE?

I got off the bus and headed toward Mom's house. It was the last place I ever thought I'd be when I woke up that morning, but it wasn't like I had a ton of options. I thought about how much I was going to miss playing pool with Lindsay and taking dance and music lessons with Jane. She was amazing on the violin and I'd been learning to play cello and it was way more fun to practice together than alone. I thought about what my classmates and teachers would think when I just never came back, and I wondered what they'd say about me. I tried to shake off my sadness, because there was nothing I could do about any of it.

I turned from Paloma onto my old cul-de-sac and started running just before Sarge's house. I ran straight to Mom's door and knocked, breathless.

It took her a while but when she did open that door, I could tell she was shocked to see me. She also was a little tipsy, but definitely not drunk. I'd gotten to the point where I knew where she was at any given moment on the intoxication scale; that afternoon, she was a solid four, which wasn't that bad at all.

"Erin, what are you doing here?" she demanded. I told her about Betty and the beatings and that I didn't know I was getting called into the office. I hadn't realized anybody could see the blood. I showed her my back and legs.

Mom covered her face with her hands.

"What did you do to make her do this?" she asked finally, so I told her about the clothes on the chair. She hugged me and asked if Dad knew this was happening, and how I got there. She told me that I wasn't going back to Betty's, and that we could "just let her show up here and we'll see what happens!" Then she let me crawl into bed with her, where we held hands and watched movies. I could have stayed right there forever. Captain Jack called at one point — his daily token show of affection — and Mom told him I was there with her. I couldn't hear screaming or cursing, so that was a good sign.

I wasn't sure how he'd react when he got home, but he was mostly amused that I'd made it back by myself and wanted to know about my new bike. I promised I'd get it back and he gave a harrumph and a sigh and went back to *Gunsmoke*. And that was about the size of it.

My dad finally called looking for me, partly because he was worried about me and partly because he was worried Betty was going to get into trouble, I figured. Mom told him about the beatings and the whip marks all over me. I don't know what he said back, but the police didn't show up, and nobody came to bring me back to Walnut Street.

I had a hard time sleeping that night. I wondered what had happened when the school called Dad, and how he'd reacted when he found out I wasn't there. I wondered what

Betty had told him about what the school said; if she'd lied about it or denied it or told him I deserved it. I wondered what they'd tell Lindsay and Jenny and Jane, and if Jenny would get twice as many beatings now because of me.

I stayed at home the next day and by the following Monday, Mom had re-enrolled me in Stanley Elementary. I was in Mrs. Jones's fifth grade class. She'd been my third grade teacher, too and I was so excited to have her again. After a few weeks of deflecting a nonstop litany of questions ("Where'd you go?" "Are you back for good?"), I slowly settled into my old life as Erin Blomgren.

It was an easy routine to fall back into, except every once in a while out of nowhere I'd get confused when I was writing my name on my paper. I wouldn't even realize what I'd done until my teacher would say, "Wait. Who's Erin Cole?"

HOLIDAY BLUES

Nothing in sight finicialy. This is going to be the poorest Christmas I believe we ever spent. Nothing for the kids is whats killing Don & I. No place to even borrow enough for them.

ONE TRACK MIND

"Just when you think you know people,
they disappoint you in ways you never thought they could."

~Unknown

Back at Stanley Elementary, one thing was certain: I had to find something to do after school so I'd have an excuse to avoid Sarge. I signed up for track and field because they had practice every day. From the first day of drills, my coach was amazed at how fast I could run. I thought that was funny because I was hardly even trying. All I had to do was picture Sarge or Timmy Labonte chasing me and there was no catching me. In fact, I'd have to hold back so I could run with the other girls. I didn't mind; I was having a blast. When I won first place in all my events at the first meet, Coach was like, "Whoa, Erin! Where did *that* come from?" I just shrugged. I didn't know how to tell him that I didn't want to make everyone else feel bad, but I also really liked winning.

I started making friends with some girls on the team, and one of them brought me a big bag of hand-me-down clothes one amazing day. I guess she'd noticed I wore the same patched pants and shoes with holes in the soles day after day and felt bad for me. I might have been embarrassed if I wasn't so overwhelmed with happiness and gratitude.

We had a huge meet coming up and it was on a weekend, so Mom said she and Captain Jack would for sure be there. They'd said they were going to come to some of my weekday meets before, but then Mom would have a few drinks too many or Captain Jack would get home from work and be too tired to go anywhere. But this time they promised. I was so excited for them to see me, because we'd been training for months and I knew I was going to win all my races. I wasn't being cocky; it was a given. Everyone knew it.

I ran to the school early so I could stretch and warm up with my team. Busloads of kids arrived from various schools, lots of them wearing expensive, official-looking track outfits. One girl had these long red ribbons in her hair. They matched her running shorts and I just couldn't get over the fact that someone had gone to all that trouble to make her look so cute when she was just *running*.

Our team had gotten matching t-shirts so for once I felt like I fit in, even in borrowed running shoes and my old lost-and-found gym shorts that had someone else's name in the little white box.

Parents were beginning to show up, many with extra snacks and drinks for their kids. I assumed those were going to be the best runners, because they had families that supported them. I knew Mom and Captain Jack wouldn't bring me anything to eat or drink, but at least they were coming.

I kept my eyes trained on the entrance to the field, wondering if my mom would be walking or in her wheelchair. I didn't care either way, I just wanted her to get there already. I still had yet to see them when the announcer asked everyone to stand for the Pledge of Allegiance. I loved this part and was sad my parents weren't there yet to see it.

The first race started. My friend Kirsten was running it and I was rooting for her, even though I knew she wasn't the fastest. When she came in at the back of the pack, her family crowded around her, comforting her and telling her not to worry, that she was doing great and she still had other races to run.

I hadn't spotted my parents yet when they called my first event, the 440-yard dash. Maybe they'd snuck in the back, or would arrive the minute I turned my head. *Please let them see me, please let them see me,* I prayed as I took my position on the starting block.

"Runners take your mark... get set... BOOM!" The starting gun rang out and I took off like a bullet train. I was as nervous as I'd ever been, but I immediately grabbed the lead and held it until I beat the second-place runner by several paces.

I scanned the crowd but there was still no sign of my parents. They must be running late, or maybe they were having trouble getting Mom's wheelchair into the truck. That happened sometimes. My next race wasn't for an hour, but still I silently begged them to hurry. Mom would be so proud of me when she saw me winning over and over.

She was coming. She *promised.*

My next race was up.

I got into position.

"Runners take your mark..." the announcer began, and I scanned the field one last desperate time.

"Get set..."

They weren't coming.

"BOOM!"

In that moment, when that gun went off, I knew that fact suddenly and completely.

I had never felt more alone.

Fueled by pain and anger and disappointment and longing, I ran like I'd never run in my life. I felt like I was the only runner on the whole track, as I couldn't feel anyone behind or beside me. I flew past the finish line and the stands erupted in clapping and cheering.

I'd crushed it again.

No one cared.

I was crushed.

I'd been so sure that winning first place over and over would give my parents something to be proud of, a reason for them to get up and out of that house and stop drinking for a few short hours. It wasn't about collecting trophies and ribbons for me; I'd have traded places with Kirsten any day of the week just for that love and approval. I walked away that day with three first-place trophies and the knowledge that my parents would never, ever be there to watch me win. If I wanted to be the best at anything, I'd have to do it for myself.

COPPER PIG

"There is no love without forgiveness,
and there is no forgiveness without love."
~Bryant H. McGill

I t was a long, tiring walk home from my track meet. I was lost in my thoughts the entire way, furious at my parents for disappointing me yet again, and even angrier at myself for letting them. I should have known better by then; after all, my entire life had been one long string of canceled plans and broken promises they'd forget they made in the first place. I just wanted so badly to believe that they could change and that I could help them do it that I set myself up for heartbreak, over and over.

The next few days were eerily quiet at home. Mom wasn't feeling well, which meant I wasn't allowed to have or voice any issues of my own. That was just the way it went. No matter what was bothering me, if I dared to raise a complaint she always had an ailment of her own that trumped it.

"Mom, my head hurts," I'd say.

"Honey could you go make me some tea? I'm getting a migraine," would be her reply.

When I slammed my finger in the door, it was, "Gosh, if I could just get this swelling in my hand to go down I'd feel so much better." I walked through life knowing that my problems were never as big or as important as whatever she was going through.

The track meet excuse was her bad knee. She was really sorry, she explained, but that knee was just giving her fits and she was afraid she might slip and fall. I'd heard it all before and dismissed her weak apology the way I always did. "Don't worry about it, it's not a big deal." *I'm not a big deal*, I added in my head.

I was getting older, though, and I was starting to let my disappointment show. "Are you drinking tonight?" I'd ask out of the blue.

"Why do you ask?" she would want to know.

I'd shrug. "Just curious." I could see this getting under her skin because now it was out there. She knew I was watching.

The Friday following the meet I came home to find Mom stone-cold sober. That hadn't happened in ages. She was sitting in her rocking chair, dressed in actual clothes and grinning like the Cheshire cat.

"I have a surprise for you," she said.

Wait, *what*? A surprise? For ME? That occurred about as often as a meteor shower.

"What is it?" I dared to ask.

"When Dad gets home, we're taking you somewhere," she told me. "You go get ready while I put on my face." That meant do her makeup, but I always thought it sounded as if she were a skeleton about to don a flesh-mask.

I heard Captain Jack pull into the driveway and wondered what he thought about this surprise, or if he even knew about it at all. Where on earth were they taking me? It was awfully late to go somewhere like Disneyland or even the park with the big slide, and I couldn't imagine them wanting to go roller skating or bowling with me. I could hardly stand the suspense.

The Captain was sober, too, which put him at around a seven on the pissed-off scale.

"You ready?" he barked at me. I assured him that I was, although I had no idea what I was supposed to be ready for.

He drove past Lucky Supermarket and then pulled into the shopping center where I'd bought Mom's crucifix. Maybe we were going to get some new clothes at Goodwill or grab a cone at the ice cream parlor. But Mom took my hand and led me in the opposite direction; straight toward the pet store.

"How about we get you that guinea pig?" she asked, pulling open the door.

"WHAAAAAAAAAAAAAAT? ARE YOU SERIOUS?" What in the name of Honey Nut Cheerios was going on here? Were these even my parents? I looked at Captain Jack and he made a hurry-up motion with his hands. Like, *Get your ass in there and get your stupid guinea pig before I change my goddamn mind.*

I led them to the cage where they kept the guinea pigs and pointed out the rust-colored one I'd had my eye on. I couldn't believe he was still there because he was by far the cutest of the bunch. My parents let me pick out a cage and a water bottle and an exercise wheel and food, and I got to sit with my new best friend in the back of the camper on the way home. Part of me kept thinking the whole thing might be a dream.

But it wasn't. We got all the way home and I had a guinea pig and he was real and he was mine. Mom named him Copper and I didn't mind one bit. I wanted her to feel like he was hers, too. Copper was a perfect pet, quiet and sweet and he'd never bite or scratch you. He did have this crazy high-pitched squeal and sometimes he'd let loose with it in the middle of the night, but that stopped when I started sleeping with him in my bed.

When Captain Jack was out, Copper went everywhere I went. He had the run of the house and would follow me from room to room and even Sinny the cat left him alone. But when my stepdad came home, Copper went right back into his cage. If I knew anything at all, it was that you never wanted to push your luck with Captain Jack.

BURIED TREASURE

The weekend tradition of dinner at Grandma B's was still going strong. After we ate, my grandma would take me and Mom into her back bedroom and show us the new things she was making. One of them was a knitted blanket she planned to trim in pompoms, like the ones that go on the back of tennis socks. She taught me and Mom how to make them and said we could take the supplies home if we wanted to make more there. That blanket needed a lot of pompoms and we were excited to help.

Grandma was surprised and delighted when we returned the next week with an entire brown grocery bag filled with those fluffy balls. The best part was feeling like Mom and I were working on something fun and creative together.

I noticed that Mom drank less when we were together, so I started helping her with cooking and cleaning. I'd vacuum and do the dishes for her in the hopes my efforts would sustain her sobriety for a day or even an hour. Something was always better than nothing.

One day I was outside watering her plants. The planter box was as awful and overgrown as ever, and I decided to take another stab at it. I was bigger and stronger now, and I thought I stood a pretty good chance of actually making an improvement this time. In fact, I knew I could.

It felt like Groundhog Day as I gathered the clippers and shovels and rakes. I remembered something Grandpa Sam had told me last time I was gardening with him, which was if you wet the soil first, it made things a lot easier. You had to *really* wet it until it was soaked through. Ideally you'd let it sit like that for a day, but I was too anxious to wait. I started at one end and I hosed the whole planter on full blast until it was almost muddy, then I went back to where I'd started.

I grabbed a huge handful of those weeds and bent them back and forth and back and forth in a sweeping motion. I'd done this four or five times when something orange caught my eye. It was deep down in the planter, wedged into the corner. I pulled the weeds back and I could see it was a cup, and it was filled with water. I was afraid to pull it out with my bare hands because I had (and still have) a crippling fear of spiders, so I found a garden glove and turned it inside out (for the same reason) before putting it on.

It was a cup and it was wedged in there good, but I managed to pull it out. There was something in it, at the bottom, something round and sparkling and —

MOM'S RIIIIIIIINNNNNNNNNNNNNNNNNNNNG!!!!!!!!!!!!

I was afraid to believe it, but it was true! I had found Mom's ring! She was going to be so happy! I poured the water out slowly and collected the ring. I had never been so excited to give someone something, except maybe Mom's wooden cross, in my life.

I ran into the house, out of breath and nearly bursting with excitement. I found Mom in the kitchen.

I held my closed fist out to Mom and said, "Close your eyes!"

Mom laughed. "No way," she said, because I got my arachnophobia from her and because of it, we were always trying to freak each other out with little balls of string or lint we'd find and pretend they were creepy-crawlies. I laughed back.

"I promise it's not a spider or a bug, please close your eyes!" I begged. She kept refusing, saying she'd given birth to me and she knew I was up to no good, and I kept pleading with her to trust me and just CLOSE HER EYES!

Finally, reluctantly, she gave in. I reached for her hand and put the ring in it, then closed her fingers around it. I watched her relax as she felt its hardness and realized it wasn't an insect of any kind. I told her she could look.

She opened her eyes. It took less than a second for her to realize what she was holding, and then she was sobbing and screaming and hugging me.

"Oh my God, Erin, where did you find this? Where was it? I can't believe it. I can't believe you found my diamond. This is incredible!" She was elated, and it was all because of me. If there was a sweeter feeling on God's green earth, I'd yet to encounter it.

Mom celebrated having her ring back with Captain Jack that night the way they celebrated anything, and I didn't mind. They weren't wasted, just happy. We watched *Wild Wild West* together and for the first and probably only time in my life, I was my mother's hero.

I GOT YOU BABE

"If grass can grow through cement,
love can find you every time."

~Cher

A couple of days before my eleventh birthday, my brother Pat called my parents and asked if he could come visit for a while. In the years since Kelly died, I'd only seen my oldest brother a handful of times when he'd stop by with a brown paper bag of goodies for me and Jen. Pat had bounced around a few different friends' houses and even lived at the water truck yard while he was driving trucks with our dad. He was between jobs and had some time and wanted to see us, Pat said. Jenny had come back to Mom's for a little while, too (although that wouldn't last long), and we were over the moon.

My sister moved into my room and gave Patrick hers. The three of us would stay up late and play cards and Yahtzee or listen to his treasured Beatles album. Poetic, philosophical John Lennon was his favorite artist of all time, something I think says a lot about my brother.

Patrick was hardly a saint, though, and he still had his old devious big-brother streak, telling me to sit against the wall while he loaded matches into his BB gun and then pretending he was going to shoot my feet. He'd get the biggest kick out of me because I'd be like, "Okay, go!" That's how much I trusted him. He would demand to know *"Who's the greatest brother on the whole entire earth,"* before he'd let you in his room. Obviously it was him, I told him, because it was true. Everything was better when Pat was around.

One of our favorite things to do was watch *Tony Orlando and Dawn* and *The Sonny and Cher Show* on TV. Cher was to me what John Lennon was to my big brother: everything. I wanted to look like her, dress like her, sing like her, be like her. She was over the top and absolutely unapologetic about it—and she could be anybody she wanted. Cher was magic in a costume and I was all in. Who got to wear a belly-baring, beaded loincloth with slits up to there and a technicolor headdress that touched the ceiling and trailed behind you like a peacock's tail at the same time? That headdress would be burned onto my soul forever, marking the beginning of my love affair with bold, dazzling design.

I remember the day I heard they were coming out with a Cher doll. I had no idea how—it certainly wouldn't be for my birthday—but I was getting one.

Some years we got a birthday present, just one, and some years we didn't. That year I was positive I wouldn't be getting one, as Mom brought up on a daily basis how much money we didn't have. Birthday or not, we knew better than to act as if we wanted anything ever; if Captain Jack thought for one second you were thinking of yourself and your own selfish wishes, he'd make you feel like the lowest piece of scum that ever walked the earth.

God forbid I ask for that Cher doll. In fact, I wasn't going to ask for anything, because Mom was starting to feel good again and Pat was home and Jenny and I were getting along. The last thing I wanted to do was make any waves and cause someone to do something crazy or leave again.

My birthday came and along with it, a gift from my amazing Grandma Blanche and Grandpa Sam. My grandpa loved to send packages through the mail, and would wrap them neatly in kraft paper before tying them up with real twine from his garage. He'd take your present to the post office himself and carefully arrange it so it would arrive at just the right time. It made my birthday so special. A lot of times he'd send something extra for Jenny on my birthday and vice versa, because he was kind and because he probably knew we didn't get much.

That year, my grandparents' gift was a stuffed turtle with a red beret on his head and bells in his feet. I named him Sonny, and he was the greatest stuffed animal I had ever owned. Mom gave me a calculator because she wanted one, and then she made fried chicken and green beans and mashed potatoes, and Jenny and Patrick and I had a really nice dinner together. Just as we were finishing up, Pat said he had something to give me.

I was surprised and delighted and couldn't believe my brother had gone out on his own and gotten me something — it didn't matter one bit what it was — and then waited all day to give it to me. I got to enjoy that warm, fuzzy feeling for about ten whole seconds.

"Well, you can just wait until everyone's done eating," the Captain hissed, trying as always to burst my bubble. "Your mother and I haven't had our dinner yet." *You disgust me* was written all over his face, and he took his sweet-ass time eating his meal, let me tell you. But I wouldn't dare try to rush them or even show one ounce of excitement or frustration. I wouldn't give him the satisfaction. Nothing could ruin my special surprise.

Finally Mom said they were done. Pat went to his room and came back with not one but two presents. What in the world? My brother handed me the smaller one first, which he'd even wrapped in newspaper. His smile lit up the whole room. I was speechless.

"Well, are you going to open it?" Mom finally asked.

I peeled off the paper slowly and opened the tiny box. Inside was a sparkly ring with a sapphire-colored stone flanked by two fake diamonds on each side. It was exquisite, and certainly unlike anything I had ever owned or worn. I slid it onto my middle finger and then held my hand out in front of me like I was the Queen of England with all my splendor and sparkle, wiggling my fingers and batting my eyelashes. In that moment, I was the fairest of them all. Even Captain Jack gave a chuckle.

"Now look what you've done," he said to my brother with an eye roll.

"I'm so glad it fits you, monkey," Pat said. "Now open the other one."

There was more? How was that even possible? I'd already opened one gift that was never coming off my hand; nothing could ever top it. My brother could have wrapped up a unicorn or a goose that laid golden eggs in that other box and I couldn't possibly love it more than I loved that ring. I was sure of it.

I peeled back the paper for a second time that night, and when I did my mind exploded right there on the spot, in my dingy, ugly living room on Ramona Place.

It was the doll.

My sweet, darling brother had gotten me the Cher doll.

She was as magnificent as I had imagined, and Jenny and I played with her all night in Pat's room while we listened to Jimi Hendrix. I felt loved and lucky and special all at the same time. My brother Patrick could do that to a girl.

A SIGN OF THE TIMES

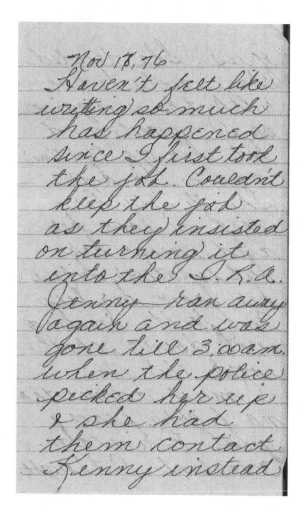

Nov 18, 76
Haven't felt like
writing so much
has happened
since I first took
the job. Couldn't
keep the job
as they insisted
on turning it
into the I.R.A.
Jenny ran away
again and was
gone till 3:00 a.m.
when the police
picked her up
& she had
them contact
Kenny instead

of us. She decided she wants to live with them again so I agreed and let her go. (3rd time) again. I hope she finds herself. I love her and miss her, but whatever helps her from her lies I'm for it. Smoking not doing school work etc; etc: I must admit tho no fights, peace & quiet. Erin calm & content. I thought

11-17-76

it would effect
her badly but
it hasn't. Keep
looking for an
inner sign. so
far none.

STREAKING WITH THE SAINTS

"The secret to happiness is freedom,
and the secret to freedom is courage."

~Thucydides

There were three main reasons people ran down the street naked in the 1970s: as a prank, for publicity, or in protest. But that night, I did it purely for fun.

It was one of those warm, magical summer evenings when a silvery moon hung low in the sky. There had been no cattle call because I was with the saints, Maggie and Patty, and Mom had said as long as we were together I could stay out after dark. A Taste of Honey's "Boogie Oogie Oogie" had just come out, and a neighbor's babysitter was blasting it in the front yard. The saints and I did cartwheels across the lawn and danced and sang and I was high on disco and freedom.

It was hot and our dance party was exhausting. One of the Fuentes brothers brought us Otter Pops and orange soda and when he left, I announced that I wanted to go streaking. The saints never would have done something so daring themselves, but they promised they'd be on the lookout for me.

I didn't think twice about it. I stripped down to my bare skin and took off down the street, feeling exhilarated and free. Maggie and Patty howled with laughter, astonished at my boldness. I probably should have thought about what would happen if I got caught, but I'm so glad I didn't.

For once in my life, I got away with feeling good and having fun.

NOTHING BUT THE TRUTH

"Whoever is careless with the truth in small matters cannot be trusted with important matters."

~Albert Einstein

Sometimes someone gives you something that changes your life. My someone was Grandpa Sam, and the something was a special sort of sketchbook. It was filled with drawings of butterflies and flowers and hummingbirds, each with a sheet of tracing paper you could lay over the top. I couldn't get over how amazing it felt to recreate these beautiful drawings over and over; to copy the perfect curve of a wing or the sharp angle of a thorn. I'd often been mesmerized watching Mom draw, but I'd never had any supplies of my own. Now that I did, anytime I wasn't running I was tracing in my room. I'd turn up my transistor radio—another gift from Grandpa—and get lost in shadows and pencil shavings for hours.

Eventually I abandoned the tracing paper and began sketching random things, either by sight or from memory. Sometimes Mom would come in and watch me the way I used to watch her and give me pointers.

"Relax your hand and just let it flow out of your mind," she'd say, and I had to stifle a laugh. If she only knew what sort of stuff wanted to fly out of my mind! Oh, no. I'd been successfully burying that stuff for years, and it needed to stay right where it was. But drawing itself? Drawing was heaven. It was Nicolette Larson's "Lotta Love" put down on paper. Hours passed unnoticed whenever I had a pencil in my hand.

Maybe it was because Jenny wasn't there to attract trouble like a magnet, or perhaps I had figured out how to stay out of Captain Jack's way; regardless of the reason, I wasn't getting knocked around nearly as often as I used to. If my parents were modestly sober I'd even still put on shows for them, parodying the Lip Quencher and Firestone commercials or imitating Ruth Buzzi. I could do a mean Doris Sidebottom, and I'd have them in stitches.

The only real problem in my immediate periphery was the predator up the street. Sarge was still around and he was relentless, asking Mom several times a week if I could come clean for him. I was running out of excuses.

"Just tell me why you don't want to go," she said for the hundredth time. I wanted to tell her so badly it ached, but I knew I had to be careful.

"I just don't want to make a big deal out of it," I said finally.

"Make a big deal out of what?" Mom asked. "Tell me, now."

Sarge had been manipulating me with fear from the beginning, but I'd gotten to the point that I was more afraid of what would happen if I *didn't* tell than if I did.

"Sarge does bad things he shouldn't be doing," I blurted.

"What does THAT mean?" Mom shouted.

"Why are you getting mad at me?" I demanded. I think we were both surprised that I had such assertiveness in me — I never, ever talked back to her — but I couldn't help it. I was tired of getting in trouble for doing nothing.

"I'm not mad," Mom promised, softening her voice. "Just tell me."

"Well, I don't want you telling anyone else, especially Don," I said. I never called him Captain Jack to her face, not even once.

"I won't tell anyone," Mom said. "Is he being a dirty old man? Is that what it is?"

"Yes," I said, relieved that I didn't have to find the words. "That's exactly what it is."

Mom said nothing.

She asked me nothing.

She nodded and sighed.

She never sent me back there again.

And that was about the size of it.

THEY BOTH STINK

Mom and Dad never spoke about their battle for legal custody of me, but I found out later that the war waged on behind the scenes for quite a while. Even Grandpa Sam — a kind man of few words and the person you'd least expect to stick his nose in anybody else's business — was paying attention. In a letter to Mom and Captain Jack (included on the following pages but which I have taken the liberty to transcribe here because his handwriting is nearly illegible), he wrote:

Dear Don & Jeri,

Have been thinking the last few days whether to write you this letter or not and do not know what your reactions to it would be.

I have noticed during the times we were down there on Thanksgiving and Xmas that Erin was an entirely different girl since she came out from the influence of Jennie [sic] and more so since she has been up here this time.

She seems more cheerful and full of fun than ever before and she and mother sit and talk all the time and more contented than ever before.

The other times she was up here with Jennie she seemed downcast and cowed and would hardly say anything and whenever she did say anything she would get a dirty look from Jennie.

From what mother told me today that you told her what Jennie has done, I would tell your lawyer all about it and also tell him about that [illegible] who lives close to you who uses pot and that they are a going to testify against you and let him investigate them.

I asked Erin today if she wanted to go live with Kenny and she said no they STINK.

I told her that I was arguing to keep her up here with us and she said O.K.

But I sure would tell that lawyer of yours all that has been said lately and not let it go by for the more information he can get against them the better he can handle it.

But please don't get mad at me for writing this but wanted to tell you what my observations have been recently.

Best of love,

Dad

San Pedro C.A.
Dec- 25- 1976-

Dear Don & Jenni:-

Have been thinking the last few days whether to write you this letter or not and do not know what your reactions to it would be.

I have noticed during the times we were down there on Thanksgiving and Xmas that Erin was an entirely different Girl since she came out from the influence of Jennie and more so since she has been up here this time.

She seems more cheerful and full of fun than ever before and she and mother sit and talk all the time and more contented than ever before.

The other times she was up here with Jennie She seemed down cast and cowed and would hardly say any thing and whenever she did say any thing she would get a dirty look from Jennie

From what mother told me today that you told her what Jennie has done I would tell your Lawyer all about it and also tell him about

that Patsy who lives close to you
who uses Pot and that they are a.
going to testify against you and let
him investigate them.

I asked Erin today if she
wanted to go and live with Kenny and
She Said no they STINK.

I told her that I was a going
to keep her up here with us and
She said O.K.

But I sure would tell that
Lawyer of yours all that has been
said Lately and not let it go by.
For the more information he can get
against them the better he can
handle it.

But Please don't get mad at
me for writing this but wanted
to tell you what my observations
have been recently,

Best of
Love
Wed

YOU'RE INTO SOMETHING GOOD

Don't even want to think about Tues. Total loss and disgust with myself. The only good thing I did was get all my vitamins and water pills down. Ate a real regular Hamburger, french fries and onion rings. Can still taste it. Mustn't think about it.

Kelly's garden was finally becoming a reality. Mom and I had been spending every spare minute we had out there, and even Captain Jack had pitched in, filling at least fifteen bags of weeds and brush in one day. Afterward, Mom planted neat rows of onions and squash and carrots and turnips and beets.

While they toasted to their hard work, I offered to ride my bike to Carl's Jr. and pick up some lunch.

Carl's Jr. was their favorite—and the only restaurant they'd ever taken me to—but I'd learned long ago never to suggest going there with Captain Jack. The workaround was to go *for* him; that way he could stay home and drink, and I could get food without being humiliated. It was a win-win.

"What's the goddamn problem in there?" he'd explode at the guy working the drive-thru window. "Awwwwwww balls! What's taking you so goddamn long? This is BULL-SHIT!" Every once in a while he'd actually get out of the drive-thru line, screech the camper into a parking spot and drag me inside with him to rough up whoever happened to be working the counter. "You don't know SHIT about how to run a goddamned restaurant," he'd slur, and I would want to die on the spot. Every customer in that place would stop chewing, and even the people outside in their cars would be staring open-mouthed at the lunatic at the counter. Sometimes the Carl's Jr. workers would threaten to call the police, but they'd always wait until they'd given me my onion rings and burger before they kicked him out, which I thought was nice.

Back at school, I still felt no urgency to excel. My sixth grade teacher Mrs. Garwood was one of the special ones who genuinely cared about her students and wanted to make sure everyone got something out of her class. We started working on a project called Industries on Parade, where you got to choose a company to write a letter to describing a good or bad experience you'd had, or making some sort of request. The idea was to get them to respond to you and maybe even send you a small token of appreciation for your efforts.

Everyone was excited about this project except me. I was downright pessimistic about the whole thing. Who was I going to write to anyway? What would I say? And most importantly, why would anyone listen to me, or take the time to reply? One kid was writing to one of the airlines, and a girl named Lacy was going to write to the skateboard company her dad worked for. Another student picked Hostess, the company that made Ding Dongs and Twinkies. That gave me an idea: I could write to Carl's Jr.

It was perfect. I would tell them how much my family and I loved their food, and that it was the only restaurant we ever went to. I could ask if anyone ever complained about the service, and reiterate that we only ever had amazing service there. I would definitely leave out the part about Captain Jack roughing up the employees when the food wasn't out in sixty seconds flat. I would be gracious and polite and appreciative, and maybe it would help undo some of my stepfather's damage. I was one of the first students to finish her letter, and I mailed it off proudly.

Responses started trickling in. A girl had written to Crayola and they replied with a box of crayons for each student in our class. The airline kid scored us a field trip to John Wayne Airport, where we all got to tour an airplane. That was one of the best replies. Lots of kids got no response at all, and I was sure I'd be in that group. Even though I knew my letter was good, I also figured they had some way of knowing that my stepdad was the ticking time bomb who routinely went off every time he visited the place. I understood why they wouldn't want to write back to me, and I didn't even blame them.

I'd all but forgotten about Industries on Parade the morning Mrs. Garwood called me to her desk and handed me a letter. It was on heavy paper and it said Carl's Jr. Corporate Offices at the top. Mrs. Garwood asked me to read it to the class, which was a lot of pressure to put on a shy kid like me.

But I was dying to know what that letter said, so I cleared my throat and I read:

> Dear Erin,
> Thank you for writing to let us know about you experience with our company. We value your opinion and feedback so that we may better serve customers just like you. On behalf of the company, we would like to treat you and your entire class to lunch on the day of your choice. Please call the number below to set up the time and date that works best. Thank you again for your letter, and please feel free to write us again with any concerns or comments you may have in the future.
> Sincerely,
> Carl Jr.

Okay, it wasn't signed by Carl himself, but it might as well have been. My head was spinning. *This shit really works? No way!* When I finished reading, my classmates were clapping and cheering. For me! My happiness was super-size that day, and again the day they brought in a greasy feast for my whole class. Forget about Burger King; in my head at least, I was the Burger Queen.

OH, CHRISTMAS SHRUB

Good day going still early. The tree looks very nice, and good feeling because it came from our yard just from pruning a cypress that was in bad need of a good cutting. We have more decorations to make and add but this year has really been enjoyable.

DEAR MRS. DRAKE

I do wish Don's new job would come thru. He is so irritable & touchy about everything, one can hardly speak with him, & don't particularly want to when he is like that.

aptain Jack lost jobs the way seven-year-olds lose teeth. And when my stepfather was out of work, he liked to fill all of his pesky free time with booze. A committed enabler, Mom wouldn't dream of letting him drink alone. It never took long for things to progress to the full-on desperation stage where they slept all day, stopped buying food and basically ceased being aware of my existence. I was as good as living on my own. I had my guinea pig Copper and that was about it.

The Industries on Parade project had planted a seed. I kept thinking maybe if I wrote someone a letter and told them what was going on in my house, they could help. I wouldn't be telling on my parents; I'd be saving them. They'd thank me for it one day, I was positive. I thought and thought about who I could write this letter to, and one day in PE I got my answer.

Mrs. Drake was the stereotypical gym teacher. She was sensible and strong as an ox and she didn't mess around. She wouldn't think twice about dress-coding you when you forgot your uniform or making you do an extra lap if she caught you chatting after she told you to pipe down. Although I didn't know her all that well, she seemed like someone who might be able to talk some sense into my absent, alcoholic parents.

I started the letter at school, but I ran out of time there so I tucked it inside one of my text books and brought it home. As usual my parents were passed out when I got there. I tiptoed in quietly and locked myself in the bathroom to finish my masterpiece. I didn't have a lock on my bedroom door, and even closing it would have seemed suspicious. The bathroom was a brilliant call because nobody would even think to bother me—

"Erin, what are you *doing* in there?" It was Mom, suddenly wide awake and banging on the door.

"I'm just peeing," I lied, startled and scared. I sounded guilty, even to me.

"You've been in that bathroom forever," she said. "I want you to come out right this minute." We only had the one bathroom; God knew how long she'd been out there waiting.

I shoved the letter back in my book with shaking hands, flushed the toilet for good measure and unlocked the door.

Mom's eyes were wild; her hair was crazy. I tried to slip past her, but she was having none of that.

"What's that?" she said, motioning to my textbook.

"Just a book from school. I was doing some reading," I replied.

"Give it to me," she said. She held out her hand and raised her eyebrows. She was serious and not about to budge.

"Why? What's wrong? I was just doing homework," I stammered, handing the thing over reluctantly. Refusing her was never an option. But how did she *know*? It was like she had some crazy sixth sense. She had to, to wake up from a drunken stupor and decide out of the blue that I was doing something devious in the bathroom.

Mom led me to the living room and ordered me to sit, so I did. I was positive she could see my heart beating out of my chest. She lowered herself next to me and fanned through my book. When she did, the letter slid to the floor. She picked it up and began reading. I sat next to her, frozen in fear.

The letter left nothing to the imagination. I started by telling Mrs. Drake that I was in her third period PE class and that I had a problem. I told her my parents drank all day and all night and that they would stay in bed for weeks at a time. I told her that whenever they were awake they'd fight and hit each other and me, and that sometimes we had food and sometimes we didn't. I told her I was lonely and that I couldn't take it anymore. I begged her to help me, to help them, to help all of us.

"What the hell is this?" Mom shouted. She couldn't have even gotten through half of my incriminating words by that point, but she certainly got the gist.

Once again, I had no choice.

I shot to my feet, ready to run, and Mom instinctively grabbed my arm. I tried to pull away and her fingernails dug into my flesh, tearing tiger stripes through my upper arm's soft underbelly. I braced myself for the pain and gave one more big yank to free my arm from her claw, and then I was out of there, out the back door and over the fence, just like Jenny had done that day a million years ago. Some things in that place never, ever changed.

I had never gotten my ten-speed back from Dad's, so I ran to a neighbor's house far up the street.

Donna opened the door with a smile but when she saw my bleeding arm, her face quickly fell.

"Erin, what happened?" she asked, overcome with concern. Donna wanted to know how she could help me, and I asked if I could call my dad. It was just the latest in the series of lesser evils that was my life. I wasn't old enough to completely take care of myself or to be alone the way I was at the house on Ramona. Going back to the wrath of Betty was better than the isolation at Mom's, even if she didn't kill me for writing that letter—which she very well might.

Please God, help me, I thought as I waited for Dad to come get me. I was going to need it. I was going back to Walnut Street.

WALNUT AGAIN

HELLO AND GOODBYE

When Dad got to Donna's house to pick me up, I could see the sadness in his eyes.

"Erin, you can't keep doing this," he told me, as if I had some choice in the matter. "You need to pick a house and stick it out." He couldn't possibly know how badly I wanted to stay in one place, or how hard it was for a twelve-year-old to try to choose between no rules and an iron fist; between being ignored and being beaten; between starving and being made to eat until you puked. One was no worse than the other; it was just a matter of how long I could tolerate the present situation before trading it in for the other.

I hadn't spoken to Dad at all since the day nearly a year before when I bolted from school and took the bus back to

Ramona, and he didn't bring up that incident or the beatings at all on the drive home. He just kept telling me that I needed to try harder and I promised him that I would. The irony was that I wanted to like Betty, and there were things that I genuinely loved about her. I loved that she got out of bed every day and had something to do, even if it wasn't an actual job. I loved that she took time to get ready when she went out. I loved that she drove a car and wore high heels and played the cello and the piano. I loved that one time when I had the flu and I crept into their bedroom in the middle of the night, she didn't yell or punish me or tell me how bad *she* was feeling. Instead, she sat up and asked me what was wrong and put me in bed next to Dad and gave me medicine and an ice pack for my head. I loved that when I came home this time, she met me with a hug and said, "It's good to have you back, kid." I didn't see that side of her often, but I knew it was there, buried deep below the layer of unhappiness that made her want to hurt and humiliate everyone in her path.

I was allowed to return to Ramona to get a few of my things. There were only three that I cared about: my guinea pig Copper, my red and blue Vans, and Sonny the turtle. The first two were exactly where they should have been, but Sonny was nowhere to be found. After searching in every possible spot twice, I knew with a profound and overwhelming sadness that Mom had hidden him from me. It was a hideous thing to do to a child; the cruelest sort of revenge. I left with my meager things and a broken heart.

Dad re-enrolled me in Fountain Valley Elementary, and I was back to being Erin Cole again. My old best friend Jane was beside herself to have me back. She was one of dozens of kids who wanted to know why I left and where I'd gone. I'd reply with some vague story about my mom being sick and quickly change the subject. It wasn't exactly a lie, I told myself. She *was* sick. Maybe we all were.

I abandoned track along with everything else I'd left at Mom's and went back to dance classes. Immediately I fell in love all over again. Just like with drawing, I could completely lose myself in movement for long hours at a time. I didn't even need a ride to Mr. Baker's studio because I had my ten-speed back. Everything would have been bordering on good if it weren't for Jenny.

My big sister still couldn't keep herself out of trouble. She'd push Betty's buttons and get in fights at school and once we woke up to find someone had spray-painted BITCH across our driveway in jet-black paint. To be honest, I thought there was a fifty-fifty chance the artist had been talking about Betty, but everyone else seemed positive that expletive was directed at Jenny. That fact was confirmed the next day when a group of eighth graders followed my sister home and repeatedly called her the b-word while they tried to beat the crap out of her right in our front yard.

Being hated in two places was too much for Jenny to handle. She was barely fourteen when she was suspended for taking a thermos full of vodka to school. I was shocked. My sister had always been as repulsed by alcohol as I was. *How long had she been drinking?* I wondered. *Was it hereditary, like cancer or some other sickness she couldn't control?* I had no one to ask; no internet to consult. Once again, I was alone with my questions and my fear.

Jenny was transferred to the local school for troubled kids. My sister attended Wintersburg Alternative for two whole weeks before she decided she'd had enough of that school and enough of all of us and she ran away for good. I later learned she spent some time on the street and some time in a random garage before she met and moved in with her boyfriend. He was much older than she was and as mean as the day is long and apparently, the guy could hit just as hard as Captain Jack.

Jenny never came home again.

T-BONED

"There are no accidents…
there is only some purpose that we haven't yet understood."

~Deepak Chopra

With Jenny gone, our roles in the house shifted. I was on dish duty day and night and Lindsay was charged with clearing the table and putting all of the food away. We worked hard to make sure we were always on top of our chores and homework so that we could continue to do the things we loved. For me that mostly meant dancing.

Soon after my return, Mr. Baker asked me if I would consider teaching a few of the studio's tiny tots ballet classes in exchange for free lessons of my own. It was a best-case scenario for me, not having to ask Dad and Betty for money for lessons, and being out of the house doing what I loved to do three additional days a week.

My life was on a definite upswing.

I rode my bike everywhere now, including the therapy Betty felt I needed to sort out the cobwebs of my childhood, as she put it (although I knew I was only going because she had the hots for my therapist, Alan). Most of the time I'd just talk about her and how awful and abusive she was; how toxic the house had become. I told Alan that I just needed to get through the next five and a half years. That was it. The day I turned eighteen I was out of there for good and never, ever looking back. Alan took a lot of notes and said very little.

I landed my first real job — one that paid in actual money and not trade — shortly after my thirteenth birthday. It was at a reading center for kids who were struggling in school or who had been absent for long periods of time for one reason or another. One kid I worked with had recently had open heart surgery; another had a learning disorder that made it difficult to connect letters to their respective sounds. It wasn't a job I would have picked for myself, but I liked it well enough. The truth was Betty knew the owner and had gotten me the gig because she thought it would be good for me to have a little more responsibility. Conveniently, I thought it would be good for me to get as far away from her as possible so it all worked out swimmingly.

The bike ride to that job was six miles each way, and it was a rough trip at times. By the end of my shift I'd be tired and it would be dark and there were some crazy drivers out there in the world. Once a car full of screaming boys blew past me, scaring me so badly I nearly fell off my bike. Another time I was pedaling furiously along the road's edge when an elderly man in a big old Buick gunned around me and then proceeded to make a sharp right-hand turn directly in front of me.

There was a single split second of awareness — big car, too close — before I T-boned the Buick's passenger side door, flew over my handlebars and rolled across the hood. My bike and I landed in a heap on the other side.

The driver could have been Captain Jack's angry older brother. He jumped out of that car, all flushed and furious, and started yelling at *me*.

I was hurt, I was bleeding and my bike was a mangled mess. The last thing I wanted or needed was another lecture on how I was doing something wrong when in actual fact, I was completely blameless.

Never in my life had I raised my voice or spoken back to an adult, but something in me snapped right there on Newland Street. I strung together every profanity I could think of as I gave the angry man directions to the DMV and suggested he go there immediately and apply for a license. Then I jumped on my wobbly-wheeled circus bike and hauled my sorry, scraped-up self home, teetering all the way.

Dad was in the kitchen when I came in.

"What the hell happened to you?" he wanted to know. He didn't say it like I must have done something to cause or deserve it; he was genuinely concerned. I told him about the idiot driver and that my bike was basically totaled.

"How did that feel?" he asked, trying to make me laugh.

"Oh, it felt amazing," I replied, rolling my eyes.

"We should probably get you a light for your bike," he said.

"There's not much left of it," I told him. "It's pretty bent up."

"You can take mine. You were getting too tall for that old one anyway."

He was right. I actually was.

We went to Kmart the next day and bought a light for my new-old bike, and all I could think was that finally someone cared if I lived or died.

DIVING IN

*"Life isn't about waiting for the storm to pass.
It's about learning to dance in the rain."*

~Vivian Greene

D espite abysmal odds and a decided lack of academic ambition, I had made it to high school. I was a dreadful, disinterested student unmotivated by anything so mundane as passing grades or grand dreams of the future. I was just getting by, buying time until my release.

Dance was everything to me, but I was missing something I'd had with track, something that took me a while to put my finger on. Finally it hit me: I missed being part of a team.

I longed for the camaraderie, the competition, and above all, the sense of belonging to something. My friend Jane suggested I join the swim team since I was always so happy in the pool. It seemed like a good enough reason to me, so I signed up.

While some swimmers I know savor the monotony of the strokes, the rhythm of identical lap after lap, to me the lane pool was like a torture chamber. It was me alone with my thoughts of home and how much I hated it there on a silent, never-ending loop.

The day I went to tell the coach I was quitting, he said, "Follow me," in a brusque tone and took off. Mr. Bray was crazy and everyone knew it. He'd gone to war and come home with a steel plate in his head, and you weren't wise to argue with him. I followed him away from the lane pool and over to the diving pool. That one had a half-dozen kids jumping and splashing from three diving boards; two one-meter boards and one three-meter.

"I want to see you jump," he said.

Jump? Me? Why? I didn't ask these questions out loud, though. Instead, I watched and listened as he explained what he wanted me to do. I had a lifetime of experience with crazy people and I knew that going along was almost always your best bet.

"Go on," Mr. Bray told me.

I went to the lowest board and waited my turn. The divers before me were all over the map. Some were elegant water-ballerinas and others were as graceful as a three-legged hippo. When my turn came up I walked to the end of the board, mesmerized by the way it gave beneath my weight. It was amazing; springy like a trampoline but also strong and powerful, like it could launch you clear across California if you let it.

"Jump," Mr. Bray ordered. "But come down with the board, don't let it slap your feet. Just do that, and keep jumping."

I did what he said over and over until I lost my balance and tumbled into the water. It was exhilarating.

I was all in.

The team welcomed me with open arms, and the other divers would show me easy tricks to try. I was fearless and daring and caught on quickly, and my new teammates respected me for it. That was a first for me, being accepted by my peers, and it was like a drug to me. I couldn't get enough. As I mastered the moves, they got progressively harder. Before long I was doing forward flips, backward flips, reverse and twists. I learned to pike and tuck and point my toes like a pro. Sometimes I'd think about Pat and that slide on Stardust and wish he could see me now. I knew he'd be beside himself with pride.

Diving is a sport that takes two things above all else, almost in equal measure: guts and trust. My teammates would teach me a new move and then say, "No matter what, *stay tucked until you hear the call.*" The call was a loud, unmistakable *HUP!* and the caller had to shout it at just the right time or you were in for a world of hurt. That's where the trust came in. Everyone would be quiet when someone was calling a dive; we had each other's backs in every sense of the word.

The sport became my obsession; the divers became my tribe.

My schedule was insane. I'd practice in the morning before school, shivering with my teammates on the pool deck at the unholy hour of four a.m. Sometimes I'd see Betty's car circling the parking lot and I knew she was checking to see if I was really doing what I said I was. I couldn't have cared less. After a full day of classes, including dance, I'd swim again for two more hours until I had to leave to make it to work on time. I had it timed down to the split second. I'd slip sweats on right over my suit, grab a snack and hop on my bike with dripping wet hair. I had to haul ass the six miles to the learning center to be on time, but it was worth it just to eke out every blissful second in that pool.

APRIL SHOWERS

My brother Patrick had briefly been married to a woman we called "the volcano" because of her volatile personality. They even had a young son together. But when the marriage imploded after less than two years, his wife took their child and left. It was a different world back then, and fathers—especially ones who were practically children themselves—weren't likely to fight a move like this. Pat paid child support faithfully even though he never saw his first son again.

He'd been working for the same trucking company for several years when he was called to work on an oil spill in El Segundo. He was taking a break down by the beach when he spotted a tall, beautiful woman strolling along the water's edge. They exchanged hellos and she continued on her way. This exact scenario played out three days in a row until on the fourth day, the skies opened up and it started pouring. Pat invited the woman—her name was April—to sit in his dump truck with him until the storm passed. It was love at first sight, he'd insist every time he told the story over the years.

April was the opposite of Pat's first wife. She was smart and stable and knew as much about music as he did. They were soul mates; he was sure of it that very first day. Unfortunately, his bosses who happened to be circling overhead in helicopters to check on progress were sure that having a woman in your truck was against company rules. They met Pat at the truck yard after his shift and fired him on the spot.

My brother didn't mind so much. He could find another job, but he would never find another April.

TRUNK SHOW

"Do not underestimate the determination of a quiet man."
~Iain Duncan Smith

t turned out having friends was a bittersweet win, because I wasn't allowed to do the things everyone else was allowed to do, like have sleepovers and go to movies or just hang out at the mall. Instead of letting me have an actual social life, Betty filled any sliver of free time I had with chores. The truth was I worked for her, and my time would never be my own as long as I lived under "her" roof.

I was still coming home to dirty dinner plates on my bed even though I hadn't been there for the meals. Likewise, I was punished for slipups I didn't make, like leaving the orange juice pitcher on top of the refrigerator. Never mind that I hadn't put it there or even noticed it; somehow I was responsible for the fact that the juice had spoiled. Betty delighted in watching me down that rotten liquid in its entirety, a punishment I found not at all surprising coming from the woman who had made me eat my own vomit.

It became a game to see if I could outsmart her. One night Betty was off at school and Dad had fallen asleep on the couch after a long day of work when my diver friend Nick called and said some kids were going to a movie. I knew I wasn't allowed to go anywhere without Betty's permission. I also knew that if

Dad were awake his response would be "ask Betty." So I whispered something about a movie in his ear, and decided to take his tired grunt as a green light to go.

I bolted out of there as fast as I could, before Betty could come home and bust me. I'd worry about the aftermath later. Plus, I'd already found her massive, secret stash of pot in the attic, so I knew I had some dirt on her.

Nick and his friend Chris picked me up on the corner and we headed to our friend Nanette's. We cracked open some beers and listened to The Pretenders and I felt freer and happier than I had since the long ago night I'd gone streaking down Ramona Street.

I was well behaved and responsible by nature and also by virtue of the fact that I was incredibly naive. I didn't really know what sort of trouble there even was to get into in the world because I'd been deprived of every opportunity to go out and find it. All I knew was it felt amazing to be with my friends.

When it was time to head to the Fountain Valley Drive-In, somehow it was decided that Nanette would sit up front with Chris and I would ride in the trunk with Nick. In addition to being mischievous fun, we'd also save two dollars apiece on tickets.

Sign me up!

It turns out, an easy way to find out if you're claustrophobic is to let yourself get locked in the trunk of a car. And an easy way to find out if you're *really* claustrophobic is to let yourself get locked in the trunk of a car with a guy who decides to open-mouth kiss you without any warning whatsoever, completely covering all your breathing holes in the process.

I pushed my friend off of me. "Oh my God, you have to stop," I told him, gasping for air. He laughed before moving in for more.

"I'm serious, I can't breathe," I said, and immediately he understood I meant it.

Nick and I watched the movie that night as friends. Even though I did have a crush on him — he was an incredible diver and I admired him greatly for that — I just wasn't ready to go down that road. It was obvious that he respected me too, because he didn't push it.

And just like that, I learned that love and loyalty didn't have to be conditional. You could say no, and stand up for yourself, and that didn't make you wrong or bad; it just made you *you*. Nick and I laughed about that night for many years the way you do with friends who care about you without any strings attached and appreciate you for exactly who you are.

When I got home that night, everyone was asleep. The next day, Betty asked me casually where I'd been the night before.

"I asked Dad if I could go to the movies and he said yes," I explained. Dad shot me a look like, *I DID?* and I nodded. Betty glared at him.

"I did," Dad told her.

It was another win for me in the ongoing battle of wits on Walnut Street.

SLEEPING IN MY SHOES

"If people are good only because they fear punishment
and hope for reward, then we are a sorry lot indeed."
~Albert Einstein

B etty decided out of the blue that I needed orthopedic shoes. I had no problems with my feet; no scoliosis or back or knee pain to speak of. Still she took me to a small, smelly shoe store for old people and because they were in the business of selling expensive shoes, they looked at my problem-free feet and agreed with Betty's amateur assessment. I went home with the ugliest brown clodhoppers I'd ever seen.

If you wanted to make sure you'd get your ass kicked in high school, those were the shoes you'd wear.

I was not going to be caught dead in them, no matter what Betty said.

I would put them on long enough to get out the door in the morning, then change into my Vans as soon as I was out of her line of sight. I thought this was a fairly bulletproof plan, but I should have known she wouldn't be able to resist checking up on me. The first time Betty dropped by the school and saw me hanging in the quad in my checkered sneakers, she sauntered right up to me.

"Oh, I see you changed your shoes," she said with a sneer. "Great. You can sleep in the orthopedic ones I bought you then. I hope you enjoy it." She followed through on her threat, too. She made me wear those god-awful shoes to bed for two weeks straight. She'd come into my bedroom and check on me periodically throughout the night, too, to make sure I hadn't kicked them off.

Sadly, Betty was as determined to catch me disobeying as I was to defy her, so I would suffer this consequence more than once. I didn't care. Knowing I'd be punished for ignoring her ridiculous rules made getting away with it that much sweeter.

GIRL MEETS BOY

*"The magic of first love is our ignorance that it
can never end."*

~Benjamin Disraeli

In ninth grade I discovered chemistry—and I'm not talking about phases of matter or ionic bonding.

His name was Mike Oliveri and he was a surfer who lived around the corner from Dad's. We met through a mutual friend and I liked him right away. He was tan and cute with long, sun-bleached hair and it was major first-rush love. Mike had already graduated high school, but he was taking a year off before starting college. He wasn't a slacker or pretty-but-dumb surfer boy; in fact, just the opposite. Mike was brilliant. His brain worked on overdrive and he was always coming up with crazy inventions and innovative business ideas. I was in awe of his creative mind and entrepreneurial spirit. I'd never been surrounded by so much motivation and I found it almost dizzying.

As Mike and I grew closer, I began to share more about my life at home. He was incredibly understanding but also angry at the unfairness of it all. His parents were so loving and supportive—he was going to open a surf shop with their blessing—and he wanted me to have the same thing. He'd be polite to Betty's face but he'd also stand up to her and call her out when she was on one of her know-it-all rants. He'd do it subtly, though, and in a way that made it look like he was genuinely interested in what she had to say.

Before long, Mike had Betty wrapped around his finger. She'd hang on his every word, just waiting for her chance to try to shine like the intellectual star she believed she was. Although the physical abuse had nearly stopped—I had seven inches and twenty pounds of lean muscle on her by this point—Betty still tried her best to control me. I wouldn't have dreamed of asking her if I could go anywhere or do anything, but with Mike around I didn't have to.

"Want to go to dinner and a movie tonight?" he'd ask me, always when Betty was in earshot. I would never say a word and Betty would never say no to him. It was perfect.

"Are all of your chores done?" she'd ask me in her nails-on-a-chalkboard manner. They always were.

"Then go ahead," she'd say, mostly to Mike.

We never went to dinner *or* the movies. Those were just the generic, cliche plans he knew my parents would approve of. We had a group of friends and we'd hang out at their apartments or go to random parties around town. I'd told Mike about the pot in the attic and one night he told me to grab some, so I did. I never even took a hit but it must have been good weed because after smoking it everyone else was laughing their asses off and eating everything in sight.

I was working myself ragged and reaping little of the rewards. Betty had opened a checking account for me, and each week when I got my paycheck she held out her hand and said the same thing: "Hand it over." There was no way in hell she was going to let me just "piss it all away," she informed me. I was allowed to keep exactly twenty bucks at a time, and the rest went into savings. Someday I'd thank her, she'd say.

(It would turn out someday she'd thank *me*, when I willingly gave them my entire savings to help pay the mortgage.)

Mike thought my work schedule was insane and I couldn't argue. He asked if I liked my job and I admitted that I hated it. Why didn't I get a different one, he wanted to know. It was the proverbial light bulb moment. *What else would I do? What else* could *I do?*

Mike laughed. I could do anything, he told me. What did I like?

I liked clothes and shoes and diving and dancing. I liked drawing and being out of the house and having freedom and outsmarting Betty. I liked Mike, and I really liked that he believed in me. I liked believing in myself for once, too.

Without a word to my warden, I applied for work at three places that seemed interesting to me: a shoe store, a bank and a restaurant called Mama Rose's. When call-backs came in from all three, I picked the shoe store. The manager turned out to be a complete dimwit, but the new, empowered me had the wits and the wherewithal to move on quickly.

Mama Rose's was exactly my speed. The restaurant was owned by Dad's friend Larry, the same guy whose pink donut boxes dotted my early years at Walnut Street. Larry had ditched the donuts and was now dishing up Italian fare alongside his wife Rose and their four kids. Mama Rose's was a true family operation and quickly became a hit.

Business grew and they added locations and I worked my way through every position in the place. I waited tables and manned the register and learned how to make pizza. I made great tips and I was in heaven there. I went to school with all the kids I worked with, so we were together night and day. We'd have dough fights and lock each other in the freezer and have a great old time, but we worked our tails off, too. Larry taught me about running a business and managing money and dealing with people and above all, what a real family looked like and what they could accomplish when they worked together and respected each other.

SEW AMAZING

The winter formal was coming. Normally such an event wouldn't even be on my radar—besides still being traumatized by Jenny's Vaseline humiliation, *what would I wear?*—but my great friend Jane and her boyfriend were going and she wanted to double-date with me and Mike. It actually sounded like something out of a movie, maybe one starring Kristy McNichol and Scott Baio or Tatum O'Neal and Shaun Cassidy, except for the *formal* part.

Jane told me not to worry.

My best friend was a girl of many talents. In addition to being tall, blonde and beautiful, Jane was a gifted artist and could bake like nobody's business. At Christmas she would spend two solid weeks making a dozen different kinds of cookies to hand out to friends and neighbors. Jane was nice to everyone but didn't let anyone push her around, a combination I both envied and admired. Together we'd choreograph elaborate original dances, performing them over and over to the theme song from *Star Wars*. As far as I could tell, there was nothing Jane couldn't do.

"I'm going to make your dress for the winter formal," she told me. "I can sew anything, just show me the style you want." I couldn't fathom possessing such an amazing skill or having the time to dedicate to it.

Jane and I went to the fabric store together to pick out our patterns and fabrics. I chose a strapless style with an accordion-pleat bodice and full, floor-length skirt and Jane got to work straight away. I'd watch her measure and pin and cut and sew and feel deep admiration. You didn't get next-level at any craft without working hard and putting in your time, and Jane definitely had done both. We'd meet regularly for fittings, changing a detail here and adding another there, until there was nothing left to fine-tune. Jane kept her own gown under wraps until the last second because she wanted it to be a surprise, but I knew it would be a knock-out. Everything Jane touched turned to gold.

Finally my friend announced she was done.

The finished product exceeded my wildest expectations.

I pranced around Jane's den like a runway model in my all-black evening gown and admired the way the silky taffeta skirt draped perfectly over my hips and how the bodice hugged my waist and highlighted my broad shoulders at the same time. I spent hours twirling in the mirror, mesmerized by the lines and the way the light played off the shimmery folds of fabric. I felt beautiful for the first time in my life.

It was magical, all of it.

I ran my fingers along the neatly sewn seams, the perfectly placed zipper, the delicate organza ruffle. I could only ever dream of making a dress like this.

BAG LADY

"Clothes aren't going to change the world.
The women who wear them will."

~Anne Klein

By the time I was fourteen I was nearing five feet eleven inches and weighed 127 pounds soaking wet. Thanks to dance, diving and biking everywhere I went, I essentially completed what amounted to a sprint triathlon every single day. I was lean and ripped. People frequently would comment on my body, but I didn't see it as an object of beauty. It was a survival machine. My workouts were a way to occupy my time and my thoughts and have an excuse not to be at home. The body they were building was strong enough to fend off attackers. That was enough for me.

The fact that I was taller, bigger and stronger than Betty didn't mean I was safe — it meant she would need to find clever new ways to control me.

Betty always seemed to be up for that challenge.

Because of my insane schedule, I was never home long enough to do my laundry. In my house, it's not like you'd ever return from a grueling day to find a tidy stack of clean clothes on your bed with a note saying, "Hey, I noticed you're super busy so I got you this time." Not once. Instead, I came home late one evening after another seventeen-hour day to find all my clothes were gone. Vanished. Clean, dirty, halfway cute or desperately out of style; Betty was indiscriminate. She had removed every last faded t-shirt, too-small skirt and frayed pair of corduroy shorts I owned from my room. It wasn't as if I had much, or that any of it was the height of fashion, but I was a teenager. Clothes were everything, and now I had nothing.

I stood in front of my closet, speechless. As the knowledge of what she'd done took hold in my brain, Betty was waiting in the wings to savor my reaction.

"Since you can't seem to take care of your clothes, I'm going to hang onto them for you," she informed me. "But I'll let you pick out one outfit." She led me to her closet, where she'd bagged up all of my things into trash bags. "Take your time and make it a good one, because you'll be wearing it for the next three weeks." I wouldn't be washing it during that time either, she added, so I could expect it to get "nice and ripe." I kept my face expressionless as she laid down her latest, nonsensical law. It took every ounce of restraint I had not to grab her and do to her what she'd done to me countless times over the years, but I managed. She wanted me to fly off in a rage, and I wouldn't give her the satisfaction. I would be the bigger person if it killed me.

I chose a pair of jeans and a blue and white top, thinking something simple and generic might go unnoticed. I left her room without a word, wondering how on earth I was going to survive this fresh hell. I had my diving sweats and dance team sweats in my gym locker but that was it.

It took two days for me to realize that while Betty could poach my clothes, I had something else, something far better, that she could never take away.

I had friends.

They noticed my repeat outfit on day two and wanted to know what was going on. At first I did what I'd always done, which was to deny and deflect. I had no interest in airing my dirty laundry — or lack of it in this case — and had been schooled in the art of secrecy since birth. "I'm so fine," was my motto; my battle cry. "There's nothing to see here, so you can take your concern elsewhere."

My friends weren't buying it. We'd bonded through dance and through diving, through terrible teachers and a detention or two. Dawn and Nancy and Nanette and Patty were all nice girls from good families and as far as they knew I was a normal kid just like them. I didn't want to wreck that facade, but I also needed help. So I told them about Betty and my punishment. To my relief, my friends didn't judge or shun me; instead they leapt to my defense and began formulating a plan.

Dawn lived closest to me and offered to meet me before school with a new outfit every day. I'd change in the bathroom after swimming and go about my day, praying Betty wouldn't do a drive-by check-up. The others offered to be on backup, and all four volunteered to take turns running "Betty Patrol," promising to find me, come hell or high water, if they saw her anywhere near campus. I only wore my prison uniform two or three times during my sentence, but the one time she showed up at Fountain Valley High to check on me was one of those days. I was long overdue for that miraculous stroke of luck.

While Betty's intent had been to mortify me, for those three weeks I got to be the fashion plate I had always wanted to be. Dawn looked and dressed like a runway model, and she gladly offered up a bottomless supply of Candies high heels and sweet little skirts and a darling array of tops. Her feet were two sizes smaller than mine so I was stuck in my Vans, but I didn't mind so much. Her clothes were far more fashionable than anything of mine that was crumpled in a ball in Betty's closet. I wore my friend's clothes proudly and reveled in the knowledge that I was both luckier and smarter than the wicked witch of Walnut Street.

SIDEWALK TALK

"Superstition is the poetry of life."

~Johann Wolfgang von Goethe

Suburban Southern California was a friendly place in the late 1970s.

"How's it going over there?" different neighbors would ask periodically, as if they knew something was going on behind closed doors but they had no idea what. Dixie was the only one I knew I could trust. She was a steel trap.

"Great, thanks," I'd say to all the others with a bright smile and continue on my way. The fact is, you never knew who Betty was in bed with, so to speak. The last thing I needed was a casual, offhand complaint getting back to her and sending her flying down Walnut Street on her broomstick.

I wondered if her back ever hurt, because I walked around town stepping on every crack I could find.

WINDOW OF OPPORTUNITY

"You can't fix yourself by breaking someone else."

~Unknown

I f Betty was a master at anything, it was pitting the kids in her care against one another. One of her many precepts was that if any of us wanted to do anything or go anywhere or enjoy even the simplest privilege, it wasn't enough to do your own chores; you had to make sure everyone else had done theirs, too.

Sometimes it seemed as if Lindsay lived to make this as difficult as possible.

Partly because she was a nine-year-old kid and partly because she was governed by a completely different set of rules, Lindsay's bedroom got pretty gross, pretty fast. She'd stuff banana peels and half-eaten sandwiches and abandoned cereal bowls beneath her bed and let them fester there for days, until the room smelled as if it were populated with moldy, rotting pelican carcasses. The peak of her bedroom's repugnance invariably coincided with the day I'd ask for permission to do something fun.

"Sure," Betty would say. "Just as soon as Lindsay's room is spotless."

On this particular day, Betty was off at one of her classes and Lindsay was feeling less than generous. Not only was she not going to help me get the job done, she was going to actively stand in my way—her way of thumbing her nose at Betty and me both. As soon as I told my sister my plan—we were going to pick up her room and then I was going to take her to the beach—she locked herself in her smelly cell and refused to come out. I pounded on her door and she ignored me. I begged her to let me in and she fired back with, "You're not the boss of me!" No matter how nicely I asked, Lindsay wouldn't budge.

Rage and frustration began boiling inside me. I was fed up with all of it: the food on my bed, the broom-beatings, the hole-digging, the humiliation. I resented the fact that Lindsay was allowed to get away with everything while I was allowed to get away with nothing. Years of control, torment and abuse bubbled to the surface all at once, blinding me with indignation.

There's no other way to say it.

I snapped.

There were only two ways into Lindsay's room: the door and the window. If she wasn't going to open the first one, I'd come in through the second.

I went out the slider to the backyard and through the graveyard of holes Jenny and I had dug. It looked like an abandoned game of emotional Whac-a-Mole. The thorny bush outside Lindsay's window was at least two feet thick and higher than the sill. It had been placed there intentionally, to thwart burglars and bad guys and revenge-seeking half-sisters.

That day, I could not be thwarted. That bush could have been built of barbed wire laden with razor blades and I'd have plowed through its branches anyway. I didn't care if I broke the window or got in trouble or scratched all the skin off my limbs. I was getting in there and Lindsay was going to pay.

Nobody else was home, so there was no one to hear my sister's screams.

"WHAT ARE YOU DOING?" she shouted as I clawed through those thorns and lifted her window up out of the frame.

"ERIN, STOP!" she yelled as I set the glass in the dirt and leaned it against the side of the house.

"STOOOOOOOOPPPPPPPPPP!" she bellowed as I climbed through the opening, wild-eyed and determined. Betty herself couldn't have stopped me at that point.

I was the Bionic Woman and the Rock'em Sock'em Robot all rolled into one as I pulled Lindsay off her bed and did what I'd been taught to do when you wanted to establish dominance: I let her have it. I slapped at her arms and her legs, leaving giant angry palm marks. I was furious and I meant business and I needed her to know it. She'd left me no choice.

For the first time in my life, I tasted power. It was tinged with dominance and dusted with revenge and it was delicious.

"Clean all that crap out from underneath your bed," I ordered as I started picking up her toys.

Lindsay, who was cowering in a corner, scrambled to comply. For an hour, we cleaned her room in silence.

"Get dressed, we're going to the beach," I told her. The beach was far — more than five miles each way — and Lindsay hated riding her bike but that was her tough luck. I fixed us two peanut butter and jelly sandwiches each and packed them up with some other snacks and we set out.

On our ride I tried to make Lindsay laugh. I'd tell her that midgets lived over the hill and we had to ride really fast or they'd come and get us. I told her I'd buy her ice cream when we got there. I needed her on my side, because we both knew what would happen if she wasn't.

Lindsay could have signed my death warrant that day. She could have told Betty what I'd done and there was a decent chance I'd have lost life or limb or both. But Lindsay wasn't a bad kid, and neither was I. We'd both seen so much abuse and neither of us had been taught a better way. We'd been groomed to be rivals, but we loved each other dearly despite all odds. On some level I'm sure Lindsay felt bad that she got away with so much more than I did, and she probably thought she deserved what I had dished out. She didn't, of course. She deserved to be loved and cherished just as I did. Without that, we were each doing the best we could with what we'd been given.

Lindsay never said a word to anyone about what happened in her room. When I needed her the most, she chose to forgive me and to protect me. It was the beginning of a new closeness that saw me through countless heartaches to come, one that I cherish to this day.

THE FOG

*"May the fleas of a thousand camels invade the crotch
of the person who ruins your day.
And may their arms be too short to scratch."*

~Keisha Keenleyside

oco and Sam were a pair of Old English Sheepdogs. They were sweet, smelly and inseparable. Much like Sinny, Dad's cat Wendy was prone to popping out litters of kittens on a whim, and whenever she did, Poco in particular would become obsessed. Dozens of times a day, that dog would sneak out to the garage and retrieve Wendy's kittens and bring them into the house, one by one. Then he'd tuck them away inside the player organ in our living room. We'd hear the hungry mewing and see Wendy roaming the house frantically looking for her babies. Meanwhile Poco would be sitting at the foot of the organ, blocking her way.

One sweltering summer, Poco and Sam got fleas. This was no ordinary infestation; it was a plague-level calamity, up there with locusts and lice and endless days of darkness. You couldn't walk through any carpeted room without your legs and feet turning black. At night I'd pull my hair down over my ears and into a low ponytail to keep the fleas out. I'd try to sleep with my pillow covering my face, but invariably a dozen or more would get trapped in there and be jumping and biting me.

Lindsay and I were losing our minds, but the adults continued to ignore the problem.

The dogs weren't allowed in Dad and Betty's room, so they got the full brunt of those blood-suckers last. By the time they did, the situation was dire. Dad set off about twenty of those drugstore foggers and when we came back, the whole house was a sea of flea corpses. I don't remember anyone ever vacuuming them up, but at least they were dead.

With the insect situation under control, Betty announced she wouldn't stand for anything like that again, and so she had sent the dogs to live with a friend of hers who had a big farm where they could run and play. We never got to say goodbye to them.

Shortly after, I spotted a letter from the veterinarian as I was bringing in the mail and I opened it. It was a bill for "euthanasia X2."

Betty had our dogs put to sleep.

JUMPING TO CONCLUSIONS

"Life is tough, my darling,
but so are you."

~Stephanie Bennett-Henry

I was wearing espadrilles with my one-piece, zip-up army jumpsuit that day. The jumpsuit had cute little epaulettes on the shoulders and gold and red patches on the breast and it was everything to me. Also it was a bitch to get on and off, although that part was just a lucky coincidence.

It wasn't often that I walked to work, but the bike I was using had a flat tire and nobody had wanted to drive me. The walk there hadn't been too bad, but now it was after my shift and I was hungry and tired and I just wanted to get home. It was dusk and I was only a little more than halfway into the trip when he came up behind me from out of nowhere. He was so close as he raced past me that I felt his breath on my ear. He had on purple and white Dolphin running shorts. That was all I noticed before he tucked into a driveway and disappeared. I was shaken to my core.

As soon as I turned onto Newland Street, I saw him again. Now, full-blown fear hit me like a punch in the gut. He was leaning up against a light pole, waiting for me. I just knew it. My heart pounding, I tried to look calm and confident as I considered my options.

I really had no choice; I had to keep walking. The alternative was to turn my back to him, and that was even scarier. There was nothing worse than a surprise attack.

I bent down and unbuckled the ankle straps that held my espadrilles on my feet, and then slipped them off. I needed to be ready to run, and I'd be twice as fast barefoot as I would in those sandals.

As the gap between us closed, he pulled the elastic of his shorts all the way down and pulled out his limp pink penis. It hung there like a deflated balloon. It was the grossest thing I had ever seen.

I picked up my pace.

"You're disgusting," I said as I passed him. I couldn't help it; I was pissed.

And then I took off. He was hot on my heels in an instant. He grabbed me in a bear hug and pulled me back and suddenly we were both on the ground, punching and kicking and scratching. Right there on the sidewalk.

Cars whizzed past us, but no one stopped to help.

Not one single person.

To this day, that fact blows my mind.

Somehow I managed to fight him off, scramble to my feet and get away. All of my track training kicked in and I ran like the wind until I came to a tract of homes. I hauled ass to the first house, praying someone would be home or else I knew I was screwed. I was in luck. The screen was closed but the door was open. I ran through the screen and slammed the door behind me, locking it quickly.

A tiny Asian woman was knitting by a window. It would have been impossible to tell which one of us was more terrified.

"Help me, please," I begged. "Can I use your phone?" She was scared and confused, clutching her knitting to her chest. Realizing that she spoke no English I held my hand to my ear, hang-ten style, and mimicked talking into it. She nodded and led me nervously to the kitchen, pointing to a wall phone. I think she was just relieved I wasn't planning to rob her.

It seemed like hours before my dad got there to take me home. He'd brought his gun. On the way home we passed a police car and Dad flagged the guy down and told him what had happened to me. To my surprise, the cop followed us to my house to take a report.

He asked me a million questions about the guy, stuff like how tall he was and what he was wearing and what color his eyes were.

"I wasn't looking at his eyes," I replied. Betty laughed at that; my father was furious. Lindsay missed the joke.

"Is that what you were wearing?" the cop asked me, sizing up my jumpsuit. I nodded.

"How low was the zipper?" he wanted to know. Lindsay and I looked at each other, stunned by his question. I wanted to ask if he was joking, but I could tell that he wasn't. He was implying that it was my fault I'd been assaulted; that somehow I'd been asking for it. But I already knew better. It was never your fault when someone attacked you out of the blue. Never.

Dad got the tire on the bike fixed before my next shift. I found a different route to work and I never saw that creep again.

CONVICTED

"I was quiet, but I was not blind."

~Jane Austen

I towered over Betty, but that wasn't the only reason we didn't see eye to eye. I had zero respect for her and not just because of the abuse and cruelty I'd suffered at her hands for so long. The fact is by this point I was old and wise enough to see who she really was. I knew about the pot she stashed in the attic and the four-foot marijuana plants she grew in the backyard. I saw the way she flirted with everyone from my therapist to the "classmates" she was always bringing home to "study" with, and the disrespectful way she talked to my dad. She even acted sexually toward my boyfriend Mike, which was the most disgusting of all, even though he knew what she was doing and despised her equally for it. The writing was on the wall and I could finally read it clear as day.

Grandma Cole, Dad's mom, had been diagnosed with tongue cancer and he was out of his mind. Dad would make the drive over to Hemet as often as he could just to sit by her bedside and hold her hand. It was during one of these vigils that Betty decided to invite her sleazy friend Ron over for a sleepover. Ron was an ex-con Betty had met during her brief employ at a halfway house for newly released inmates. Ron had been shot in the stomach four times while robbing someone, but he was fine now and he liked to have a good time.

"You're on the couch tonight," Betty told me, as if I was supposed to believe that Ron would be sleeping in my room. Even Lindsay was on to her antics by this point.

At bedtime, Betty trotted off to her room and Ron went to mine. Predictably, five minutes later Lindsay and I heard the shuffling of doors and feet.

"I'm going to go get my pillow," I announced. Lindsay followed me. We tiptoed back to my bedroom and I knocked quietly. Of course there was no response; there was nobody in there. We opened my door to find Ron's clothes strewn about, and I realized he must have dashed across the hall naked. We stood outside Betty's door long enough to hear the waterbed in full rocking motion before I dragged Lindsay back to the living room with my pillow and confirmation of what I already knew: Betty was screwing around behind my father's back.

I'd like to say I thought long and hard about ratting her out, but I didn't. I called Dad right away at my grandma's house and told him what Lindsay and I had seen and heard. He got quiet and then he said he'd talk to me more when he got home.

It really didn't occur to me that he might be devastated by this news. In fact, part of me even hoped he'd be relieved like I was that we finally had a solid excuse to get rid of her. They weren't even married. It would be a piece of cake. But when Dad walked in the next day, he was completely wasted. I'd never seen him drunk in my life and the sight of him like that frightened me and brought back a world of awful memories. He stumbled to the couch and I followed him.

"It's okay, we can do this," I told him. "I can help you. I can get a better job and we can move somewhere else and we can totally make it work. We don't need Betty! She's not even working or helping anyway. All she does is hit us and boss us around. We've got this, Dad. It'll be me and you and Lindsay and we're going to be so fine!"

In my young, innocent mind, it really was that simple.

I walked around on eggshells the next day, waiting for Betty to drop the hammer on me. Obviously Dad was going to tell her what he knew and *how* he knew, and she was going to be out for blood. I just needed to stay strong until she was gone. I had to, for Dad.

A solid week went by, and nothing at all had happened. I was a nervous wreck the entire time. Then one afternoon when Lindsay and I came inside from playing at the neighbor's, Betty was waiting for us inside the foyer.

"The next time either of you have a problem with me," Betty hissed, "try saying it to my face." And then she walked away.

I wondered if Dad knew all along about Betty's affairs, because he didn't kick her out after all. Maybe the sadness I'd seen wasn't because she was cheating, but because she didn't even have the decency to be discreet about it. Or maybe it was because he knew he was too weak to ever leave her.

It was official. Betty's smug face wasn't going anywhere. It was time to start plotting my escape.

GETTING MY KICKS

"We can only bend so far before we break."
~Gabrielle Travis

M y friend Nancy was having problems at home. From my vantage point it looked like she had it pretty damned good, but I figured I probably wasn't hearing the whole story. Nancy swore it was so bad she needed to get out of there, so she was moving in with her boyfriend Brett.

It turned out that Brett's parents weren't too hip on the whole living-together plan so Nancy's idea was this: she'd keep her clothes at my house, that way she wasn't technically *living* there, she was just crashing there from time to time. The parents seemed okay with that, so I agreed to house her things, which I stored neatly in my closet.

Nancy worked at a killer clothing store and she had a rock star wardrobe packed with all the early 1980s staples I dreamed of owning. I said I'd be happy to house them for her. I guess Nancy and I were both guilty of failing in the thinking-it-through department that day.

I always kept my room spotless to keep the wrath of Betty at bay, but I should have known she'd go snooping in there anyway. What I couldn't have guessed, however, was that she would steal all six bags of Nancy's clothes right out of my closet.

When I came home and discovered they were gone, I flipped. I ran through the house until I found Betty in her office.

"What did you do with Nancy's clothes?" I demanded.

"They were in my house, so they're *my* clothes now," she replied, her voice dripping with saccharine.

"What?" I said, incredulous. Surely I had heard her wrong. "What are you talking about?"

"If they're hers, then why are they in my house?" Betty wanted to know.

I scrambled for a response. "We're going to trade some stuff so I was going to go through it," I said.

"I don't buy it, so I guess they're mine," she snapped in the self-satisfied tone she was famous for.

I was shaking with resentment and rage. How could I possibly tell my friend that Betty had stolen all of her clothes? It was one thing for Betty to torture me, to steal my clothes; that I could handle. But to hurt me by hurting my friends was beyond cruel — even for her.

Dad was in the living room. I was so furious I could barely see straight, but I tried to pull it together enough to make my appeal.

"Please help me, Dad," I begged. "They're not even my clothes. They're my friend's and they cost a lot of money. Why is Betty allowed to go into my room and take whatever she wants? Why am I not allowed to have any privacy at all? My room is clean. I do everything she asks me to do. She's trying to make my friends hate me! *WELL IT'S NOT GOING TO WORK!*"

The last line came out a full-decibel roar. So much for keeping it together.

"You watch your mouth!" Dad exploded. He'd never heard me raise my voice before and he was hearing my anger, not my words.

I couldn't believe this was happening. I ran to my room, desperately wanting the satisfaction of slamming the door with all my might, but we weren't allowed to close our bedroom doors, ever. Even in my blind fury, I couldn't defy her.

Seconds later her hideous face was filling my doorway.

"Tough life, isn't it, bitch?"

She wouldn't.

She didn't.

But she would.

She did.

With a smug, sarcastic smile, that lying, cheating, stealing, no-good trailer trash had just called me a bitch.

To my face.

It was the very last possible straw.

I pulled my foot back and I kicked that door as hard as I humanly could.

It hit her square in the face.

"KENNNNNNNNNNNNNNNNNNNNNNNNNN!" she howled, in a shout undoubtedly heard 'round the neighborhood. "SHE HIT MY FACE!!!!!!!!!!"

I hadn't even moved a muscle when Dad burst through my door.

"Erin, what the hell did you do?" he demanded.

"I didn't hit her, the door did," I cried. "Dad, you have no idea what goes on in this house. None! She does awful, unbelievable things to all of us. Please. You have to hear me out."

The look on his face was pure disbelief, yet he knew me well enough to know I wouldn't lash out without a really good reason, so he sat on my bed with a heavy sigh and I lowered myself next to him. For the next two hours, I spilled the entire sordid story. I didn't know if Betty was listening and I didn't care. I told him about all of the abuse, physical and mental. I told him she was the only reason I ever ran away. I asked him why Betty was allowed to get away with being so awful, with the dishes on the bed and the Vaseline for Jenny and the countless other humiliations. He had no answer. I told him I had no privacy in that house, no dignity, and that I didn't get a shred of love or support or physical affection from anyone.

"You hug Lindsay and ask her about her day and you spend time with her, but I might as well be invisible," I told him. He looked sad and tired.

"I had no idea," Dad said. "I'm so sorry, Erin. You're right. We do need to spend time together. Let's make that happen."

His words were music to my ears. He had heard me and even more importantly, he believed me. He had apologized and acknowledged me and he told me he wanted to hear it all, even the things I told him I couldn't say when I knew Betty could bust through the door at any minute and kill us both.

I nodded and he hugged me. I could count on one hand how many times that had ever happened. It felt so good, so safe, that I wanted to stay there forever.

CLOTHES CALL

"Winning isn't everything, but wanting to win is."
~Vince Lombardi

Dad took me to work that Saturday. We spent an entire glorious day together and I filled him in on the rest of the gory details of my life at home. He said that he was so very sorry that it had gotten so bad. Dad promised me things would get better and that he'd start standing up for me, and I believed him. I asked him if he knew where Nancy's clothes were and he told me she had stuffed them in the tiny front trunk of her VW Bug.

I had to get those clothes back.

Nancy and I came up with a plan. I knew Betty's school schedule so we waited for her early one evening down the street in Nancy's boyfriend Brett's black Falcon. As soon as she pulled out of the driveway Brett zoomed up on her tail. When she got to the first stop sign, he pulled up right next to her. His door was inches from hers and he was revving his engine menacingly.

"Pull over," I yelled out the window. Betty ignored me and drove off. Brett took off after her, swerving dangerously close to her on all sides. I could see the look of terror on her face and I have to admit, I was loving every second of it.

"PULL OVER," I shouted at a light, "AND GIVE NANCY BACK HER THINGS!"

Again Betty took off. Over in the Falcon, we were rolling with laughter. We had all night and we figured eventually she'd either give up or run out of gas. We'd been playing the cat-and-mouse game for close to a half hour when Betty pulled up outside the Fountain Valley Police Department. She killed her engine and dashed inside, so we did the same thing.

"I'm being harassed!" she was saying to a group of police officers when we got inside. "By them!" She pointed at me and my friends. I smiled politely.

"No, she isn't," I said. "She actually stole something that belongs to my friend and we're just trying to get it back." I turned to Betty. "I'm so glad you came here. I actually was planning to call the police myself, so thanks for saving me the trouble."

"Did you take this girl's things?" one of the cops asked her.

"They were in my house, so they're mine," Betty spat.

"Did you buy these things with your money?" he pressed. Betty mumbled something that sounded an awful lot like no.

"Well, then you're going to need to give them back to her," he ordered.

I thanked the policeman before continuing.

"I've lived with her for a long time, and you might want to come and check out our house. She's got a big bag of pot in the attic and I think that might explain her erratic behavior. She's high all the time." If looks could kill, my blood would have been all over that police station that night.

A cop followed us outside and watched as we moved Nancy's things from one car to the other (although to my great disappointment he didn't arrest her *or* follow her home to investigate my hot pot tip). Betty hopped in the Bug and sped off, fuming.

When I got home, Dad was up waiting for me. Betty had told him what I'd done; her version of it at least.

"You put me in a really bad position," he said.

"Are you serious?" I asked.

"I tried to stick up for you," he insisted, "but your mouth just keeps getting you in trouble, Erin. You disrespected her, and she won't live here as long as you're here."

"What are you saying?" I asked him.

"You need to go," Dad said. He couldn't even look at me.

I was sixteen years old, his own flesh and blood, and he was effectively kicking me out on the street. He'd had a choice, me or Betty, and he picked her.

And that was about the size of it.

THE NEIGHBORS'

NOBODY'S DAUGHTER

*"When everything goes to hell,
the people who stand by you without flinching –
they are your family."*

~Jim Butcher

D ad wasn't a monster; he was just weak and defeated and powerless over Betty. Still, he wasn't going to let me be some street urchin so he arranged for me to move in with his friend Jack Deluca's family. It was awkward and strained for countless reasons, but at least I had a roof over my head.

Jack and his wife Virginia lived on Walnut Street, too, just a few houses down from Dad's. They had two sons my age I went to high school with and many years earlier they'd had a daughter as well. Julia was just eighteen months old when she died of SIDS while in the care of a babysitter. Virginia never really recovered from that loss, and when I moved in she went on and on about how happy she was to finally have a girl in the house again.

"Would it be okay if I called you Julia?" she asked me soon after I arrived.

"I'll just be Erin if that's okay," I told her.

The Deluca family were kind to me and gave me my own room and I was invited to eat with them whenever I was home, but still I was too shy to ever open a cupboard and fix myself a snack or help myself to so much as a piece of fruit. I knew I couldn't stay there long.

One day there was a banging on their front door. It was Betty. She apparently had just learned I was living there and she insisted that I leave immediately. I wasn't welcome on that street, she shouted, and she wanted me gone. Jack Deluca calmly told her that she could get her own ass off of his property or he'd be happy to take care of that for her.

It was one of life's sweetest victories.

My other neighbor Dixie Merrill heard through the neighborhood grapevine that I'd moved out of Dad's house, and she showed up at the Delucas' one day with an envelope full of money.

"It's yours," she told me. "You earned it. I was just holding onto it for you."

Between Dixie and the Delucas, I felt cared for and supported and I was on my way to being independent. Virginia was a literal lifesaver. She brought home stacks of forms and told me we were going to apply for money for college. She scored me a $2,500 grant and another $1,500 in loan money and helped me open a savings account of my own—one Betty wouldn't have access to.

Jack took a more tough-love approach with me, informing me that nobody was going to drive me around forever and it was time for me to get my driver's license. He tossed a driver's ed handbook at me and told me I had two weeks to study. Jack was patient but firm as we practiced around town, calmly asking me if I was planning to slow down or just slam into the car in front of us, and suggesting I turn the wheel nice and easy when switching lanes instead of dive-bombing like a maniac. Although I was positive I was going to fail the driving test, I wound up passing with flying colors.

The Delucas were crazy about Christmas. They gave me more presents than they bought their two sons combined.

There were stacks of gifts with my name on them under their giant tree, filled with clothes and toiletries and nicknacks and a gold nugget diamond ring. Such excess made me feel guilty and uncomfortable, and I struggled to react appropriately as I opened gift after grueling gift.

Virginia was heartbroken when I told her I was moving out. I explained that I had a girlfriend named Julie who lived across the street from the high school who was living alone and needed a roommate. I wanted to help Julie out, I explained. I was sure it was for the best; the right thing to do.

In actuality I didn't know Julie at all. But everything else I told Virginia was true and the fact was, as warm and wonderful and gracious as the Delucas were, I had to get away from Walnut Street. I had finally found my voice and learned to listen to my gut, and it was telling me that I could do this; that the only person I could count on was myself. It was a colossal leap of faith and I was terrified, but I figured as long as I did the exact opposite of everything I'd ever seen and known and done in the past, I would be okay.

THE FOUNTAINS

THE ANATOMY ASYLUM

"She was unstoppable.
Not because she did not have failures or doubts,
but because she continued on despite them."

~Beau Taplin

'd seen Julie Lanphear around school but we'd never actually met before the day she came up and told me she'd heard through a mutual friend that I might need a place to live. Julie's mom had moved to Upland to be with her fiance, but Julie wanted to finish out senior year at Fountain Valley High School, so she'd stayed behind. Now she was looking for someone to help cover her rent. Julie was seventeen and I was still just sixteen, and you could do things like that in the 1980s. Anyway, our personalities clicked on the spot and I could tell we were going to be great friends. We agreed to meet after school so I could check out her place.

Julie's apartment was as nice as any I'd ever seen. It had two bedrooms and a perfectly furnished living room and a kitchen with a dishwasher and everything. Julie had moved into the master, leaving her nice twin bed in the other bedroom for me. She told me all I needed to do was pay my $200 rent on time and buy my own food.

Food? Who needed food?

The Fountains apartments were on the corner of Slater and Bushard, directly across from FVHS. This was convenient as I was now without a bike and determined to graduate, even though my grades were downright lousy. None of my siblings had managed to even make it to high school and I had promised myself I wouldn't let anything stop me from getting my diploma.

Fountain Valley High had phone booths on campus, so I started calling Mom to check in on her. It was something I'd never have dared to do from Dad's house and now that I was hearing her voice I began missing her—and worrying about her—all over again. I told her I would call and visit more often. She said that would be nice and she seemed to mean it.

Meanwhile, I was loving every second of my new independence. My classes were hard but I found that without the distraction of Betty hovering nearby (or just lingering in my subconscious), I was able to handle the load remarkably well, even with work and diving and dance team. My grades actually improved, even though there was no one cracking the whip but me—or maybe because of it.

Now that I had rent to pay, I cut my dive team practice to mornings only so I could work in the afternoons. My shift at Mama Rose's didn't start until 4:30 so I had some free time in the afternoons—and I knew exactly how I wanted to fill it.

Aerobic dancing was all the rage and Richard Simmons' oddly named Anatomy Asylum had just opened in town. The Asylum (tagline: "Isn't it time you were committed?") promised people a place to "lose weight, look good and feel great," and somehow I'd scored a free two-week pass. I took a dozen different high-impact classes and nearly lost my mind. I filled out an application and was offered an interview, which consisted of me leading the two older hiring managers in an impromptu aerobics class. I taught the whole hour from memory and was hired on the spot.

Between my two jobs, I was taking home $400 a month, which might as well have been $4,000. I'd never seen that kind of money before, no less been allowed to decide what to do with it, and I felt like a millionaire. I was halfway responsible, always putting away the first $200 I earned for rent, but invariably I'd blow the other half faster than a kid in a candy store.

Clothes were my weakness already, and now I needed cute workout wear on top of everyday stuff. I'd buy tights and thongs and leg warmers and headbands like they were going out of style, and of course I always had to have the latest Reeboks, which were not cheap. Neither was music back then. My classes were packed because I played the best tunes—Prince and Lisa Lisa & Cult Jam and Michael Jackson and Sylvester—and I was forking over $20 a piece for custom mix tapes. I was a reckless spender at times and often found myself with just a few dollars here and there for food. I wasn't particularly bothered by this. After all, you could get Top Ramen and popcorn and oatmeal for next to nothing, and I was used to getting by on crumbs. Food was a luxury I'd have one day, I was sure of it. Besides, there wasn't a morsel on earth that could taste as delicious as flesh-colored tights and freedom.

MEANWHILE, BACK AT THE RANCH

Feb 21, 82
Two weeks since
I had to give up
my job. Same old
reason. Even after
he promised he
wouldn't drink,
at least until I
was home, he
picks me up
at 6:30 and so
drunk. At least
he took the back
streets and we,
made it safe
, and its been
that way every
time he picks

me up. I can't
handle it. I'm
perinoid and it
scares me. I don't
know why he is
trinking so heavy
now. We need
every dime. Last
weekend was bad.
Fri. nite all nite
Sat. morn. at 5:30 AM
pass out by 1:00 PM
up at 4:00 PM drink-
ing. out again
by 6:30, Sun morn
up and at it
by. 9:00 a.m. drunk
bad by 12:00 noon.

HOME

Mike and I were growing apart.

The age difference was definitely a factor. Even though I was living on my own and working two jobs, I was still a high school senior and Mike was a man, with zero interest in high school things. Plus I was making new friends and had new interests and my world was expanding in every exciting direction. The last thing I wanted was anyone or anything holding me back. I was desperate for a fresh start, one that had nothing whatsoever to do with Walnut Street.

Ending things with Mike was one of the hardest things I had ever done. He was a good man, and he'd been there for me during some of my darkest days. He knew as much as anyone ever had about my miserable home life and he loved me anyway. Mike begged me to give us another chance, but I knew there was no going back. I never wanted to hurt or disappoint anyone but I couldn't keep getting sucked back into my old life. I wanted to pack it away in a tidy box, tape that thing shut, throw it off the pier and watch it sink to the bottom of the ocean.

At school two of my popular friends from dance team talked me into trying out for a part in *Guys and Dolls* with them. We went to the auditions together and I couldn't believe the turnout. There were jocks and cheerleaders and nerds and band kids and I was excited and terrified. The director was going to give everyone a few minutes to memorize some lines, she told us, and then one by one we were going to get up and sing and dance while everyone else watched.

Say *what*?

I had always been the invisible kid. My shyness had bordered on crippling at times. And now I was going to get up on a stage and stand right there in the spotlight and draw attention to myself? *On purpose?* Even on dance team I was all about blending into the background. I was tall, and tall was always in the back, never the lead.

But that was the old me.

The new me was emboldened by my autonomy. I was physically strong and gaining more confidence with each passing day. I made my own money and paid my own bills and I knew how to survive. I was an entirely different person than I'd been just a few months earlier, and the new me could and would try anything. When my name was called, I marched up on that stage like I owned the place and I sang and danced my heart out. I recited my memorized lines as if I were born to be a performer. Afterward my friends told me I crushed it and kids I didn't know were smiling and congratulating me. It would be a week before I officially saw my name on the cast list, but I walked out of that audition on cloud nine.

That musical became my world. Other than diving and track (which at the end of the day are both still mostly solo sports), I had never been an integral part of any team effort—who wanted to depend on anybody else, and who needed the pressure of everyone depending on *you?*—and the camaraderie was intoxicating. The playing field was leveled in performing arts, and if you had talent and drive, even girls like me were welcome. I was becoming friends with cheerleaders and popular girls and it was one of the best experiences of my life. I had found my passion and my people, and I was part of something that was so much greater than the sum of its parts.

I was home.

GRILLED GOVERNMENT CHEESE

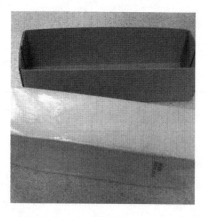

I talked to Mom often now. She was proud of how I was getting on and wanted to know what I was doing for food. When I told her about the ramen and the popcorn she said I needed protein and wanted me to come over so she could put together a care package for me. She was still into Adelle Davis as much as she could be while receiving government assistance.

Decades of financial troubles had finally caught up with Mom and Captain Jack, and they'd sold the house on Ramona and moved into a trailer park called Orangewood. It was basically an asphalt parking lot with some doublewides parked shoulder to shoulder, but it was clean and surprisingly spacious and better, in my opinion, than the chain-link fences and child molesters they'd left behind on Ramona Place.

The government was helping them out, delivering a big box of powdered milk, butter, eggs, bread and cheese to their door once a month. The cheese was about the same size around as a Kraft single, except it came in a giant brick that wasn't sliced at all. It was pasteurized and processed and said GOVERNMENT CHEESE in giant block letters on the wrapping, and I was pretty sure it was the best thing I had ever tasted. Mom put a little bit of everything in my care package, including a sawed-off chunk of that cheese, and Julie drove me over to the park to pick it up.

I wasn't sure what to expect when we got there and I was glad I had my roommate with me. Sometimes when I'd call Mom from school she'd be wasted and sad early in the morning and our conversation would ruin my day. Plus there was always something hurting her, so I was prepared for that, too. But Mom had pulled it together for our visit, even though I knew she wasn't keen on having company, particularly new people. She'd done her hair and makeup and she was actually sober. She looked great and kept saying how proud she was of me. She even wanted to call Grandma Blanche right then and tell her how great I was doing on my own.

It was the visit of a lifetime, and Julie and I went home with more food than we had ever had in our apartment at one time and made the most amazing grilled cheese sandwiches. I showed my roommate a trick I had learned from our friend Janet who worked at the Sizzler. If you buttered the bread and then sprinkled grated parmesan cheese (the kind that was made with wood chip filler but we didn't know that then) on top before you grilled it, it came out tasting exactly like the Sizzler's cheesy bread which we both agreed was culinary Nirvana.

Our only problem was trying to slice that brick of cheese. We had exactly one knife and it was worthless for anything other than spreading mustard or opening envelopes. Trying to shave off a decent, uniform slice of the government stuff would bruise your hand.

"Julie, will you *please* cut the cheese for me?" I'd beg.

"Happy to," she'd reply and then let loose with a loud cheek squeak. We would die laughing. Nobody could cut the cheese like Julie.

HEAVY HITTING

Moving out on my own was hands-down the best decision of my sixteen-year-old life. Julie and I were equally respectful and responsible and we kept our apartment clean and tidy. We didn't have much free time, but when we did one of our favorite things to do was to invite our friends over and dare each other to jump naked in The Fountains' community pool. Julie — who wasn't an athlete and had a few extra pounds on her frame — would laugh and roll her eyes whenever the rest of us called it *skinny dipping*. Eventually she dubbed her own version *chunky dunking*, which everyone agreed was hilarious.

I could walk to school and work from our apartment but if I wanted to go anywhere else, my choices were to take the bus or bum a ride. The grant money Virginia had helped me secure was tucked safely away, and as much as I liked having that security blanket, I decided that buying a car would be investing in myself and my future. I could look for better jobs and of course I would need a car when I started taking college classes. I found a darling red VW Bug—it was the car my dad owned so I assumed it was a reliable choice—for $1,800, making sure I left myself enough money to insure the thing.

As much as I relished my freedom, I never went crazy or abused it. In the back of my mind, I was aware of the fact that I was too young to be out on my own and that technically Dad still had custody of me until I turned eighteen. I was one stupid move or bad choice away from being sent back to Walnut Street and I never forgot that fact. Lots of kids at Fountain Valley High were going to raging parties with drinking and drugs but those things held no appeal to me. I went to one low-key party where I had a single beer and was home by eleven. Even if I'd been tempted to let loose, I was teaching Anatomy Asylum classes at five and six in the morning, a schedule that wasn't exactly conducive to late nights out. In a way, I had set my own curfew to keep myself safe.

It was working.

Even though I had a car, my friend Kerry nicknamed me the "white knuckle driver" because still I was petrified any time I was behind the wheel. Whenever we went anywhere, I'd crawl my way to her house like a grandma and then have her drive wherever we were going. Then I was offered a job at the new Anatomy Asylum in Garden Grove. It was a fifteen-minute commute each way which made me insanely nervous, but it was an amazing opportunity I couldn't turn down. I'd be working at the front desk as well as teaching two different types of classes, regular high impact aerobics and a special class for very overweight clients, Richard's personal passion.

The second class was exclusively for people who were more than fifty pounds overweight. It was a dramatic departure for me because it wasn't just about changing their bodies but also about making a mental shift. At the end of each workout, I was required to close the class with some sort of inspirational message, which could have been awkward considering our surface dynamics: I knew they were heavy; they knew I was thin. People taking my class for the first time would say, "Really? This skinny seventeen-year-old girl is going to *inspire* me?" But I knew about pain and sadness and struggle, I promised them. I knew about bargaining and desperation and blaming and wishing things were different. I knew about wanting so badly to change your life that you'd swear you would do whatever it took to make that happen, no matter how hard or painful the process was. I knew that sometimes you'd fail and other times things would have to get beyond bad, they'd have to get gut-wrenchingly miserable, before you got to the point where you were ready to risk trying and failing again. I'd tell them to close their eyes and take a deep breath, and that when they exhaled, they were breathing out every single thing that was holding them back. I asked them to forgive themselves, right there in that moment and in that room, for the mistakes they made yesterday or last month or ten years ago, and to think about one thing that they were amazing at today that made them special or unique or happy. I would do it along with them. I'd squeeze my eyes closed as tightly as I could and I would mentally congratulate myself for working and finishing school and making incredible friends and paying my own bills and taking care of myself.

"Today is all you have," I'd remind them at the very end of each class. "So, be good to you, because you deserve it."

I knew in my heart we all did.

FORESHADOWING

"There is nothing to writing.
All you have to do is sit down at a typewriter and bleed."

~Ernest Hemingway

Life at The Fountains was magical. The best part was that I was keenly aware of it. Every time something totally crazy, funny, fabulous or fun happened, I would say, "This is definitely going in the book." I said it so often that my friends would bring it up, too.

"This *has* to go in the book!" they'd shout.

It was funny at the time, but somewhere along the line it stopped being a joke.

My life was a parade of bizarre, hilarious, heartbreaking tragedies littered with great friends, tough, spirited siblings and more than a few laugh-out-loud moments. It all had to go in the book.

"Don't forget to put cutting the cheese in there," Julie would say.

I promised her I wouldn't.

#METOO

"Change happens when the pain of staying the same is greater than the pain of change."

~Tony Robbins

'll call him Craig.

We worked out at the same gym and he was the whole proverbial package. He was charming and funny and smart, with a gorgeous face and a personality as big as his biceps. Craig was the guy everyone wanted to be around; the life of the party; a living people-magnet. It took me about five minutes to develop a massive crush on Craig, and to my delight, he liked me back.

Craig was a wrestler. Initially at least, his massive physique made me feel protected and safe. He was the first person—man or woman—I opened up to fully. I told him about my awful, abusive childhood and I thought I could see the concern in his eyes. It felt so amazing to share this part of me with someone finally. I had turned a huge emotional corner. We were inseparable almost immediately.

It always started out as "joking around."

"Let's wrestle," Craig would say, scooping me up with his massive hands and tossing me like a newborn kitten to the floor before pinning me there. "Say uncle," he'd jeer as he smashed my face into the ground. I would cry and tell him that he was hurting me and beg him to stop, but he'd just laugh and hold me there longer. When he finally tired of tormenting me, he'd walk away without a backward glance. If I dared to act angry or upset by this mistreatment—which I did often—he would give me the silent treatment for days, a punishment I knew well. I'd done something to anger him and I was going to pay for it. That was just the way it went.

Craig never split my lip open or gave me a black eye like you see in the movies. He was careful that way. He'd pelt me with ice cubes from across the room—"It's a game! Isn't this fun?"—until there were welts all over my body. Or he would stand on one of my feet and twist his own has hard as he could, putting all of his body weight into the malicious move. The pain was excruciating; my foot would ache for days. It was my fault, always. Cue the silence.

"This is ridiculous," I told him once after two weeks of wordlessness. "You can't ignore me forever. Hello? Can you please talk to me?"

I guess I pressed back one time too often. In a blur I couldn't make sense of then or now, Craig spun and grabbed me by the shoulders, smashing my head into the wall and holding me there. My legs and feet dangled limply beneath me.

"I told you I don't fucking want to talk," he spat in my face. I hung there speechless, staring into his hateful eyes. "Just remember, I never hit you," he said finally before releasing his grip. I slid to the floor, a sudden realization flooding my body: I had a choice. I didn't have to take this. I could walk away and never see him again.

The next day, that's what I did. That was the last time I was ever physically abused.

I didn't know back then that abused children often grow up and repeat the cycle, unconsciously choosing the miserable yet familiar. Up until Craig slammed me into that wall, that's exactly what I had done. That day was a wake-up call. Craig may have looked good on paper, but behind closed doors, he was physically cruel and emotionally heartless and I knew I deserved more. I may not have known exactly what that looked like, but I was keenly aware that it was something I had never experienced before. I thank God every day for giving me the grace and the courage to keep searching for it.

MORE THAN A SPRING FLING

"Never, ever underestimate the importance of having fun."

~Randy Pausch

"We're going to Palm Springs for spring break," Janet and Kerry squealed. "You *have* to come, it's going to be a blast!"

They were my friends from school and the three of us were glued at the hip. Janet was in dance with me and Kerry and I would go visit her at the Sizzler and gorge on the salad bar. It was all-you-can-eat and with our budget, it was like a Christmas feast every time we went.

Palm Springs, though? It might as well have been Pluto.

I'd never been to the desert or on a vacation of any sort before, ever. "How much would it cost?" I asked. "Where would we stay?" *Could I actually be the type of person who took vacations?* The last question stayed inside my head.

We were just going to wing it, they told me. Our friends Roger and Ed from school were going, along with some guy named Bryan I didn't know, and it was going to be amazing. I desperately wanted more fun in my life, and I was determined to choose that for myself. I got co-workers to cover my Anatomy Asylum shifts and took the whole weekend off. I had no idea where we would sleep or what we would eat, but those weren't the biggest concerns of the day anyway. It was all about what we would wear and how much fun we would have when we got there; the rest would work itself out. It always did.

We piled into Janet's tiny red Honda and hit the road. Madonna had just released her eponymous debut album and we blasted that thing the entire ride, belting our lungs out. I felt as if I were in a movie. It was the story of three best friends who didn't have a care in the world heading out for the time of their lives; "Burning Up," "Borderline" and "Lucky Star" made up the unforgettable soundtrack.

Janet drove to a run-down little hotel that cost $75 a night for our shitty little room. The place had air-conditioning and a decent pool, though, which was all that really mattered since it was at least 108 degrees in the desert. We ditched our things, threw on our swimsuits and bolted for the pool, where we did the only thing three teenage girls would dream of doing in this situation: we lathered up with baby oil and positioned our chairs to ensure maximum skin damage.

We were three slabs of human bacon sizzling in the sun when out of nowhere, it started raining ice water.

"Let the games begin," Roger said as we shrieked and laughed and splashed our own drinks back at the boys. They had brought a cooler full of Bartles & Jaymes and we all talked and sipped in between much-needed dips in the pool.

There was instant chemistry between me and this new guy Bryan. He was eighteen and a football player at my school and just looking at him gave me butterflies in my stomach. I didn't expect to feel that ever again after Craig, but Bryan was different. He was sweet and polite and lived in Green-brook, an upscale neighborhood in Fountain Valley that had its own clubhouse. He was shocked to learn that I lived in an apartment with another student and no parents and wanted to know more, but I was determined to keep things light and fun that weekend. I told him that was a story for another day and jumped into the pool. I wasn't about to go there again.

After a while my friends and I went back to our room and got dressed to the nines, and then the boys took us out for dinner. They had their own credit cards which was crazy to me and they refused to let us pay for anything. This worked out well since my reserves were lean, to say the least. It was a magical night and I was convinced that nothing could ever top it, but the weekend just got better and better. While Bryan and I had plenty of opportunities to get physical, he didn't even try to make a move. I'd been around the bases by this point, but I loved that he wanted to take things slowly and get to know me before trying to close the deal. It made me like him even more.

Back at home, Bryan and I quickly became an official item and I was over the moon and around it nine times. My new boyfriend still lived at home like most eighteen-year-olds, and I would swing by and leave mushy cards on his doorstep, along with other small tokens of my massive crush. Our affection was mutual and magnificent. I was on top of the world.

Finally, and for the first time, my life was nothing short of wonderful and as much as I wanted to stop the clock, time was flying. Julie's lease at The Fountains was about to expire and the school year, our last, was winding down. Kids were talking about college and jobs and the big, amazing trips they were taking to celebrate. Some were planning to backpack across Europe and take cruises to Mexico. Jane and a bunch of my other friends were going to Hawaii, a holiday that was still light years beyond my reach. I was envious but I told myself I was closer to a trip of that sort than I had ever been in my life. I was going to graduate high school—a first for my siblings— and find a perfect new place to live. I'd get an amazing job and be wildly successful and someday I was going to have all of the luxuries in the world, like fancy vacations and designer clothes and a refrigerator full of food. I was sure of it.

HUNTINGTON BEACH GARAGE

BUSHES AND BED

"Health is like money, we never have a true idea of its value until we lose it."

~Josh Billings

Summer was one last three-month hurrah that flew by in a flash. Our lease was coming up and Julie was going to move back in with her mom and new stepdad to save money. The reality that I would soon be homeless weighed heavily on my mind around the clock, especially because my work schedule left me little time to look for a new place to live. Even though Bryan was supportive and concerned, I felt alone and afraid.

I started putting out feelers. It turned out my two friends Cathy and Tony were in the same boat, so we decided to look for something together. Tony heard about a house in Huntington Beach that sounded promising and we went together to look at it.

The house was not in great shape. It was a two-bedroom, one-bath, and every square inch of it was dirty and dated. The owners optimistically called the detached garage a third "bedroom" because it had a long closet along one wall, although there was no heat or bathroom out there. It was pretty awful, and all any of us could afford. Tony was in; Cathy agreed if she could have one of the inside bedrooms. I reluctantly took the garage.

It's only temporary, I told myself, feeling utterly dejected. It was old and cold and the grass was a wreck, which to me still was and always would be a sign of any home's happiness. I knew I'd never want to have friends over; that it would be a place to store a few things and maybe stay out of the rain and nothing more. I vowed to work harder than ever and get myself out of that hellhole as soon as humanly possible.

The garage was miserable on the best of all days. Southern California may be famous for its delightful weather, but even a balmy eighty-degree day can be followed by a forty-degree night. I slept in layers, wearing my workout tights and a bulky sweater under thick onesie pajamas. When I had to use the bathroom in the middle of the night, I'd have to creep across the dead, black lawn and through one of the bedrooms, open the creaky bathroom door and then strip down to nearly nothing just to tinkle. Then I'd have to re-dress and dart back out through the pitch dark to my icebox of a room, where I was positive an axe-murderer would be waiting for me.

I learned to hold it like a professional.

Bryan was the one thing I had going for me. He was always trying to make me feel better about my situation and would stay over whenever his work and school schedule allowed it. I lived for those nights, for both the company and the body heat. Knowing how much I despised the cold, for Christmas Bryan painted me a giant life-size fireplace on a floor-to-ceiling piece of plywood. The fireplace itself was brick and the insert was a brilliant, blazing fire set against black background. It was up there with Patrick's Cher doll on my short list of best-ever gifts. It would have taken the top slot if only it had actually worked.

Winter didn't just bring frost; it also brought the flu. I was hit with a wicked strain that I was forced to work through, because I'd blown through my savings. If I didn't work I didn't get paid and if I didn't get paid I couldn't make my rent. Maybe because I never took off my workout tights, the flu was followed in short order by a raging bladder infection. Between the crippling pain and the urgency to urinate every ten minutes, I was barely sleeping. I was loathe to spend the money but finally I couldn't take it anymore and I dragged my sorry self to the doctor.

Within days of starting antibiotics, I was feeling almost normal again. I couldn't believe how quickly that medicine had worked. It was so expensive that even though the doctor had specifically told me to finish the bottle I thought I probably should save the rest of the pills in case I ever got sick again, so I stopped taking them and tucked them safely away.

The infection came back with a vengeance. I reluctantly took the rest of the pills but this time they didn't help. I called my mom, because I didn't know what else to do and because moms are supposed to know how to handle these things. She told me to be careful taking any sort of pain pill because they made her deathly ill, and to drink lots of cranberry juice. She said I was scaring her and that I needed to get back to the doctor because she didn't know what she would do if she lost another child. It always came back to that, every time.

It cost me every penny of savings to get myself another round of antibiotics, which the doctor prescribed alongside some Vicodin for the pain. He told me I could take one every four hours and I was in so much agony I couldn't wait to get started. I popped the first pill before I even got in my car and I'm not sure how I even made it back to my garage. The only thing keeping me awake was the dizzying queasiness in my gut I had to actively concentrate on keeping down while I was driving.

It was probably a good thing that I had inherited Mom's intolerance for narcotics.

I made it home and no sooner had I crawled into my bed than a fresh wave of nausea hit. I'd dash outside to the bushes to throw up and then hobble back to bed. Then I'd do it all over again. Bushes, bed. Bushes, bed. Bushes, bed, bushes, bed, bushes, bed. In the morning, I threw the rest of the Vicodin away. I couldn't afford to miss one more day of work, and that stuff clearly did not agree with me.

A low-grade illness lingered all winter, but I powered through it. I had no choice. Many nights it was just me and my misery and Rudy, a neighbor's black lab who adopted me. Somehow Rudy knew that I was sick and alone and he started coming to my garage just after dark almost every night. I'd let him in and he'd sleep in my bed with me and make me feel safe. During the rainy season, his muddy paws would track wet dirt inside my already stale garage and I'd dry him off and let him climb into bed with me and keep me warm. In the morning he'd go home and be somebody else's dog; somebody who could afford to feed him but I was sure loved him a little less than I did.

HAVE YOURSELF A DIRTY LITTLE CHRISTMAS

"Christmas isn't a season.
It's a feeling."

~Edna Ferber

ach Anatomy Asylum branch had its own unique vibe that was a mixture of the people who worked there and the clientele. At the Fountain Valley location my co-workers were mostly kids from my high school, and probably half the regulars were families I knew from around town. Everything about that branch was fun, upbeat and boringly normal. I'd heard the Orange branch was similar, although I only taught one early morning class there so I hadn't been able to confirm that myself. But something about the Garden Grove location was straight-up off. And by something I mean everything. The people who worked out there were just different and I was always asking my roommate and co-worker Tony to look out for me.

I got a commission anytime I signed up new clients, and a family of four was a score, so initially I was thrilled to meet the

Hunts. Jeremy was a photographer and his wife Susan worked in his studio, where they told me they even had a playroom set up for their two kids so they could take them to work. I thought that was amazing. Jeremy wanted to know if I had ever modeled and I told him that I hadn't and he said that was a shame, which was flattering.

The Hunts became Asylum regulars. Susan was a mousy brunette, dowdy and conservative. Obviously the life of that party, Jeremy was friendly and outgoing and relentless about telling me how badly he'd love to shoot me. I'd thank him for the compliment and reiterate that I wasn't interested in modeling. My plate was already overflowing, I explained, and it just wasn't my thing. He would say, "Yeah, of course, I totally get it," but that never stopped him from bringing it up.

One day Jeremy told me he was looking for someone to work the front desk at his studio. He asked how much I earned at the Anatomy Asylum and then he told me his position paid more, so we made arrangements for me to tour his Costa Mesa warehouse. When I arrived, Jeremy showed me around and described the job and since it sounded easy enough and the salary was a nice step up, I accepted the position. I could keep teaching classes at the Asylum, where I made really good money, so between the two gigs I'd easily be covering my bills. I congratulated myself on putting myself out there and looking for new opportunities and making things happen in my life.

Jeremy and Susan had a lot of friends. In fact, the studio seemed to have a revolving door, with people coming and going constantly despite the fact that very little in the way of photography seemed to be transpiring there. Day after day I greeted a parade of suits and surf bums, soccer moms and cops. It was strange, but then again what did I know about the picture-taking business? Maybe everyone needed headshots for something. I really had no idea.

December rolled around and the Hunts invited me to their annual Christmas party. In fact, Susan made a big deal out of making sure I knew I was invited. Most of the time I got the feeling she didn't like me very much, so I was surprised and again, flattered. I said I'd love to go. I had never been to a proper holiday party and I wondered if they'd have an ornament or white elephant gift exchange, both of which sounded so fun to me. I was so excited I even splurged on a new dress for the occasion. It was sparkly organza and had a full skirt and cost two weeks' rent, but I worked hard and I decided my first official corporate party justified the expense.

When I arrived at the studio the night of the soiree, you could hear the music from a block away. I entered the building, excited and a little nervous, to Teena Marie's "Lovergirl." The song was hugely popular at the time and one of my favorites but surprising nonetheless. *What an interesting choice to celebrate the season of Jesus's birth*, I thought as I passed by my empty desk and made my way back toward the source of the music.

The cavernous warehouse was awash in pulsing lights, and the first thing that registered was bodies. Naked bodies. Not just arms and legs but backs and breasts and bare asses everywhere. The place was teeming with flesh and more flesh. *Why am I seeing naked people right now?* Despite the fact that warning lights were flashing in my brain, I was a master at hiding my feelings, so I continued to walk as if nothing were amiss.

I made my way around the perimeter of the room, scanning the crowd. I was looking for a familiar face and willing my eyes to take in something—anything—other than what they were positive they were seeing.

On the outside, I was the picture of composure. But on the inside, my head was on the verge of exploding with a resounding *NOOOOOOOOOOOOOOOO*.

Because I had just realized that the people weren't just naked; they were having sex.

It was a massive orgy. People were having sex everywhere—standing and on the floor and on swings suspended from the ceiling—and in every possible position you can think of. And they weren't just faceless people; they were the very same suits and soccer moms and surfer bums and cops I'd seen coming and going for the past few weeks. *I was watching policemen have sex! Was that some sort of crime?* I was so scared, and so naive, I didn't know where to look or what to do.

Everywhere I turned, naked men and women were poking and prodding each other and spinning on stripper poles; just as many were standing or milling around just watching this X-rated spectacle. I casually made my way through this sea of sex in my pretty new party dress, wondering if anyone had noticed me or would try to stop me if I bolted for the door.

"Beautiful dress," a guy said to me, all nonchalant. He was wearing a G-string and nothing else and I'd just seen him dancing on one of the poles.

"I'm sorry," I stammered, pleading with my eyes. "I don't belong here. I need to leave." I didn't think he necessarily could or would help me, but I wanted to be talking to someone and not just standing there awkwardly and staring. The nearly naked man laughed.

"Aw, don't worry, girl, you're fine," the stripper-pole guy insisted. "Just hang out. You don't have to participate, just have a drink and enjoy the show."

Enjoy the show?

I smiled weakly, trying to screw up the courage to turn and make a run for it. I was afraid now that I'd seen what was going on, I was somehow an accomplice to it all and I wouldn't be allowed to exit of my free will. But I knew that I had to at least try so I turned without another word to my half-naked friend and calmly made my way back toward the door on wobbling legs. The crisp, wintry air slapped me in the face and I dashed to my car and sped the hell away from that crazy place.

I never saw Jeremy or Susan again, and I promptly quit teaching at the Garden Grove Asylum as well. I also never told anyone about what happened at that party, not even Bryan, because I was mortified by the whole experience and I just wanted to bury it in the past and pretend it never happened.

I had learned a valuable lesson that night, though. I'd known all along there was something about Jeremy and Susan Hunt that I couldn't trust; my only mistake was not trusting myself.

BANK ON IT

"Anybody who thinks money will make you happy
hasn't got money."
~David Geffen

needed a new job. I had been getting by on my old salary,
but only barely. I knew I needed to make more money this
time around and I figured what could be better than working
at a bank? I'd be surrounded by cash all day every day, plus I
had all of that change-making experience from Mama Rose's.
It was perfect.

The little money I had was housed at Downey Savings, so
that's where I applied. I was hired as a teller immediately and
when I asked about my schedule, the manager laughed. "It's
banker's hours," she told me. I had no idea what that meant or
when to show up so I called the bank and casually asked what
their hours were; the lady on the other end of the line told me
ten to six. I decided I should arrive for my first shift at least a
half hour early, so I did.

I was correct.

My new co-workers welcomed me warmly and set about
teaching me the ropes. My official training lasted for two
weeks and covered everything from customer service to dealing with holdups. If it happened, there was a button to press
and then you'd hear these cameras start clicking like crazy and

the manager would press another button that locked all the doors on the spot. Simple as that.

The whole conversation floored me. Bank robberies sounded so wild, wild West. "*People still did that?*" I asked the girl training me. She shrugged and said she'd never seen one personally and we moved on to recording night deposits.

Bank hours were long but almost everyone I worked with made the time pass easily. Anna was a notable exception. She sat at the window right next to me and she was rude and condescending to everyone she met, even customers. No matter how friendly I was to her, Anna couldn't seem to wipe the sourpuss from her face. I got used to it and went about my duties.

One of those duties consisted of counting huge stacks of cash. You could only have $5,000 in your drawer at any one time, so once you hit that threshold you had to count it and take it to the vault teller. I had my window closed one day and had just counted my money. I stood up to make my way to the vault when I noticed a guy step out of the long line and approach Anna's window.

"I don't have an account here," I heard him say in a friendly voice that was barely above a whisper, "but I do have a thirty-eight caliber and it works, so give me all your cash and do it fast."

The only thing I could think was *don't panic.* Without making eye contact with the guy and as casually as I could, I walked to the window where a vault teller named Janice sat. My manager Sharon happened to be standing there and I quietly told her we were being robbed. Sharon mouthed to Janice one word: LOCKDOWN.

The click of the cameras was loud and sounded like a woman tapping her long acrylic fingernails on glass. I thought this was a terrible system — surely the guy knew we were on to him — but there was no stopping it now. Janice took the money from me without counting it—which was strictly against rules—and shoved it into the vault.

I could still hear the CLICK CLICK CLICK and saw Sharon manually lock the doors. I looked around for the guy with the thirty-eight but he'd already bolted—thankfully, in my opinion. The last thing I wanted was to be locked *inside* with him, another part of the bank's holdup plan I didn't think was especially wise.

Within minutes the entire building was swarming with what appeared to be the entire Fountain Valley Police Department. I was worried I might recognize some of them from the Hunts' Christmas orgy, but fortunately none of those faces rang even the faintest of bells.

After a while bank robberies became like earthquakes or wildfires: something that occasionally happened but usually you survived. I'd live through eight of them during my stint in banking, twice when I was only in the branch long enough to pick up my paycheck. There would always be an investigation, and Ponch and Jon would make us tell them every detail of our day, as if what we had for lunch had anything to do with the crime that had been committed. They almost always caught the guys, though, a fact that made me feel better about the whole thing. I liked it when any story had a happy ending.

TWO TRUTHS AND A LIE

afternoon. I'm really mad at Don. I went in to get a snack for lunch (he was asleep) quickly woke, he got mad at me for eating any thing and cursed me out so I came back here. Two can play that game. I'll just see about this kind of action. Its kids stuff! I know its the booze. Its eating his brain!

"**E**rin, it's your mom. Again."

I had no idea how many Downey Savings employees' mothers called them shitfaced at work day after day, but my guess was not many. I'd told her that I wasn't allowed to take personal calls while I was on the clock, that I would check in with her on my lunch break—and I did. But as it had been for as long as I could remember, whenever Mom had a need, forever and always it trumped mine.

"Are you okay?" I asked her.

"Something's wrong with me and I don't know what it is." She was sauced as usual.

I hesitated here, because I was at work... and because I was tired of her games... and because I was beginning to understand that you can't save someone who doesn't want to be saved.

"But don't worry about it," Mom said sarcastically in response to my silence. "I can take care of myself."

"Mom, what is it? What's wrong?" I couldn't keep the irritation out of my voice.

"It's bad, Erin," she slurred. "I can't get up and I don't know why."

My reaction was ages in the making.

"Really, Mom?" I asked, furious. "Do you think maybe it's because you drink yourself sick all day every day? You've been wasted every time I've spoken to you for weeks. Actually, make that years. No wonder you don't feel right!"

"Erin, if you don't come right now... I don't think I'm going to make it."

"I'm on my way," I told her.

My boss was annoyed but I promised I'd be back in an hour. Her look dared me to break my word.

The smell of urine hit me first; it always did, entering their mobile home. I knew the stench from my childhood of course, but mercifully it wasn't something I ever got used to. I stifled a gag and went inside anyway.

Mom was sprawled out on the living room floor, completely passed out. Captain Jack was hovering nearby, a mumbling, pickled mess. He was half-angry and half-apologizing for the sorry state of all of it; my mother, the mobile home, their very existence. The man who once made me cower in fear was so pathetic to me that for a moment I was torn between pity and rage.

Rage won.

"What in the hell is wrong with you guys? Look at yourselves! You're pathetic!"

I dropped to my mother's side to assess her condition while Captain Jack launched into his hackneyed platitude routine.

"You shape up or you ship out!" he roared. "That's all she wrote. I tried to get her up but I couldn't. And that's about the size of it!"

I ignored him, grabbed the phone and called 911. What was my emergency, the operator wanted to know.

"My mother is passed-out drunk… she doesn't think she's going to make it… no, she's not conscious now… yes, she's breathing… sure, I'll stay on the line while you send help…"

I held the phone while the Captain continued muttering under his liquor-soaked breath. Mom started to come to so I told her what was happening; that I had called an ambulance and that she was a mess and she needed to get help. My words were matter-of-fact but my tone told her I was fed up.

"You called an *AMBULANCE*?" she howled. "I'm fine! That's ridiculous! Just help me to bed."

"You don't need to go to bed, you need to go to the hospital!" I told her, covering the phone's mouthpiece. "Have you looked in the mirror? You look awful. You called me for help and I'm helping you!"

At this announcement, Mom got a frenzied second wind and struggled to a sitting position. "Damnit, Erin… so help me God… if you don't hang up that phone, you're going to pay for it. ALL of it! The doctor bills and the hospital bills and the ambulance and every last bit!"

"So be it," I told her. "You need help and I'm not leaving until you get it."

When the policeman and EMTs arrived and the repulsive odor of the place hit them like a punch, the look on their collective faces said it all. I was mortified. How could I let them get so bad? It was my fault; it had to be.

"Shut the goddamn door before the cat gets out!" Captain Jack shouted at the responders. The police officer looked incredulous.

"We're leaving the door open," he told the Captain sternly.

"I guess you're the boss," Captain Jack replied with a sarcastic laugh. "Do it your way."

The cop pulled me aside, where I apologized profusely. He wanted to know if I lived there, and what was going on, and how long it had been like this. Were they doing drugs or just drinking? How often did I visit them?

I began to sob, something I never, ever did in front of other people, particularly strangers.

"Not very often," I explained guiltily. "You can see why."

I was a blubbering mess by this point. When I told him that my mother was pissed that I'd called for help, his sad smile nearly pushed me over the edge.

"Addicts always get mad when they have to go to the hospital, because they know they won't be able to drink. I'll be honest. Your mom's in bad shape. It was good that you called. You did the right thing." He nodded toward at Captain Jack. "Now, what about him?"

"What are you looking at me for?" the Captain screamed. "I told her to stop drinking a week ago!"

A *week* ago? I just shook my head.

"Sir, can you walk?" the cop asked him.

"I'm a Marine, goddamnit! I don't need your help. I'm a MAN!"

Oh, here we go, a voice inside my head said. But I couldn't hear it one more time, and I was no longer afraid of him.

"Yeah, you're a man, all right," I fumed. "You're a hell of a man. Just look at you! You're disgusting. You're a drunk and a coward and a pathetic excuse for a human being! You make me SICK!" I was crazy with exasperation and indignation, hurtling every insult I could think of at the wretched failure who had stolen my mother from me. The cop put his hand on my arm and gently told me to stop.

The EMTs had Mom on a stretcher now. I cried as they took her away, because it was over. My mother loved alcohol and the abusive enabler she was married to, and she would never and *could* never love me. She wasn't capable of it. I was an inconvenience, a reminder of her sadness. No matter how many times I tried to save her, to convince her that I was worth changing for, it would always end the same way.

I followed the EMTs out of the mobile home to a soundtrack of Captain Jack's marine-banter howling and pulled the door shut behind me without another word.

The hospital called me a few hours later and told me that Mom had one of the most severe cases of cirrhosis of the liver they had ever seen. The doctors didn't think she was going to make it through the night. The voice on the phone said something about scar tissue and fluid build-up and inducing a coma but I didn't hear any of it; only that she might not make it. Could that really be possible? Her nonstop drinking was such a part of her that it hadn't occurred to me that it might actually kill her. I knew alcohol made her mean and detached and sleepy and weak, but she had survived so much already. Surely she'd pull through this, too?

They needed me to sign some papers, the man on the phone said. Could I come right away? I didn't even want to see her. I was so tired of being the parent, of coming to the rescue, of being let down and then getting sacked with the blame. I was furious at her for putting me in this position again and pissed at myself for being so angry at the woman who had given me life. I drove to the hospital, signed the papers and left, racing to get back to Bryan's before he got home from night school.

Bryan had moved out of his parents' house and was living with a couple of roommates. I stayed at his place every chance

I could get, because it was far nicer than my decrepit garage and because I loved him. And even though I believed he loved me back, I never told Bryan when I had to clean up after Mom and Captain Jack. He would never know the devastation of what I had seen, smelled and felt that night, or that I had cried my eyes out in front of strangers, which was absolutely against my life rules. He wouldn't understand. In my mind, he would judge me, or even worse, pity me. He'd realize that his family was wonderful and mine was awful and that I had nothing to bring to the table. Bryan couldn't wait to have children, and these two would be their grandparents. How could I break his heart with that news? So I said nothing and continued on as if nothing were amiss.

Mom was in the hospital for a month. I didn't visit her but we spoke on the phone on a few occasions; each time she was angry and defiant, wanting to know exactly who I thought was going to pay all of her medical bills. I'd tell her to calm down and just focus on getting well—because surprisingly, that was happening. She was gaining strength and had even been able to walk a few steps. One day she called me to tell me they were sending her home; as in back to the mobile home and Captain Jack and round-the-clock happy hour. For perhaps the first time in our relationship, I voiced my concerns.

She was stronger in her mind and feeling better than she had in years, Mom promised me. She wasn't going to put up with any more from Captain Jack, and if he wouldn't stop drinking, she was going to leave him. The doctors told her that if she drank again, she would die, no question about it.

"Do you want to die, Mom?" I asked her.

"No," she said. "I don't. I just never wanted my life to turn out this way. I'm tired of scraping for every dime. I can't ever even enjoy a meal out or go to a movie. I sit home with him while he drinks, day and night. It's not much of a life."

It was the first time in as long as I could remember that Mom and I were having a real conversation. I wasn't about to ruin it by pointing out that up until now she'd been Captain Jack's number-one drinking buddy. If she wanted to stay sober, I'd do whatever it took to help her.

When they released her, Mom was transported home by ambulance and told to take it easy. Her doctors encouraged her to get in-home care but Captain Jack wanted no part of that. He promised he'd be a top-notch caretaker, a vow Mom told me he broke within minutes of her return to the festering trailer.

I knew she was telling the truth because I'd hear him bellowing in the background whenever I called to check in, and he rarely had the decency to hide his irrational ire.

"You were lying around on your ass for a month, what about me goddamnit? I'm tired of this shit! I know, I'm the bad guy. Go ahead and tell Erin how it's all my fault. Tell her I said thank you very much. THANK YOU FOR SHOWING UP FOR ME! I CHANGED YOUR DIAPERS, YOU KNOW, AND THAT'S ABOUT THE SIZE OF IT!"

Other times he'd revert to karaoke-Captain Jack, crooning in the background while we tried to chat.

"Awwwww, Jeri, come on. Let's just have a little fun. *When Ireland was Ireland and England was a pup...*"

He was pulling out all the stops, trying to lure her back to her old pal, alcohol. Mom swore up and down she was clean and planned to stay that way. Each time we talked, she sounded stronger and more determined. We talked about her moving out, and what her new life without Captain Jack could look like. She still had hopes and dreams and plans; she wanted to cook and make beautiful art and sew fabulous things. I told her she could move in with me; that we'd figure out a way to make it work. She said that Captain Jack was drinking a lot less and acting a lot better and that she wanted to give him another chance, but she'd let me know if that changed. I believed all of it. It seemed like she was really listening to reason and hearing the truth, and I was filled with hope and possibility for her. I went to the mobile home and scrubbed and scoured until my fingers nearly bled, and had the house looking and smelling as good as it was ever going to get by the time I finished.

When I left that day, Mom gave me a hunk of government cheese and a pack of butter. We joked about how hard would it be for them to actually slice the stuff, and I told her I thought most families probably just passed the whole block around and took turns gnawing big bites off of it. We laughed and hugged and I went home with my cheese and a lighter, happier heart than I'd had in years.

"Erin, you have a call on line one." My manager gave me a look — *not this again* — but I smiled confidently. Things were different now.

Except they weren't.

It was Mom and she wasn't just drunk, she was out of her mind wasted. I could barely understand her garbled words, only something about Don drinking everything in sight and when was I coming over because she needed to see me.

"Mom, you're drunk," I said quietly, cupping my hand over the phone so my co-workers wouldn't hear me.

"I am not drunk," she hissed. "I haven't even had a sip! YOU DON'T KNOW WHAT THE HELL YOU'RE TALKING ABOUT!" The last part was almost unintelligible.

I slipped the phone back into the cradle wordlessly and returned to my teller window with my heart completely shattered. Sadness and anger and frustration welled up in me until I thought I might explode. The pain was unimaginable. If she had plunged a sword straight through my heart, it couldn't have hurt any worse.

IS IT HOT IN HERE?

July 16, 84 Mon. 5:30 P.M.

Couldn't sleep and Don drinking a gain. A pint 2 days in a row or evenings in a row. He still has those nitmares. Turning the lites on and telling me there is a man in the closet with a rifle; and you can't tell him other wise. He just can't hold it any more.

I wish this heat spell would break.

SONNY SIDE UP

"Money can buy you a fine dog,
but only love can make him wag his tail."

~Kinky Friedman

ixie Merrill's daughter Sherri was now a tennis pro at the Tropicana hotel in Las Vegas. She also was a sales rep for several different sportswear lines, and for the past three years she'd asked me to model at the Vegas sports apparel show. Initially—after the Christmas orgy fiasco—I'd been hesitant. But I knew I could trust Sherri, and it had turned out to be a fantastic recurring experience, not to mention a nice chunk of change in my pocket.

This time Sherri asked me if I wouldn't mind carpooling with two other models. My old VW Bug had finally bitten the dust and I had a brand-new Suzuki Samurai I couldn't wait to put some miles on. I said I'd be thrilled to drive. I picked up Ariana, a gorgeous Gwen Stefani lookalike, right in my neighborhood and we grabbed Christine, an equally stunning brunette, just outside of Los Angeles and we headed east. We were young and carefree and became fast friends, laughing and joking the entire ride.

At the show, we were outfitted in gorgeous, over-the-top, fur-trimmed ski bunny outfits that easily cost a month's rent payment apiece. We'd been given a dinner stipend on top of our modeling rate, but when some guys on the sales team begged us to let them take us out, we thought that sounded fun and accepted the offer. It turned out, the guys wanted a lot more than dinner companions. When the married company president made a move on Ariana, we put the brakes on that idea and left. We were young but we weren't dumb, and none of us had any interest in playing tonsil hockey with some old geezer. We went back to our hotel room, got dolled up and went out dancing. We had the time of our lives.

Men offered to buy us drinks left and right, but I watched my own intake like a probation officer. I wasn't a teetotaler, but I also knew I had to be careful. I had seen what the aftermath of a night of drinking could do far too often, and I wanted nothing to do with that. My friends, on the other hand, weren't quite as cautious. The next day they were miserable, running to the bathroom every few minutes to rid their bodies of the alcoholic toxins they'd consumed.

By the third day, I was dying to get home. I missed Bryan and I reeked of cigarette smoke to the point I could hardly stand myself. Ariana had decided to fly home so it was just me and Christine as we headed out across the desert.

Parched and getting low on fuel, we pulled into a combo gas station/mini-mart called Sunshine Liquor. Outside the store a woman was sitting with a box of brand-new puppies. They looked like tiny pigs, all pink and squealing. Their mother had been hit by a car, the woman explained, and two had already died. She didn't know when they'd last eaten. They were only four days old, Boxer and Pit Bull mix she thought, and their eyes hadn't even opened yet. Was there any chance I could take one? Please?

I couldn't say no. I picked out the fattest pink pup, figuring it had the best chance of survival, and wrapped her in a pair of my sweatpants. I named her Sonny after Sunshine Liquor, not even realizing yet it was also the name of the beloved stuffed turtle of my childhood. The lady gave me a box and a grateful smile and we hit the road again.

The trip was excruciating. Sonny was ravenous and howled the entire time. I stopped at a grocery store at one point and bought a bottle and some milk, but the nipple was too big for her tiny mouth. Christine held my unruly new puppy and shushed her as I raced toward home.

I dropped my friend off and drove straight to the veterinarian's office on my street. Sonny was still wailing her head off. The vet took her in and examined her, and then told me her chances of survival were slim. He gave me a tiny bottle filled with goat's milk and I shoved it into her mouth. The room fell silent. We watched as Sonny hungrily downed the entire bottle. That was an excellent sign, the vet told me. I left with more goat's milk and the realization that I had to go tell my boyfriend what I'd done.

I didn't know how Bryan would react, so I left my new puppy sleeping in the car when I arrived. Bryan was sweet and affectionate and happy to see me, wrapping me in a giant hug and kissing my neck and insisting that he'd missed me like crazy. I replied that I had a surprise for him and told him to close his eyes and that I'd be right back.

I returned with the box and set it in front of him.

"Open," I said.

Bryan's face contorted oddly.

"What the hell is that?" he asked.

"It's a puppy!" I explained.

"Is it alive?" he wanted to know. I assured him that she was. I told him the whole story about Sonny's mother being killed and the noisy ride home, all the while praying that Bryan would fall in love with her as I had.

"Please, can we keep her?" I asked with sad puppy dog eyes of my own.

"I don't want any stupid dog," Bryan said.

My heart sank. I begged and pleaded and promised I'd do everything, feed her and pick up after her and take her for walks, but Bryan stood firm.

"I just don't want some mangy dog running all over this house," he said. And because Bryan was the boss, I had to leave it at that.

That night I woke up every two hours to feed her. When Bryan got up to go to work at 4:30, he found the two of us on the couch. I'd fallen asleep feeding her and Sonny was curled in the crook of my arm like a tiny fur ball. Bryan bent down and kissed my forehead.

"Okay, babe," he whispered. "We can keep her. But you're training her and I mean it." I smiled the biggest smile of my life and carried my new baby back to bed with me, where I snuggled her as if I'd birthed her myself. I was beside myself with happiness. I'd finally gotten my Sonny back.

BILL OF WRONGS

*"A small debt makes a man your debtor,
a large one your enemy."*

~Proverb

Mom and I weren't speaking at all. Every few weeks she'd try to call me and act like nothing had happened, and she was always drunk when she did. It was easy to hang up on her.

Then one day she called me and she sounded clear-headed. I could tell five seconds into any conversation exactly how many drinks she'd had, and this time she was stone-cold sober.

"I'm drowning in medical bills," she told me. "I don't know what to do. I'm getting late notices every day and I don't have any money to pay them." She sounded so stressed out that once again, I wanted to help her.

"Just pick one at a time," I told her. "Maybe Medi-Cal can help? Did you call them?"

"I told you that you shouldn't have called 911," Mom said angrily. "These bills are your responsibility, not mine."

"What was I supposed to do?" I demanded. "You told me you were going to die. And you were right! I'm not going to feel guilty for getting you the help you needed. You need to grow up and accept responsibility for yourself!"

When I hung up the phone, I was shaking. I couldn't believe she was going to try to pawn her bills off on me. It was an all-new low, even for her.

About a month later, my boss Sharon called me into her office.

"I hate to tell you this, but I have to garnish your wages," she told me.

"What?" I stammered. "What does that even mean?"

"Apparently you have some outstanding bills, so instead of waiting for you to pay them, the collectors are having the money taken straight out of your paycheck until all the money is paid back."

Foolishly, I couldn't fathom what this might be about. I paid all of my bills on time and in full, and I was proud of that fact. Sharon shuffled through some papers.

"There are a bunch from Garden Grove Medical Center and one for emergency services," she said. "It looks like they're all for Geraldine Blomgren."

"There has to be some mistake," I said. Sure, Mom didn't have any money, and she never missed an opportunity to blame me for calling for help that day. In fact, she'd said point-blank that because I had, her bills were *my* responsibility. Still I struggled to believe it had come to this.

I studied the papers Sharon gave me. There was no mistake. I'd signed the hospital paperwork. I'd called the ambulance. My mother's medical bills totaled more than twenty thousand dollars and I was solely responsible for every last penny.

DONCASTER

GOING TO THE CHAPEL

Bryan bought a house in Huntington Beach on a street called Doncaster Drive. It was a nice place close to the ocean and I was convinced that owning a home at his age meant he was solid and dependable and made good choices. When he asked me to move in with him, I didn't hesitate. It was the next logical step.

At the time, I only knew our relationship in the context of others I'd seen; by that unsophisticated yardstick, I had it all. Bryan was handsome and dependable and he came from a good family. His dad was a doctor and his mom was a nurse and they were warm and loving and overwhelmingly supportive. He didn't drink. He knew how to fix things and had already established a solid plumbing career. Like many of the men who had littered my past, he could be controlling and self-centered, but that was all I had ever known and it was still the nicest a man had ever treated me. Our unspoken pact was I was lucky to have landed him; he was Mr. Wonderful and I was his plus-one. I accepted this because I knew I could certainly do a lot worse. In fact, I was pretty sure this was the best relationship I would ever get; I *could* ever get. So when he gave me a slim gold ring with a tiny diamond in it and asked me to marry him, I said yes. I felt as if I'd won a prize. Bryan had picked me over every other girl in the world.

Finally, I was loved.

My new husband didn't know my whole story; after Craig, nobody did. I had told Bryan my parents were alcoholics and my childhood had been difficult at times, but I was always vague about all of it. I wasn't trying to hide the truth, I just didn't want anybody's pity.

"Woman, I want you barefoot, pregnant and in the kitchen," he liked to say. Another refrain was, "I want an offense *and* a defense." All I could think was, *That's twenty-two kids and I don't even want* one! In fact, I didn't even like other people's children. Having any in my care was a lousy idea, period. "I will never get a divorce," he added. Since he was the boss, I believed him.

I loved him, too, but it's possible that I loved his mother more. Irene was like a mom straight out of a movie. She was classy and elegant and thin and beautiful and the consummate hostess. She loved to throw elaborate dinners and all-day "open houses" where she'd be cooking the entire time. She taught me to make egg rolls and brisket and perfectly steamed green beans, and her chocolate-chocolate chip cake made you think you had died and gone to heaven.

My own mom, on the other hand, was going downhill fast. She continued to call me, always a half bottle in. She refused to acknowledge her own drinking, and insisted that the medical bills — *her* medical bills — that I'd be paying for the next decade were one hundred percent my responsibility. It was a losing battle and I finally accepted that. I had let it go; let *her* go. She and Captain Jack were drunk and broke and neither of those two things was ever going to change. I stopped taking her calls or visiting her altogether. The void was painful and strangely suffocating, because despite everything that had happened, she was still my mother and I still loved her.

I had barely spoken to Dad since I'd moved out, but nevertheless I wanted him to walk me down the aisle. I was still hurt that he'd chosen Betty over me and I always would be, but I couldn't help longing for these simple rites of passage, these semblances of normalcy. I went to his house on Walnut Street and asked him in person, and he said he'd be honored. He wanted me to go upstairs and say hello to Betty while I was there.

"Don't you think it's been long enough?" he asked.

Forever wouldn't have been long enough. I could have lived the rest of my life without ever laying eyes on the woman who had abused and humiliated me for so many years, but instead I agreed. I marched upstairs, fueled by anger and resentment.

Betty was on the phone. "What do you need, Erin?" she demanded in a bored, entitled tone when she hung up.

"I need answers," I told her. I asked her what had ever happened in her life that made her want to brutalize and torment defenseless children. I brought up the beatings, Jenny's suicide attempt, the Vaseline, cheating on Dad, the dishes on my bed, sleeping in my shoes, the endless, awful digging, all of it.

She denied half of her own actions, and blamed me and Jenny and Lindsay for the rest.

"You were animals!" she hissed. "I taught you manners, I taught you how to cook and clean. I was good to you!"

"You call making me eat my own vomit and wear one outfit for weeks at a time being *good to me*? You curled Jen's hair and made her put on makeup before you let Dad take her to the hospital. She could have died!"

"The real world is cruel," Betty spat. "I did you a favor."

I wanted to hit her, to hurl obscenities at her, to hurt her the way she'd hurt all of us more times than I could ever count, but I refused to stoop to her level. I'd said what I needed to say, and she knew where she stood with me. That was enough. She was my past and Bryan was my future, and thankfully his family more than made up for what mine lacked.

My future mother-in-law threw me a wedding shower unlike anything I had ever seen or could have imagined. There were easily a hundred people there, mostly family friends I had never met who filled our entire living room with gifts. I didn't even know what half of the items I was opening were. "I can't wait to show you how to use this," Irene would say with a warm hug, and I couldn't wait either.

Irene took me to Mon Amie Bridal to look for a dress. It was like stepping into another world — one where everyone was happy, and everything was clean and pristine and sparkling white. I had long ago decided that I was only going to surround myself with good, positive people and things that brought me joy, and Mon Amie had both in spades. The women who worked there were stylish and warm and gracious. The gowns were gorgeous. The air smelled like fresh-cut lilies and promise. I was still teaching aerobics and working at the bank, but I asked for a job application anyway.

To my delight, I was called in almost immediately for an interview. Dreaming of my future career in couture, I trotted into the shop in a tiny, plaid schoolgirl skirt, over-the-knee socks and a Julia Roberts smile.

"Why do you want to work here?" the shop matriarch asked me kindly.

"I love everything about this place," I told her. "And I want to work hard at something I love and spend my days with smart, creative people."

"You're hired," she replied. "And don't ever wear that skirt again."

I had never felt comfortable around adults before, and I was sure these women—all of them older and most of them moms—would judge or despise me or in some way find me lacking. It was going to be a temporary thing, I told myself. I'd do it as long as I could stand it, or as long as they could stand me. But that wasn't what happened at all. Almost immediately, my co-workers took me under their collective wing, nurturing and mothering and mentoring me. It took me a while to believe it was real; that I was actually worthy; whole; loved.

On paper, I had it all. I'd landed a husband and a position as a stylist at the equivalent of adult Disneyland. It was a dream job in the fashion industry, and I was surrounded by wonderful, inspiring women and getting paid to cultivate my creative side. I moved quickly through the ranks until I was managing the accessories department and being tapped to style the salon's most prestigious clients. To the outside world, I wasn't just on my way—I was already there.

But inside I was still a little lost. Imagine dropping a naked Mongolian medicine man into New York's Central Park and telling him to build himself a mansion. That was me entering into marriage and adulthood. I had no skills, no tools, no plans, and I didn't speak the language. I didn't know what a healthy partnership looked like from any angle; all I knew was that I wanted to be cherished and protected. At the same time, I was an adult now, and I was determined not to let my miserable childhood define me. I was strong and capable and motivated and compassionate. I had some scars, but I also had a shiny set of pots and pans, a fondue pot and a whole new family, so I was pretty sure I was good to go.

The Beginning

DANBURY

EPILOGUE:
ONE FOR THE BOOKS

" This is definitely going in the book."

That was Karin's response. She'd been my best friend for sixteen years, and we'd seen and done it all together. We had celebrated birthdays and holidays, mourned break-ups and bad haircuts, and traveled to New York, Washington DC, Texas, Seattle, Slovenia, Italy and Greece. I'd brought her into the bridal business, where she did an amazing job running the sales side of my company. We were as close as sisters, and we swore up and down that one day we were going to have babies together.

It was a fairly bold proclamation considering Karin was a lesbian and I'd had both of my fallopian tubes removed in an emergency surgery following a doomed pregnancy. But now Karin was holding up her end of the bargain. She'd explored her heterosexual side long enough to a) determine she was pretty sure she was indeed gay and b) get herself pregnant. She was eight months along and the story she insisted was *definitely going in the book* was this one:

It was 2001. At thirty-six, I had survived my first marriage, a brutal ectopic pregnancy and the nine-eleven terror attacks. My bridal business was thriving and I was remarried and living in a darling little French chateau-style house on Danbury Lane in Irvine when the phone rang.

"Hey," she said. It was Jenny. My heart skipped a beat because with my sister — then, now and possibly forever — you just never knew.

"Hi, honey," I said. "How are you?" And then I held my breath.

Jenny wanted to ask me a question, she said; was I sitting down?

My panic-alarm was screaming and beads of sweat began breaking out along my hairline.

"What is it, Jen? Are you okay? Just tell me, please."

I was clutching the phone and saying silent prayers for one simple reason: history. Jenny's life had taken us both over some seriously rocky terrain over the years; terrain that tested our collective strength, trust, endurance and faith. She could be calling to ask for anything at all: bail money, a place to live, Pat's mailing address, protection from thugs, a liver. My head was spinning.

"Jenny, what do you need to ask me?" I begged.

"Are you still on that list to adopt a baby?" she asked finally.

"Yes, why?" I replied.

There was a long silence.

"Oh my God, you're pregnant," I said. It wasn't a question. My hesitations were countless and complicated. Jenny wasn't married. She had teenage twins she struggled to mother on a daily basis. She was impulsive and reckless and had inherited our mother's thirst for alcohol. She was Jenny.

"Yes, I'm pregnant," Jenny said. "And I was thinking maybe you'd want me to have this baby for you."

There were a million reasons to take my time replying; a million and one reasons to say no. I saw none of them. Not the turmoil or the drama or years of separation we'd suffered together and alone. All I saw was a baby. My baby.

"Are you sure?" I whispered.

"I'm sure," Jenny insisted.

"And you understand what this entails? Because at the end of it, you're going to be giving up a baby."

"I want to do this for you, Erin," Jenny said.

"I can't imagine what this is going to look like," I told her. "But yes. I want the baby."

Jenny promised she would stay absolutely clean for the duration of the pregnancy. It was challenging and painful and I'll forever be grateful that she kept her word.

My daughter Isabella Grace was born on August 9, 2001; through the miracle of IVF her sister Holland Grace followed five years later. I gave them both the same middle name because it was only by the grace of God, who had kept his promise to watch over me, that I ever had them at all. And that is the size of everything.

This is the rest of my story, the short version at least:

I created my first commissioned accessory line for Mon Amie Bridal in 1999. Since then my original designs have sold in upscale bridal salons in Dubai, London, Italy, Korea, Turkey, Australia, Ireland and across the United States.

In 2003, I opened the Erin Cole Couture Bridal Salon in the popular 17th Street Promenade in Costa Mesa. In 2016, I launched my own line of couture wedding gowns.

My parents passed away within six months of each other when I was twenty-four. As far as I know, Betty and Captain Jack are still alive. We do not speak.

Jenny has five grandchildren and lives in a beautiful part of Montana with her dogs and her demons. She loves cooking and jet-skiing and works tirelessly to have a good relationship with her adult twins, Christy and Katie, who are like daughters to me.

Lindsay lives in Fullerton with her long-term boyfriend and books gigs at a trendy punk rock club. She recently earned her phlebotomy degree and despite every possible odd, she's an amazing mom to Jack, the sweetest, funniest kid ever.

Pat and April had one son, Sean, and had been married for thirty-six years when she passed away in 2017 after a painful four-year battle with breast cancer. April was the light of my sweet brother's life; the strong, solid wife he cherished and deserved.

I was married again, and now I'm not.

A lot of amazing, awful, heartbreaking, hilarious and unbelievable things happened along the way, too.

They're definitely going in the next book.

ABOUT THE AUTHORS

ERIN COLE is an author, designer, artist, entrepreneur and survivor. She began her career in the bridal industry as a stylist at the age of twenty-three; today her original gowns and accessories are sold in upscale salons around the world. Erin lives in Newport Beach, California, with her two beautiful daughters, and enjoys drawing, painting, tennis, traveling and creating. Together with her co-author and soul sister, she is excited to launch a new line of everyday jewelry, Erin Cole 364. *The Size of Everything* is her first book.

JENNA McCARTHY is an internationally published writer, TED speaker, former radio DJ, and the author of more than a dozen books for readers of all ages. A former magazine editor and contributor, Jenna's work has appeared in countless publications around the world. She recently relocated with her fabulous family to Austin, Texas, where she hikes, writes, lounges by the pool and enjoys icy air-conditioning for the first time in her adult life. Even though they were born on opposite coasts, are different ages and look nothing at all alike, Jenna is convinced that her co-author is in fact her separated-at-birth twin. *The Size of Everything* is her favorite book.

COMING SOON FROM ERIN COLE & JENNA MCCARTHY

Knot Anymore™ is a one-of-a-kind jewelry collection
designed to raise awareness and funds
to fight child abuse and neglect.

www.erincole.com

14822955R00236

Made in the USA
Lexington, KY
14 November 2018